PRAISE FOR DEBORA̶̶̶̶̶AN'S *UNORTHODOX*

AN INSTANT *NEW YORK TIMES* BESTSELLER
ONE OF *O* MAGAZINE'S "10 TITLES TO PICK UP NOW"

"Imagine Frank McCourt as a Jewish virgin, and you've got *Unorthodox* in a nutshell: Wretched upbringing in an ethnic enclave yields bright new talent. Hers is a search for happiness, not a hookup; it's a sensitive and memorable coming-of-age story in the tradition of Anzia Yezierska's 1925 *Bread Givers* and Betty Smith's 1943 classic, *A Tree Grows in Brooklyn*."

—*Pittsburgh Post-Gazette*

"Eloquent, appealing, and just emotional enough . . . No doubt girls all over Brooklyn are buying this book, hiding it under their mattresses, reading it after lights out—and contemplating, perhaps for the first time, their own escape."

—HuffingtonPost.com

"A surprisingly moving, well-written and vivid coming-of-age tale."

—*The Jewish Week*

"[Feldman's] matter-of-fact style masks some penetrating insights."

—*The New York Times*

Unorthodox

The Scandalous Rejection of My Hasidic Roots

Deborah Feldman

Simon & Schuster Paperbacks
New York   London   Toronto   Sydney   New Delhi

*The names and identifying characteristics of everyone in this
book have been changed. While all the incidents described in
this book are true, certain events have been compressed, con-
solidated, or reordered to protect the identities of the people
involved and ensure continuity of the narrative. All dialogue
is as close an approximation as possible to actual conversations that took place, to the best of my recollection.*

———————

 Simon & Schuster Paperbacks
An Imprint of Simon & Schuster, Inc.
1230 Avenue of the Americas
New York, NY 10020

This Simon & Schuster trade paperback edition March 2020

SIMON & SCHUSTER PAPERBACKS and colophon are registered trademarks of
Simon & Schuster, Inc.

All photographs courtesy of the author.

For information about special discounts for bulk purchases,
please contact Simon & Schuster Special Sales at
1-866-506-1949 or business@simonandschuster.com.

The Simon & Schuster Speakers Bureau can bring authors
to your live event. For more information or to book an event,
contact the Simon & Schuster Speakers Bureau at
1-866-248-3049 or visit our website at www.simonspeakers.com.

Designed by Nancy Singer

Manufactured in the United States of America

10 9 8 7 6 5 4

Library of Congress Cataloging-in-Publication Data
   Feldman, Deborah.
Unorthodox : the scandalous rejection of my Hasidic roots / Deborah Feldman.
     p.   cm.
   1. Feldman, Deborah, 1986–   2. Jews—New York (State)—New York—Biography.
3. Hasidim—New York (State)—New York—Biography.   4. Hasidim—New York
(State)—New York—Social conditions.   5. New York (N.Y.)—Religion. I. Title.
F128.9.J5F525 2012
974.7′044092—dc22   2011001386
[B]

ISBN 978-1-4391-8700-5
ISBN 978-1-9821-4820-1 (pbk)
ISBN 978-1-4391-8702-9 (ebook)

A Note from the Author

Satu Mare, or Satmar, in Yiddish, is a city on the border of Hungary and Romania. So how did a Hasidic sect come to be named after a Transylvanian town? Well, on his mission to rescue prominent Jews from certain death during World War II, Hungarian Jewish lawyer and journalist Rudolf Kasztner saved the life of the rabbi from that city. This rabbi later immigrated to America and amassed a large following of other survivors, forming a Hasidic sect that he named after his hometown. Other surviving rabbis followed suit, naming their own sects after the towns they had come from in an effort to preserve the memory of the shtetls and communities that had been wiped out in the Holocaust.

Hasidic Jews in America eagerly returned to a heritage that had been on the verge of disappearing, donning traditional dress and speaking only in Yiddish, as their ancestors had done. Many deliberately opposed the creation of the State of Israel, believing that the genocide of the Jews had come as a punishment for assimilation and Zionism. Most important, though, Hasidic Jews focused on reproduction, wanting to replace the many who had perished and to swell their ranks once more. To this day, Hasidic communities continue to grow rapidly, in what is seen as the ultimate revenge against Hitler.

Prologue

On the eve of my twenty-fourth birthday I interview my mother. We meet at a vegetarian restaurant in Manhattan, one that announces itself as organic and farm-fresh, and despite my recent penchant for all things pork and shellfish, I am looking forward to the simplicity the meal promises. The waiter who serves us is conspicuously gentile-looking, with scruffy blond hair and big blue eyes. He treats us like royalty because we are on the Upper East Side and are prepared to shell out a hundred bucks for a lunch consisting largely of vegetables. I think it is ironic that he doesn't know that the two of us are outsiders, that he automatically takes our existence for granted. I never thought this day would come.

Before we met, I told my mother that I had some questions for her. Although we've spent more time together over the past year than we did in all my teenage years put together, thus far I've mostly avoided talking about the past. Perhaps I did not want to know. Maybe I didn't want to find out that whatever information had been fed to me about my mother was wrong, or maybe I didn't want to accept that it was right. Still, publishing my life story calls for scrupulous honesty, and not just my own.

A year ago to this date I left the Hasidic community for good. I am twenty-four and I still have my whole life ahead of me. My son's future is chock-full of possibilities. I feel as if I have made it to the starting line of a race just in time to hear the gun go off. Looking at my mother, I understand that there might be similarities between us, but the differences are more glaringly obvious. She was older when she left, and she didn't take me with her. Her journey speaks more of a struggle for security than happiness. Our dreams hover above us like clouds, and mine seem bigger and fluffier than her wispy strip of cirrus high in a winter sky.

As far back as I can remember, I have always wanted everything from life, everything it can possibly give me. This desire separates me from people who are willing to settle for less. I cannot even comprehend how people's desires can be small, their ambitions narrow and limited, when the possibilities are so endless. I do not know my mother well enough to understand her dreams; for all I know, they seem big and important to her, and I want to respect that. Surely, for all our differences, there is that thread of common ground, that choice we both made for the better.

My mother was born and raised in a German Jewish community in England. While her family was religious, they were not Hasidic. A child of divorce, she describes her young self as troubled, awkward, and unhappy. Her chances of marrying, let alone marrying well, were slim, she tells me. The waiter puts a plate of polenta fries and some black beans in front of her, and she shoves her fork in a fry.

When the choice of marrying my father came along, it seemed like a dream, she says between bites. His family was wealthy, and they were desperate to marry him off. He had siblings waiting for him to get engaged so that they could start their own lives. He was twenty-four, unthinkably old for a good Jewish boy, too old to be single. The older they get, the less likely they are to be married off. Rachel, my mother, was my father's last shot.

Everyone in my mother's life was thrilled for her, she remembers. She would get to go to America! They were offering a beautiful, brand-new apartment, fully furnished. They offered to pay for everything. She would receive beautiful clothes and jewelry. There were many sisters-in-law who were excited to become her friends.

"So they were nice to you?" I ask, referring to my aunts and uncles, who, I remember, mostly looked down on me for reasons I could never fully grasp.

"In the beginning, yes," she says. "I was the new toy from England, you know. The thin, pretty girl with the funny accent."

She saved them all, the younger ones. They were spared the fate of getting older in their singlehood. In the beginning, they were grateful to see their brother married off.

"I made him into a mensch," my mother tells me. "I made sure he always looked neat. He couldn't take care of himself, but I did. I made him look better; they didn't have to be so ashamed of him anymore."

Shame is all I can recall of my feelings for my father. When I knew him, he was always shabby and dirty, and his behavior was childlike and inappropriate.

"What do you think of my father now?" I ask. "What do you think is wrong with him?"

"Oh, I don't know. Delusional, I suppose. Mentally ill."

"Really? You think it's all that? You don't think he was just plain mentally retarded?"

"Well, he saw a psychiatrist once after we were married, and the psychiatrist told me he was pretty sure your father had some sort of personality disorder, but there was no way to tell, because your father refused to cooperate with further testing and never went back for treatment."

"Well, I don't know," I say thoughtfully. "Aunt Chaya told me once that he was diagnosed as a child, with retardation. She said his IQ was sixty-six. There's not much you can do about that."

"They didn't even try, though," my mother insists. "They could have gotten him some treatment."

I nod. "So in the beginning, they were nice to you. But what happened after?" I remember my aunts talking about my mother behind her back, saying hateful things.

"Well, after the fuss calmed down, they started to ignore me. They would do things and leave me out of it. They looked down on me because I was from a poor family, and they had all married money and come from money and they lived different lives. Your father couldn't earn any money, and neither could I, so your grandfather supported us. But he was stingy, counting out the bare minimum for groceries. He was very smart, your *zeide,* but he didn't understand people. He was out of touch with reality."

I still feel a little sting when someone says something bad about my family, as if I have to defend them.

"Your *bubbe*, on the other hand, she had respect for me, I could tell. No one ever listened to her, and certainly she was more intelligent and open-minded than anyone gave her credit for."

"Oh, I agree with that!" I'm thrilled to find we have some common ground, one family member whom we both see the same way. "She was like that to me too; she respected me even when everyone else thought I was just troublesome."

"Yes, well . . . she had no power, though."

"True."

So in the end she had nothing to cling to, my mother. No husband, no family, no home. In college, she would exist, would have purpose, direction. You leave when there's nothing left to stay for; you go where you can be useful, where people accept you.

The waiter comes to the table holding a chocolate brownie with a candle stuck in it. "Happy birthday to you . . . ," he sings softly, meeting my eyes for a second. I look down, feeling my cheeks redden.

"Blow out the candle," my mother urges, taking out her camera. I want to laugh. I bet the waiter thinks that I'm just like every other birthday girl going out with her mom, and that we do this every year. Would anyone guess that my mother missed most of my birthdays growing up? How can she be so quick to jump back into things? Does it feel natural to her? It certainly doesn't feel that way to me.

After both of us have devoured the brownie, she pauses and wipes her mouth. She says that she wanted to take me with her, but she couldn't. She had no money. My father's family threatened to make her life miserable if she tried to take me away. Chaya, the oldest aunt, was the worst, she says. "I would visit you and she would treat me like garbage, like I wasn't your mother, had never given birth to you. Who gave her the right, when she wasn't even blood?" Chaya married the family's oldest son and immediately took control of everything, my mother recalls. She always had to be the boss, arranging everything, asserting her opinions everywhere.

And when my mother left my father for good, Chaya took control of me too. She decided that I would live with my grandparents, that I would go to Satmar school, that I would marry a good Satmar boy from a religious family. It was Chaya who, in the end, taught me to take control of my own life, to become iron-fisted like she was, and not let anyone else force me to be unhappy.

It was Chaya who convinced Zeidy to talk to the matchmaker, I learned, even though I had only just turned seventeen. In essence, she was my matchmaker; she was the one who decided to whom I was to be married. I'd like to hold her responsible for everything I went through as a result, but I am too wise for that. I know the way of our world, and the way people get swept along in the powerful current of our age-old traditions.

August 2010
New York City

1

In Search of My Secret Power

Matilda longed for her parents to be good and loving and understanding and honourable and intelligent. The fact that they were none of those things was something she had to put up with. . . .

Being very small and very young, the only power Matilda had over anyone in her family was brainpower.
—From Matilda, *by Roald Dahl*

My father holds my hand as he fumbles with the keys to the warehouse. The streets are strangely empty and silent in this industrial section of Williamsburg. Above, the stars glow faintly in the night sky; nearby, occasional cars whoosh ghostlike along the expressway. I look down at my patent leather shoes tapping impatiently on the sidewalk and I bite my lip to stop the impulse. I'm grateful to be here. It's not every week that Tatty takes me with him.

One of my father's many odd jobs is turning the ovens on at Beigel's kosher bakery when Shabbos is over. Every Jewish business must cease for the duration of the Shabbos, and the law requires that a Jew be the one to set things in motion again. My father easily qualifies for a job with such simple requirements. The gentile laborers are already working when he gets there, preparing the dough, shaping it into rolls and loaves, and when my father walks through the vast warehouse flipping the switches, a humming and whirring sound starts up and builds momentum as we move through the cavernous rooms. This is one of the weeks he takes me with him, and I find it exciting to be surrounded by all this hustle and know that my father is at the center of it, that these people must wait for him to arrive before business can go on as usual. I feel important just knowing that he is important too. The workers nod to him as he passes, smiling even if he is late, and they pat me on the head with powdery, gloved hands. By the time my father is done with the last section, the entire factory is pulsating with the sound of mixing machines and conveyor belts. The cement floor vibrates slightly beneath my feet. I watch the trays slide into the ovens and come out the other end with shiny golden rolls all in a row, as my father makes conversation with the workers while munching on an egg *kichel*.

Bubby loves egg *kichel*. We always bring her some after our trips to the bakery. In the front room of the warehouse there are shelves stocked with sealed and packed boxes of various baked goods ready to be shipped in the morning, and on our way out, we will take as many as we can carry. There are the famous kosher cupcakes with rainbow sprinkles on top; the loaves of babka, cinnamon- and chocolate-flavored; the seven-layer cake heavy with margarine; the mini black-and-white cookies that I only like to eat the chocolate part from. Whatever my father selects on his way out will get dropped off at my grandparents' house later, dumped on the dining room table like bounty, and I will get to taste it all.

What can measure up to this kind of wealth, the abundance of sweets and confections scattered across a damask tablecloth like goods at an auction? Tonight I will fall easily into sleep with the taste of frosting still in the crevices of my teeth, crumbs melting into the pockets on either side of my mouth.

This is one of the few good moments I share with my father. Often he gives me very little reason to be proud of him. His shirts have yellow spots under the arms even though Bubby does most of his laundry, and his smile is too wide and silly, like a clown's. When he comes to visit me at Bubby's house, he brings me Klein's ice cream bars dipped in chocolate and looks at me expectantly as I eat, waiting for my remarks of appreciation. This is being a father, he must think—supplying me with treats. Then he leaves as suddenly as he arrives, off on another one of his "errands."

People employ him out of pity, I know. They hire him to drive them around, deliver packages, anything they think he is capable of doing without making mistakes. He doesn't understand this; he thinks he is performing a valuable service.

My father performs many errands, but the only ones he allows me to participate in are the occasional trips to the bakery and the even rarer ones to the airport. The airport trips are more exciting, but they only happen a couple of times a year. I know it's strange for me to enjoy visiting the airport itself, when I know I will never even get on a plane, but I find it thrilling to stand next to my father as he waits for the person he is supposed to pick up, watching the crowds hurrying to and fro with their luggage squealing loudly behind them, knowing that they are all going somewhere, purposefully. What a marvelous world this is, I think, where birds touch down briefly before magically reappearing at another airport somewhere halfway across the planet. If I had a wish, it would be to always be traveling, from one airport to another. To be freed from the prison of staying still.

After my father drops me off at the house, I might not see him again for a while, maybe weeks, unless I run into him on the street, and then I will hide my face and pretend not to see him, so that I don't get called over and introduced to whomever he is speaking to. I can't stand the looks of curious pity people give me when they find out I am his daughter.

"This is your *maideleh*?" they croon condescendingly, pinching my cheek or lifting my chin with a crooked finger. Then they peer at me closely, looking for some sign that I am indeed the offspring of this man, so they can later say, "*Nebach*, poor little soul, it's her fault that she was born? In her face you can see it, she's not all here."

Bubby is the only person who thinks I'm one hundred percent all here. With her you can tell she never questions it. She doesn't judge people. She never came to conclusions about my father either, but maybe that was just denial. When she tells stories of my father at my age, she paints him as lovably mischievous. He was always too skinny, so she would try anything to get him to eat. Whatever he wanted he got, but he couldn't leave the table until his plate was empty. One time he tied his chicken drumstick to a piece of string and dangled it out the window to the cats in the yard so he wouldn't have to stay stuck at the table for hours while everyone was outside playing. When Bubby came back, he showed her his empty plate and she asked, "Where are the bones? You can't eat the bones too." That's how she knew.

I wanted to admire my father for his ingenious idea, but my bubble of pride burst when Bubby told me he wasn't even smart enough to think ahead, to pull the string back up so he could place the freshly gnawed bones back on the plate. At eleven years old, I wished for a more shrewd execution of what could have been an excellent plan.

By the time he was a teenager, his innocent mischief was no longer charming. He couldn't sit still in yeshiva, so Zeidy sent him to Gershom Feldman's boot camp in upstate New York, where they ran a yeshiva for troublesome kids—like regular yeshiva, only with beatings if you misbehaved. It didn't cure my father's strange behavior.

Perhaps in a child, eccentricity is more easily forgiven. But who can explain an adult who hoards cake for months, until the smell of mold is unbearable? Who can explain the row of bottles in the refrigerator, each containing the pink liquid antibiotics that children take, that my father insists on imbibing every day for some invisible illness that no doctor can detect?

Bubby still tries to take care of him. She cooks beef especially for him, even though Zeidy doesn't eat beef since the scandal ten years ago, when some of the kosher beef turned out to be not kosher after all. Bubby still cooks for all her sons, even the married ones. They have wives now to take care of them, but they still come by for dinner, and Bubby acts like it's the most natural thing in the world. At ten o'clock each night she wipes down the kitchen counters and jokingly declares the "restaurant" closed.

I eat here too, and I even sleep here most of the time, because my mother never seems to be around anymore and my father can't be depended on to take care of me. When I was very little, I remember my mother used to read books to me before I fell asleep, stories about hungry caterpillars and Clifford the big red dog. In Bubby's house the only books around are prayer books. Before I go to sleep, I say the Shema prayer.

I'd like to read books again, because those are the only happy memories I have, of being read to, but my English isn't very good, and I have no way of obtaining books on my own. So instead I nourish myself with cupcakes from Beigel's, and egg *kichel*. Bubby takes such particular pleasure and excitement in food that I can't help but get caught up in her enthusiasm.

Bubby's kitchen is like the center of the world. It is where everyone congregates to chatter and gossip, while Bubby pours ingredients into the electric mixer or stirs the ever-present pots on the stove. Somber talks take place with Zeidy behind closed doors, but good news is always shared in the kitchen. Ever since I can remember, I've always gravitated toward the small white-tiled room, often fogged with cooking vapors. As a toddler I crawled down the one flight of stairs from our apartment on the third floor to Bubby's kitchen on the second floor, edging cautiously down each linoleum-covered step with my chubby baby legs, hoping that a reward of cherry-flavored Jell-O was in it for me at the end of my labors.

It is in this kitchen that I have always felt safe. From what, I cannot articulate, except to say that in the kitchen I did not feel that familiar sense of being lost in a strange land, where no one knew who I was or what language I spoke. In the kitchen I felt like I had reached the place from which I came, and I never wanted to be pulled back into the chaos again.

I usually curl up on the little leather stool stashed between the table and the fridge and watch as Bubby mixes the batter for chocolate cake, waiting for the spatula that I always get to lick clean. Before Shabbos, Bubby stuffs whole beef livers into the meat grinder with a wooden pestle, adding handfuls of caramelized onions every so often and holding a bowl underneath to catch the creamy chopped liver oozing out of the grinder. Some mornings she mixes premium-quality Dutch cocoa and whole milk in a pot and boils it to a bubble, serving up a rich, dark hot chocolate that I sweeten with lumps of sugar. Her scrambled eggs are swathed in buttery slicks; her *boondash*, or the Hungarian version of French toast, is always crisp and perfectly browned. I like watching her prepare food even more than I like eating it. I love how the house fills with the scents; they travel slowly through the railroad-style apartment, entering each room consecutively like a delicate train of smells. I wake up in the morning in my little room all the way at the other end of the house and sniff expectantly, trying to guess what Bubby is working on that day. She always wakes up early, and there are always food preparations under way by the time I open my eyes.

If Zeidy isn't home, Bubby sings. She hums wordless tunes in her thin, feathery voice as she skillfully whisks a fluffy tower of meringue in a shiny steel bowl. This one is a Viennese waltz, she tells me, or a Hungarian rhapsody. Tunes from her childhood, she says, her memories of Budapest. When Zeidy comes home, she stops the humming. I know women are not allowed to sing, but in front of family it is permitted. Still, Zeidy encourages singing only on Shabbos. Since the Temple was destroyed, he says, we shouldn't sing or listen to music unless it's a special occasion. Sometimes Bubby takes the old tape recorder that my father gave me and plays the cassette of my cousin's wedding music over and over, at a low volume so she can hear if someone's coming. She shuts it off at the merest sound of creaking in the hallway.

Her father was a *Kohain*, she reminds me. He could trace his legacy all the way back to the Temple priests. *Kohains* are renowned for having beautiful, deep voices. Zeidy can't carry a tune for the life of him, but he loves to sing the songs his father used to sing back in Europe, the traditional Shabbos melodies that his flat voice distorts into tuneless rambles. Bubby shakes her head and smiles at his attempts. She's long since given up trying to sing along. Zeidy makes everyone sing out of tune, his loud, flat warblings drowning out everyone else's voice until a melody becomes impossible to distinguish. Only one of her sons inherited her voice, Bubby says. The rest are like their father. I tell her I was chosen for a solo in a school choir, that maybe I did inherit my strong, clear voice from her family. I want her to be proud of me.

Bubby never asks how I'm doing in school. She doesn't concern herself with my activities. It's almost as if she doesn't really want to get to know me for who I truly am. She's like that with everyone. I think it's because her whole family was murdered in the concentration camps, and she no longer has the energy to connect emotionally with people.

All she ever worries about is if I'm eating enough. Enough slices of rye bread spread thickly with butter, enough plates of hearty vegetable soup, enough squares of moist, glistening apple strudel. It seems as if Bubby is constantly putting food in front of me, even at the most inappropriate of moments. Taste this roast turkey at breakfast. Try this coleslaw at midnight. Whatever's cooking, that's what's available. There are no bags of potato chips in the pantry, no boxes of cereal even. Everything that is served in Bubby's house is freshly made from scratch.

Zeidy is the one who asks me about school, but mostly just to check if I'm behaving myself. He only wants to hear that I'm conducting myself properly so no one will say he has a disobedient granddaughter. Last week before Yom Kippur he advised me to repent so I could start the year anew, magically transformed into a quiet, God-fearing young girl. It was my first fast; although according to the Torah I become a woman at age twelve, girls start fasting at eleven just to try it out. There is a whole world of new rules in store for me when I cross the bridge from childhood to adulthood. This next year is a sort of practice run.

There are only a few days left before the next holiday, Sukkot. Zeidy needs me to help build the sukkah, the little wooden hut we will all spend eight days eating inside. To lay the bamboo roof, he needs someone to hand him each stick as he perches on top of the ladder, rolling the heavy rods into place on top of the freshly nailed beams. The dowels clatter loudly as they fall into place. Somehow I always end up with this job, which can get boring after hours of standing at the foot of the ladder, passing each individual rod into Zeidy's waiting hands.

Still, I like feeling useful. Even though the rods are at least ten years old and have been stored in the cellar all year, they smell fresh and sweet. I roll them back and forth between my palms, and the surface feels cool to the touch, polished to a sheen by years of use. Zeidy lifts each one up slowly and deliberately. There aren't many domestic tasks that Zeidy is willing to take on, but any form of work related to the preparation for the holidays he makes time for. Sukkot is one of my favorites, since it is

spent outdoors in crisp fall weather. As the days begin to taper, I soak up
every last remnant of sunshine on Bubby's porch, even if I have to wrap
myself in multiple layers of sweaters to keep off the chill. I lie on a bed arranged from three wooden chairs, tilting my face up to the sun that falls
haphazardly through the narrow alley between a cluster of back-to-back
brownstone tenements. There is nothing more soothing than the feeling
of a pale autumn sun on my skin, and I linger until the rays peer weakly
above a bleak, dusty horizon.

Sukkot is a long holiday, but it has four days in the middle of it that are
somewhat nonceremonious. There are no laws about driving or spending money on those days, called Chol Hamoed, and they are generally
spent like any other weekday, except that no work is allowed, and so
most people go on family trips. My cousins always go somewhere on Chol
Hamoed, and I'm confident that I will end up tagging along with some
of them. Last year we went to Coney Island. This year, Mimi says we will
go ice-skating in the park.

Mimi is one of the few cousins who are nice to me. I think it's because her father is divorced. Now her mother is married to some other
man who's not in our family, but Mimi still comes to Bubby's house a lot
to see her father, my uncle Sinai. Sometimes I think our family is divided
in half, with the problems on one side and the perfect people on the
other. Only the ones with problems will talk to me. No matter, Mimi is
so much fun to be around. She is in high school and gets to travel on her
own, and she blow-dries her honey-colored hair into a flip.

After two antsy days of my helping Bubby serve the holiday meals,
carrying the trays of food from the kitchen to the sukkah and back, Chol
Hamoed is finally here. Mimi comes to pick me up in the morning. I
am dressed and ready, having followed her instructions perfectly. Thick
tights and a pair of socks on top, a heavy sweater over my shirt to keep
me warm, puffy mittens for my hands, and a hat as well. I feel swollen
and awkward but well prepared. Mimi is wearing a chic charcoal-colored
woolen coat with a velvet collar and velvet gloves, and I am jealous of
her elegance. I look like a mismatched monkey, the weight of the mittens
dragging my arms down comically.

Ice-skating is magical. At first I wobble unsteadily on rented skates, grasping the wall of the rink tightly as I make my way around it, but I get the hang of it very quickly, and once I do, it's like I'm flying. I push off with each foot and then close my eyes through the smooth glide that follows, keeping my back straight like Mimi said to. I have never felt so free.

I can hear the sound of laughter, but it sounds distant, lost in the rush of air whipping past my ears. The sound of skates scraping over the ice is loudest, and I become lost in its rhythm. My motions become repetitive and trancelike and I wish life could be like this all the time. Every time I open my eyes, I expect to be somewhere else.

Two hours pass, and I find that I am ravenous. It is a new kind of hunger, perhaps the hunger that comes from delicious exhaustion, and the emptiness inside me, for once, is pleasant. Mimi has packed kosher sandwiches for us. We hunker down on a bench outside the rink to eat them.

As I munch enthusiastically on my tuna on rye, I notice a family at the picnic table next to us, specifically a girl who looks my age. Unlike me, she appears suitably dressed for ice-skating, with a much shorter shirt and thick, brightly colored tights. She even has furry earmuffs on.

She sees me looking at her and slides off the bench. She holds out a closed palm to me, and when she opens it, there's candy, in a shiny silver wrapper. I've never seen candy like that before.

"Are you Jewish?" I ask, to make sure it's kosher.

"Uh-huh," she says. "I even go to Hebrew school and everything. I know the aleph-bet. My name's Stephanie."

I take the chocolate from her cautiously. Hershey's, it says. *Hersh* is Yiddish for "deer." It's also a common Jewish name for boys. The *ey* tacked on the end makes it an affectionate nickname. I wonder what kind of man Hershey is, if his children are proud of him when they see his name stamped on candy wrappers. If only I were lucky enough to have a father like that. Before I can open the chocolate bar to see what it looks like inside, Mimi looks over with a stern face and shakes her head from side to side in warning.

"Thank you," I say to Stephanie, clenching my fist around the bar until it disappears from sight. She tosses her head and runs back to her table.

"You can't eat the chocolate," Mimi announces as soon as Stephanie is out of earshot. "It's not kosher."

"But she's Jewish! She said so herself! Why can't I eat it?"

"Because not all Jews keep kosher. And even the ones that do, it's not always kosher enough. Look, see that mark on the wrapper? It says OUD. That means it's kosher dairy. It's not *cholov Yisroel* dairy, which means the milk that went into it didn't have the proper rabbinical supervision. Zeidy would be horrified if you brought this into his house."

Mimi takes the chocolate from my hand and drops it into the garbage can next to us.

"I will get you another chocolate," she says. "Later, when we get back. A kosher one. You can have a La-Hit wafer; you like those, right?"

I nod, placated. As I finish my tuna sandwich, I gaze thoughtfully at Stephanie, who is executing jumps on the rubber floor. The serrated front points of her skates make dull thuds each time she lands, her poise perfect. *How can you be Jewish and not keep kosher?* I wonder. *How can you know the aleph-bet but still eat Hershey's chocolate? Doesn't she know any better?*

Aunt Chaya has her most disapproving face on. She's sitting next to me at the holiday table, teaching me how to eat my soup without slurping. Her glare is frightening enough to provide incentive for a fast, effective lesson. I live in fear of attracting her attention; it's never positive. Aunt Chaya has always been behind every major decision made about my life, even if I don't really see her very often anymore. I used to live with her, back when my mother had just left for good, driving off in her little black Honda while everyone on the street poked their heads out the window to witness the spectacle. Perhaps she was the first woman in Williamsburg to drive.

I was very unhappy living at my aunt Chaya's. She would yell at me every time I cried, but the more I tried to stop, the more the tears would fall, betraying me. I begged to come live with Bubby, and even though my grandparents were old and had finished raising their children a long time ago, eventually I was allowed to move back. Zeidy still takes advice from Chaya about how to raise me, and I wonder what makes her the expert, with three daughters who took off their seamed stockings as soon as they graduated from school, and moved to Borough Park after they got married.

Before Sukkot, Bubby sent me up to Chaya's apartment on the fourth floor to help her clean for the holiday. Chaya had laid out mousetraps, because despite twice-weekly visits from the exterminator, we have always had a mouse problem, just like everyone else who lives in an old house in Williamsburg. Chaya always smears extra peanut butter on the sticky yellow trays and slips them under the furniture. When I got there, she was checking all the traps. She steered one out from under the stove with a broom, and there, making pitiful chirping sounds, was a mouse, squirming desperately on the tray. There was no way to remove it once it was stuck, I realized, but still I longed for a more merciful solution, like catching a bug and releasing it on the street. But before I could say a word, Chaya picked up the trap with two hands and folded it in half in one quick, slapping motion between her two palms, instantly crushing the mouse to death.

I gaped for a moment. I had never seen anyone get rid of a mouse with such relish. When Bubby found one, it was usually already dead, and she wrapped it in plastic bags and took it down to the garbage can in the front yard. A few months ago I opened one of my dresser drawers and found a family of mice nesting in a folded sweater of mine: nine pink, writhing creatures, each the size of my thumb, skittering happily amidst a hillock of shredded aluminum foil and paper that I supposed their mother had provided. I let them stay for a week without telling anyone of my discovery. One day they were gone. I had, stupidly, just allowed ten more full-grown mice to frolic freely in our house, while Bubby fretted constantly about how to get rid of them.

It's not that I like mice. I just don't like killing things. Zeidy thinks that compassion like mine is inappropriate, misplaced. It's like having compassion is a good thing, but I don't use it right or something. I feel bad for things I shouldn't feel bad for. I should have more compassion for the people who are trying to raise me, he says. I should work harder to make him proud.

All my aunts and uncles are hard on their children, it seems to me. They berate them, embarrass them, and yell at them. This is *chinuch*, child rearing according to the Torah. It is the parents' spiritual responsibility that their children grow up to be God-fearing, law-abiding Jews. Therefore, any form of discipline is all right as long as it is for that purpose. Zeidy often reminds me that when he is delivering a harsh lecture to a particular grandchild, it is only out of a sense of obligation. Real anger is forbidden, he says, but one must fake it for the sake of *chinuch*. In this family, we do not hug and kiss. We do not compliment each other. Instead, we watch each other closely, ever ready to point out someone's spiritual or physical failing. This, says Chaya, is compassion— compassion for someone's spiritual welfare.

And Chaya has the most compassion for my spiritual welfare of anyone in my family. Whenever she visits Bubby, she watches me like a hawk, pointing out what I'm doing wrong every few minutes. My heart beats quickly when I'm around her; its rhythm thrums loudly through my ears, drowning out the sound of her voice. It's not that no one else in the family criticizes me. Aunt Rachel is always looking at me like there's dirt on my face that I forgot to clean off, and Uncle Sinai slaps at my head when I get in his way. But Chaya looks right at me when she talks to me, her mouth hard with something close to anger that I don't quite understand. She is always dressed in expensive matching suits and shoes, somehow managing to avoid getting wrinkled or dirty even while serving and cleaning up. When I get a fine spray of soup on my collar, she makes a clicking noise with her tongue in disdain. I get the distinct sense that she takes pleasure in the fear she evokes in me; it makes her feel powerful. None of the others seem to notice how I feel about them, but she knows that she frightens me, and she likes it. There are times when she even pretends to be nice, her voice oozing sugary sweetness but the glint in her narrowed, pale blue eyes hinting at something else, asking me if I want to help her bake cherry pie, then scrutinizing me carefully as I knead the pastry dough in the big steel bowl, waiting for the slightest slipup.

Chaya is the only true blonde in the family. Although I have two other aunts who wear blond wigs, everyone knows their hair turned ashy long before they were married. Only Chaya has the coloring of a genuine blonde: fair, even-toned skin and eyes the color of blue-tinted ice. It is very rare in Williamsburg for someone to be a natural blond, and I can tell Chaya takes pride in her beauty. Sometimes I squeeze lemon juice on my head and run it through my strands in the hope that they will lighten, but no change is apparent. Once I put Clorox cream on one section, and it worked, but I was worried that people would notice because it looked too obvious. It's forbidden to dye one's hair, and I couldn't have borne the gossip that would have ensued if anyone were suspicious of my new gold streaks.

Chaya has convinced Zeidy to let her take me to another psychiatrist. We have already been to two, both of them Orthodox Jews with offices in Borough Park. The first one said I was normal. The second one told Chaya everything I said to him, so I clammed up and refused to talk again, until he gave up. Now Chaya says she will take me to a woman doctor.

I understand why I need to see a doctor for crazy people. I expect I may be crazy too. I keep waiting for the day when I will wake up foaming at the mouth like my great-aunt Esther, who is epileptic. After all, Chaya implies that it runs in my mother's side of the family. Surely, with my unfortunate genetic inheritance, I can hardly hope for mental health. What I don't understand is, if these doctors can help, why didn't they send my parents to one? Or if they did, and it didn't work, why would it work on me?

The woman's name is Shifra. She has a paper with a chart on it that she calls an enneagram. It's a list of nine different personality types, and she explains to me that you can be one of the nine personality types but still have "wings" in the other personalities, so you can be a five, with four and six wings.

"The four is the Individualist," she tells me. "That's what you are."

How quickly she has put me in a box, within the first ten minutes of our meeting. And is there something so wrong with being an individual, being self-sufficient and private as she says? Is that the neurosis that Chaya wants to drive out of me, so she can make me more like her: rigid, disciplined, and, most of all, conforming?

I storm out of the session early. Surely the "doctor" will use this as proof that I am indeed a problem to be solved, a disorderly personality to be rearranged. I walk up and down Sixteenth Avenue, watching the women and girls doing their preparatory shopping for Shabbos. The smell of old herring wafts up from the grimy gutters and I wrinkle my nose. I don't understand why I can't be like these other girls, in whom modesty is so ingrained that it runs in their veins. Even their thoughts are still and quiet, I can tell. With me, you can see on my face what I'm thinking. And even if I never speak the thoughts out loud, you can tell that they are forbidden. In fact, I'm having a forbidden thought right now. I'm thinking that I'm not expected back in Williamsburg for another hour and a half, and just a few blocks north is the public library I have passed so many times before. It's safer for me to sneak in here, in a neighborhood where no one knows me. I don't have to be so scared of being recognized.

In the library, it is so quiet and still that I feel my thoughts expand in the space that the tall ceiling provides. The librarian is arranging a display in the children's section, which is blessedly empty. I like the children's section because there are places to sit, and the books are already picked out for me. The librarians always smile when they see me, silent encouragement in their eyes.

I don't have a library card, so I can't take books home with me. I wish that I could, because I feel so extraordinarily happy and free when I read that I'm convinced it could make everything else in my life bearable, if only I could have books all the time.

Sometimes it feels like the authors of these books understand me, that they wrote these stories with me in mind. How else to explain the similarities between me and the characters in Roald Dahl's tales: unfortunate, precocious children despised and neglected by their shallow families and peers?

After I read *James and the Giant Peach*, I dreamed of rolling away in the womb of a fruit from Bubby's garden. It seems to me that in the literature revolving around children, children who are strange and misunderstood like me, at some point something comes along to transform their lives, to transport them to the magic netherworld to which they truly belong. And then they realize that their old life was just a mistake, that they were extraordinary all along and meant for bigger and better things. Secretly, I too am waiting to fall down a hole into Wonderland, or pass through the back of a wardrobe into Narnia. What other possibilities could I consider? Surely I will never be at home in this world.

I cross my legs in delicious anticipation when I read about Matilda discovering her power in class one day, in that desperate turning moment that every story seems to have, when it is thought that all hope is lost and then suddenly it shows up again, from somewhere unexpected. Will I too one day find that I have a power that has been kept secret from me? Does it lie dormant within me right now? It would make sense then, all of this, if I were like Matilda and I went home with Miss Honey in the end.

There is always a happy ending in children's books. Because I have not yet begun to read adult books, I have come to accept this convention as a fact of life as well. In the physics of imagination, this is the rule: a child can only accept a just world. I waited for a long time for someone to come along and rescue me, just like in the stories. It was a bitter pill to swallow when I realized that no one would ever pick up the glass slipper I left behind.

An empty vessel clangs the loudest. That's the adage I hear continuously, from Chaya, from the teachers at school, from the Yiddish textbooks. The louder a woman, the more likely she is to be spiritually bereft, like the empty bowl that vibrates with a resonant echo. A full container makes no sound; she is packed too densely to ring. There are many proverbs repeated to me throughout my childhood, but this one stings the most.

I try, but I can't help my natural impulse to talk back. It's not smart, I know, for me to always want to have the last word. It results in a world of trouble that I could easily save myself from, if I could only learn to keep quiet. Yet I cannot allow another's mistake to pass by unnoticed. I must comment on the grammatical slipups and misquotations of my teachers out of an unexplained duty to the truth. This behavior has branded me a *mechitsef*, an insolent one.

I go to Satmar school now. Chaya decided which class to put me in; she is the principal of the elementary division. The other students were initially jealous of me, assuming I had unlimited grace, but the truth is it's another opportunity for Chaya to keep tabs on me and report back to my grandparents. She says she put me in the smart class, so that I would feel challenged. There are twelve sixth-grade classes, and each of them is known for a particular trait. The girls in my class are dedicated and studious and don't understand my desire for excitement.

I'm tapping my pencil quietly on my desk as the teacher elaborates on the Torah portion of the week. I simply cannot endure this for hours on end, listening to her drone on in her usual monotone. If only she would care to make it a little more exciting, so I wouldn't find it so difficult to sit still. Well, if she won't provide excitement, I will.

Two weeks ago someone discovered a dead mouse under the radiator. There was a mad frenzy as everyone tried to leave the classroom at once. The stench was overwhelming. I remember Chaya came down from her office on the fourth floor to see what the commotion was all about. She walked slowly toward the back of the classroom, her square-heeled pumps echoing loudly on the wooden floor, her arms crossed behind her very straight back. She tossed the scarf that covered her short blond wig over her shoulder before bending down to check under the radiator. When she stood back up, there was a withered gray lump dangling from her gloved hand. Beside me, someone choked back a scream. Chaya dropped the dead creature into a Ziploc bag, her lips pursed and eyebrows raised in contempt. Even the teacher looked visibly shaken, her face white. I was the only one who wasn't speechless with surprise.

I cannot explain my aunt. She is not a blood member of my family, and I know very little about her past. All I know is that her children, like her, are strange. They all have the same cold manner, the same rigid posture and attitude. And she is proud of them for that and wants me to be the same. It is as if she thinks that I will never feel pain and so will always be able to perform as is expected of me. Sometimes I think she is right. But I am not prepared to erase the possibility of joy from my existence, and to live like her means to give up on emotion. I am convinced that my ability to feel deeply is what makes me extraordinary, and that is my ticket to Wonderland. Any day now there will be a tincture on my nightstand, with the label Drink Me attached. Until that happens, I am stuck in this classroom. I must come up with a way to make the time pass more quickly.

If only another mouse were discovered. As my pencil taps gently on the desk, an idea comes to me like a delicious chill shooting up my spine.

What if—no, I couldn't possibly. But perhaps—no, the risk is too great. To claim to see a mouse where there is none? But if I pulled it off, who could ever point fingers at me? Is it mischief to be startled out of one's seat by the sight of a mouse skittering across the floor? One could hardly call it premeditated. My limbs tickle now, in nervous anticipation. How would I execute this prank? That's it—I will drop my pencil. Then, when I bend down to pick it up, I will jump onto my chair, shrieking in horror. I will cry out "Mouse!" and that's all it will take.

My stomach lurches as I slowly roll the pencil toward the edge of my desk, watching it clatter to the ground while I make sure to look as bored and sleepy as possible. I reach down under my desk to pick it up, and for a moment I pause underneath it, in an instant of tortured hesitation, before I leap up on my chair. "*Aaaah!*" I scream. "*A mouse! I saw a mouse!*"

In an instant the classroom is alive with screaming as the girls jump onto their desks in an effort to avoid the threatening rodent. Even the teacher looks horrified. She sends the class monitor to get the janitor. Meanwhile there will be no more studying until the janitor has inspected the classroom and pronounced it mouse-free, as I know he will.

Still, he interviews me, trying to figure out the mouse's path, and the possible hole it could have disappeared into, never once appearing to doubt my claim. Is it because he can't possibly imagine a good Satmar girl concocting such mischief? Or is it because the fear and shock in my face are partly real? Even I am taken aback by my own daring.

At recess time, my classmates crowd around me in morbid curiosity, demanding to hear every detail of the sighting. "Your face was so white!" they remark. "You looked truly terrified." What an actress I am. A white face and trembling hands to go with my scream. To think what I can do with a skill such as this—the ability to convince others of emotions I don't really feel! It is a thrilling thought.

Later, when Bubby and Zeidy hear about the incident from Chaya, they laugh about it. Only Chaya turns to me with a suspicious look in her eye, but she doesn't say anything. For the first time, I feel triumphant, and I look back at her calmly. This, then, is my power. Perhaps I cannot move things with my mind, like Matilda, but I can pretend; I can act so convincingly that no one will ever be able to discover the truth.

• • •

"Bubby, what's a virgin?"

Bubby looks up at me from where she is kneading dough for kreplach on the cast-iron tabletop. It's a humid day, perfect for getting dough to rise. The steam rising from the stove fogs up the rain-splattered windows. My floury fingers leave smudges on the glass bottle of olive oil with its picture of an artfully draped woman snaked around the words *extra virgin*.

"Where did you hear that word?" she asks. I notice her shocked expression and realize I've said something bad, so I stutter anxiously in response, "I d-d-don't know, Bubby, I don't remember . . ." I turn the olive oil around so that the label is facing the wall.

"Well, it's not a word for little girls to know," Bubby says, and goes back to rolling the delicate potato-flour dough with her bare hands. Her pink cotton turban is askew, so that the glittering rhinestone set into the knot is over by her right ear, and a thatch of white fuzz is visible. When I'm married, I'm going to wear the fashionable turbans, made out of terry cloth and piled elegantly into a square knot on top of my head, and my neck will be shaved clean, even though Bubby says her neck itches all the time when it's shaved closely.

Bubby loves to tell the story of how Zeidy asked her to shave her head. Two years after they were married it was; he just came home one day and said, "Fraida, I want you to shave off all your hair."

"Husband of mine," she retorted indignantly, "you went crazy in the head or what? It's not enough for you that I cover my hair with a wig, even when my own mother didn't bother back in Europe, but now you want me to shave it all too? Never in my life did I hear of such a *frumkeit*, of such a religion, that says a woman has to shave her head."

"But, Fraida," Zeidy entreated, "the rebbe said! It's a new rule. All the men are telling their wives to do it. You want me to be the only man whose wife doesn't shave her hair? *Nu*, an embarrassment like that you want to bring down on our family? You want the rebbe should know that I couldn't get my wife to follow the rules?"

Bubby sighed dramatically. "*Nu*, what is this rebbe? My rebbe he never was. Your rebbe he never was either, before the war. Suddenly we have a new rebbe? And tell me who is this rebbe that he said I have to shave my hair, when he never even met me? A more modest, devout woman he has never met before, tell him, even if I have a little hair on my head."

Still, after multiple appeals, Bubby finally capitulates and takes a razor to her head. She always tells me, "The shaving you think was such a big deal? Not a big deal at all. I got used to it so fast! And honestly, it's so much more comfortable, especially in the summer."

It was nothing in the end, she says. Sometimes it sounds like she is trying to convince herself and not just me.

"Why did the rebbe decide that the women have to shave their heads," I always ask, "if nobody did that in Europe?"

Bubby hesitates for a moment before answering. "Zeidy tells me that the rebbe wants us to be more *ehrlich*, more devout, than any Jew ever was. He says that if we go to extreme lengths to make God proud of us, he'll never hurt us again, like he did in the war." And here she always falls silent, sinking into reminiscent misery.

I look at Bubby now, bent over her ever-present work, and watch as she adjusts her turban with a floury hand, leaving a white streak on her forehead. She begins cutting squares out of the flattened sheet of kreplach dough and fills them with farmer cheese, then folds the squares in half to form triangular pockets. I drop the kreplach into a pot of boiling water on the stove, watching them jostle each other for space at the top. I wish I could take back my question, or at least say *a gut vurt* to Bubby, something that will reassure her that I'm a good girl who doesn't use bad words. All I ever have are questions, though. "*Oy vey*," Bubby says with a sigh when I start asking questions, "why do you always need to know everything?" I don't know why, but it's true, I just *need* to know. I want to know about that book she keeps hidden in her underwear drawer, the cheap paperback with the pouty woman on the cover, but I know it's hidden for a reason, that it's a secret, and I have to keep it.

I have secrets too. Maybe Bubby knows about them, but she won't say anything about mine if I don't say anything about hers. Or perhaps I have only imagined her complicity; there is a chance this agreement is only one-sided. Would Bubby tattle on me? I hide my books under the bed, and she hides hers in her lingerie, and once a year when Zeidy inspects the house for Passover, poking through our things, we hover anxiously, terrified of being found out. Zeidy even rifles through my underwear drawer. Only when I tell him that this is my private female stuff does he desist, unwilling to violate a woman's privacy, and move on to my grandmother's wardrobe. She is as defensive as I am when he rummages through her lingerie. We both know that our small stash of secular books would shock my grandfather more than a pile of *chametz*, the forbidden leavening, ever could. Bubby might get away with a scolding, but I would not be spared the full extent of my grandfather's wrath. When my *zeide* gets angry, his long white beard seems to lift up and spread around his face like a fiery flame. I wither instantly in the heat of his scorn.

"*Der tumeneh shprach!*" he thunders at me when he overhears me speaking to my cousins in English. An impure language, Zeidy says, acts like a poison to the soul. Reading an English book is even worse; it leaves my soul vulnerable, a welcome mat put out for the devil.

I'm not myself today, which explains my slip of the tongue. There's something new under my mattress this week, and soon (when Bubby doesn't need my help with the kreplach) I will shut the door to my room and retrieve it, the wonderful leather-bound volume with its heady new-book smell. It's a section of the Talmud, with the forbidden English translation, and it's thousands of pages long, so it holds the promise of weeks of titillating reading. I can't believe I will finally be able to decode ancient Talmudic discourse designed specifically to keep out ignoramuses like me. Zeidy won't let me read the Hebrew books he keeps locked in his closet: they are only for men, he says; girls belong in the kitchen. But I'm so curious about his learning, and what exactly is written in the books he spends so many hours bent over, quivering with scholarly ecstasy. The few bits of watered-down wisdom my teachers supply in school only make me hunger for more. I want to know the truth about Rachel, Rabbi Akiva's wife, who tended her home in poverty for twelve years while her husband studied Torah in some foreign land. How could the spoiled daughter of a rich man possibly resign herself to such misery? My teachers say she was a saint, but it has to be more complicated than that.

Why would she marry a poor, ignorant man like Akiva in the first place? It couldn't be that he was good-looking, because then she wouldn't agree to his twelve-year trip. There has to be a reason, and if no one will tell me, then it's my job to find out.

I purchased the Schottenstein translation of the Talmud last week at the Judaica store in Borough Park. The small shop was empty, lit only by the weak strands of sunlight filtering in through the grimy windows. The silver dust bunnies seemed suspended in the beams of light, floating slowly upward with the force of a weak draft from a heating vent. I hid in the shadows of the staggering bookshelves as I mumbled to the bookseller that the book was for my cousin, that I had been asked to purchase it. I wondered if my nervousness was evident; surely my deception was written on my forehead, just as Zeidy always warned me it would be. *"Der emes shteit oif di shteren,"* Zeidy says. "No matter how convincingly you lie, your forehead gives you away." I imagine words etched into my skin, glowing like neon in the dark, my lanky brown bangs swept upward by a sudden breeze.

There is only one man ever working in that tiny bookstore on New Utrecht Avenue, as I have gleaned from the many reconnaissance trips I have made. He is old, with shaky hands and eyes that blink unsteadily, and as he wrapped the large, ungainly book in brown paper, I couldn't quite believe I'd gotten away with it. Maybe this man couldn't read foreheads, or I had succeeded in looking stupid, keeping my eyes flat and lifeless. He took my sixty dollars, most of it in singles and earned from babysitting jobs, counting it slowly before nodding his head. "It's *gut*," he said: I could go. I tried to exit the shop nonchalantly, and it was only once I was all the way down the block that I started skipping in uncontained joy. The illicit thrill of what I had just done made my knees tremble on the bus ride home to Williamsburg. Surely anyone could see the mischief I had been up to. The men sat in the front section of the bus, thankfully turned safely away from me, but the women with their kerchief-wrapped heads and thick stockings seemed to stare accusingly at me and the hefty parcel in my lap.

Walking down Penn Street, I clutched the brown paper package to my chest, my legs jerky and electrified by a mixture of fear and triumph. I

avoided the gaze of passersby, terrified of running into a suspicious neighbor. What if someone asked me what I was carrying? I skirted young boys
careening by on shabby bicycles and teenagers pushing their younger
siblings in squeaky-wheeled prams. Everyone was outside on this balmy
spring day, and the last half block seemed to take forever.

At home I rushed to hide the book under my mattress, pushing it all
the way in just in case. I smoothed the sheets and blankets and draped
the bedspread so that it hung to the floor. I sat down at the edge of the
bed and felt guilt wash over me so suddenly that the strength of it kept
me pinned there.

I wanted to forget that this day had ever happened. All through
Shabbos the book burned beneath my mattress, alternately chastising
me and beckoning to me. I ignored the call; it was too dangerous, there
were too many people around. What would Zeidy say if he knew? Even
Bubby would be horrified, I knew.

Sunday stretches ahead of me like an unopened *krepela*, a soft,
doughy day encapsulating a secret filling. All I have to do is help Bubby
with the cooking, then I will have the rest of the afternoon free to spend
as I please. Bubby and Zeidy have been invited to a cousin's bar mitzvah
today, which means I will have at least three hours of uninterrupted privacy. There is still a slab of chocolate cake in the freezer that I'm sure
Bubby, with her spotty memory, won't miss. Could this afternoon get any
better?

After Zeidy's heavy footfalls fade down the stairs, and I watch from
my second-floor bedroom window as my grandparents get into the taxi, I
slide the book out from under the mattress and place it reverently on my
desk. The pages are made of waxy, translucent paper, and they are each
packed with text: the original words of the Talmud as well as the English
translation, and the rabbinical discourse that fills up the bottom half of
each page. I like the discussions best, records of the conversations the
ancient rabbis held about each holy phrase in the Talmud.

On the sixty-fifth page the rabbis are arguing about King David and
his ill-gotten wife Bathsheba, a mysterious biblical tale about which
I've always been curious. From the fragments mentioned, it appears that
Bathsheba was already married when David laid his eyes upon her, but he

was so attracted to her that he deliberately sent her husband, Uriah, to the front lines so that he would be killed in war, leaving Bathsheba free to remarry. Afterward, when David had finally taken poor Bathsheba as his lawful wife, he looked into her eyes and saw in the mirror of her pupils the face of his own sin and was repulsed. After that, David refused to see Bathsheba again, and she lived the rest of her life in the king's harem, ignored and forgotten.

I now see why I'm not allowed to read the Talmud. My teachers have always told me, "David had no sins. David was a saint. It is forbidden to cast aspersions on God's beloved son and anointed leader." Is this the same illustrious ancestor the Talmud is referring to?

Not only did David cavort with his many wives, but he had unmarried female companions as well, I discover. They are called concubines. I whisper aloud this new word, *con-cu-bine,* and it doesn't sound illicit, the way it should, it only makes me think of a tall, stately tree. The concubine tree. I picture beautiful women dangling from its branches. *Con-cu-bine.*

Bathsheba wasn't a concubine because David honored her by taking her as his wife, but the Talmud says she was the only woman David chose who wasn't a virgin. I think of the beautiful woman on the olive oil bottle, the extra-virgin. The rabbis say that God only intended virgins for David and that his holiness would have been defiled had he stayed with Bathsheba, who had already been married.

King David is the yardstick, they say, against whom we are all measured in heaven. Really, how bad can my small stash of English books be, next to concubines?

I am not aware at this moment that I have lost my innocence. I will realize it many years later. One day I will look back and understand that just as there was a moment in my life when I realized where my power lay, there was also a specific moment when I stopped believing in authority just for its own sake and started coming to my own conclusions about the world I lived in.

At the time, the problem with losing my innocence was that it made it difficult to keep pretending. Inside me a conflict was brewing madly between my own thoughts and the teachings I was absorbing. Occasionally this tension would boil over my smooth facade, and others would try to remove me from the flames of curiosity before I went too far.

I don't hear the alarm go off on Monday morning, and when I finally wake up, it's 8:40 and I don't have time to do anything but get dressed and fly out the door. I pull on the thick black stockings that Bubby washed yesterday and dried on the porch clothesline; the fabric is stiff and cold from the chilly autumn air and won't conform to my legs, wrinkling unattractively around my knees and ankles. In the bathroom I peer into the cracked mirror under the light of a fluorescent bulb and poke at the blackheads on my nose. My hair is squashed and limp, my eyes storm gray beneath swollen eyelids.

I've forgotten to put a shirt on beneath my sweater. There's a new rule about no knits directly on the body. Now that we are growing up, my teachers say, we have to be careful to avoid clingy fabrics. I could get in trouble, but it's ten minutes to nine and if I leave now, I will make it just in time to be let into the cafeteria for morning prayers. I can't afford to be late today; I already have too many demerits stacked against me. Forget the blouse.

I race into school just as the junior secretary is about to close the door to the prayer room. She sighs when she sees me, and I know she can't decide whether to let me in or make me wait in the principal's office for a late note. I squeeze past her through the half-open door with a sheepish smile. "Thanks," I say breathlessly, ignoring her scowl.

Downstairs an eighth grader has already been chosen to lead the prayer session. I slide quickly into one of the empty spots in the back rows, next to Raizy, who is still running a comb through her knotted brown hair. I keep my eyes down, in the general direction of the prayer book on my lap, but unfocused, so that the words are blurred on the page. I move my lips to look like I'm praying when the senior secretary walks down the aisle, checking to see if we are all following along. Raizy slips the comb underneath a page in her prayer book and chants loudly along with the others.

We are praying to the God of our people, whom we call *Hashem*, literally, "the Name." The true name for God is devastatingly holy and evocative; to utter it would represent a death wish, so we have safe nick-names for him instead: the Holy Name, the One, the Only, the Creator, the Destroyer, the Overseer, the King of All Kings, the One True Judge, the Merciful Father, Master of the Universe, O Great Architect, a long list of names for all his attributes. For the sake of this divinity I must surrender myself each morning, body and soul; for this God, my teachers say, I must learn silence so that only his voice can be heard through me. God lives in my soul, and I must spend my life scrubbing my soul clean of any trace of sin so that it deserves to host his presence. Repentance is a daily chore; at each morning prayer session we repent in advance for the sins we will commit that day. I look around at the others, who must sin-cerely believe in their inherent evil, as they are shamelessly crying and wailing to God to help them expunge the *yetzer hara*, or evil inclination, from their consciousness.

Although I talk to God, it is not through prayer. I talk to him in my mind, and even I will admit that I do not come to God humbly, as I should. I talk to him frankly, as I would to a friend, and I'm constantly asking him for favors. Still, I feel like God and I are on pretty good terms, relatively speaking. This morning, as everyone sways passionately around me, I stand calmly in the sea of young girls, asking God to make this day a bearable one.

I'm very easy to pick on. The teachers know I'm not important, that no one will defend me. I'm not a rabbi's daughter, so when they get angry, I'm the perfect scapegoat. I make sure never to look up from my siddur during prayer, but Chavie Halberstam, the rabbi's daughter, can elbow her friend Elky to point out the toilet paper stuck to the teacher's shoe and it's as if nothing happened. If I so much as smirk, I'm singled out immediately. This is why I need God on my side; I have no one else to stick up for me.

The minute I walk into my fourth-floor classroom this morning, I'm accosted by Mrs. Meizlish, our Yiddish teacher. Her unibrow is knitted in anger. I call her Mrs. Meizel, or Mrs. Mouse, behind her back. I can't help it; her name practically begs to be made fun of, and there's something about the way her upper lip lifts over her two front teeth that makes her look genuinely ratlike. She doesn't like me very much.

"You're not wearing a shirt under your sweater," Mrs. Mouse barks at me from behind the heavy steel desk at the front of the classroom, twisting her head toward me so that her thick black braid whips behind her like a tail. "Don't even think about going to your desk. You're going straight to the principal's office."

I back away slowly, half glad at being banished. If I'm lucky, the principal will be busy all morning, and I will get to sit in her office instead of bungling through Yiddish period. It's a fair trade-off. Sure, I'll get a yelling; maybe I will even get sent home to change. If Zeidy isn't home, I could while away most of the afternoon in the name of "changing." Perhaps finish this new book I'm reading, about an Indian girl who falls in love with an American colonist in the seventeenth century. But there's always a chance he could be at the house. Then he will want to know why I was sent home from school, and I can't bear the look of crushed disappointment on his face when he finds out I'm not the model student he wants me to be.

"*Nu*, Devoireh," he groans pleadingly. "You can't be a good girl for your *zeide*, so I can have a little *nachas*, a little pride, from you?" His Yiddish is heavy and European-accented and has an ever-present wrenchingly sad rhythm that makes me feel old and tired whenever I hear it.

Maybe I shouldn't ask this of God, this wish to be sent home to change just to avoid a couple of hours of school, not if there's a chance I might have to sit down to a lecture about obedience and honor at the dining room table.

Rebbetzin Kleinman's office is a mess. I press one shoulder against the creaky door to shove it open, moving boxes of envelopes and pamphlets away from the doorway so I can tiptoe inside, careful not to tip over any of the open boxes perched at the edge of her desk. There seems to be no free space for me to sit down; the one other chair is a wooden stool piled with prayer books. I perch on the edge of the windowsill, the section where the paint isn't peeling too badly, and prepare for a long wait. I have a special prayer for these occasions, Psalm 13, my favorite, and I always repeat it thirteen times in these situations. "Consider and hear me, Hashem," I mumble quietly in Hebrew. Dramatic pleas, but desperate times call for desperate measures. Also, it's the shortest psalm in the book, thus the easiest to memorize. *Please let me not be in enough trouble to have Zeidy notified,* I pray silently. *Let her just give me a scolding and I will never forget to wear a shirt again. Please, God.* "How long shall my enemy be exalted over me . . ."

Outside the secretaries are gossiping loudly, devouring the snacks they confiscated during morning prayers from the few kids who hadn't managed to eat breakfast and had hoped for a chance to get something into their growling stomachs before first period. The next break isn't until 10:45. "How long will you hide your face from me, Hashem . . ."

I hear footsteps out front, and I straighten up quickly as the principal heaves her considerable bulk into the office, red-faced with the effort. I finish up that last round of the psalm in my head: *"I will sing unto Hashem, because he has dealt bountifully with me."* It takes her a few minutes to get settled into the enormous armchair behind her desk, her breathing loud and labored even after she has been seated.

"So," she says, turning to look at me appraisingly, "what are we going to do about you?"

I smile sheepishly. It's not my first time in this office.

"Your teacher says you're having trouble following the rules. I don't understand why you can't be like everyone else. No one else seems to have any problems wearing shirts under their sweaters. Why do you?"

I don't answer. I'm not supposed to answer. All her questions are rhetorical; I know that from experience. I'm just supposed to sit quietly with my head down and my expression humble and contrite, and wait it out. After a few moments, she'll wind down and become more affable, looking for a compromise. I can tell she's tired of having to discipline me. She's not one of those principals who enjoy the thrill of the chase, like the one who used to make me stand outside her office for hours in the sixth grade.

The verdict is in.

"Go home and change," Rebbetzin Kleinman says, sighing in defeat. "And don't let me catch you breaking the modesty rules again."

I slip out of her office gratefully and take the four flights of stairs two at a time. The moment when the spring sunshine hits my face is like the taste of Zeidy's kiddush wine, my first breath of fresh air a long, slow tingle down my throat.

At the intersection of Marcy Avenue and Hooper Street, I cross over to the other side without even thinking about it, to avoid the massive Catholic church that graces the corner. I keep my eyes averted from the seductive statues staring at me through the gated enclosure. To look directly at the church grounds is to look at evil, Bubby says when we pass this corner; it's an open invitation to Satan. I cross back over at Hewes Street, quickening my pace because I can feel the eyes on my back, and I picture the stone figures coming to life, lumbering down Marcy Avenue, shattering a little with every step.

I hug my arms, rubbing them to get the goose bumps to go down. In my rush I almost collide with a man walking in the other direction, mumbling prayers to himself, his earlocks swinging. I have to step awkwardly into the gutter to avoid him. Funny, I notice suddenly, there are no other women on the street. I've never been on the street at this time of day before, when all the girls are in school and mothers are busy cleaning house and preparing dinner. Williamsburg seems hollow and empty. I quicken my pace, jumping over the puddles of dirty water shopkeepers spill out into the street. The only sound is the harsh echo of my own staccato footsteps on the cracked asphalt.

I take a left turn on Penn Street, passing Mr. Mayer's grocery on the corner, and leap up the steps to my brownstone home. Pushing open the heavy double doors, I listen for any sound but hear none. I close the doors gently just in case. My shoes make faint clicking noises as I climb the staircase, but if Zeidy is in his office downstairs, he doesn't hear them. I take the key from under the doormat that Bubby leaves for me when she goes away, and sure enough, the lights are off and the house is quiet and still.

I change quickly, buttoning a long-sleeved blue oxford shirt all the way to the top so that the collar is tight against my neck. I put the sweater back on over the shirt and pull out the two collar points so that they rest neatly on the navy blue wool, and I turn twice before the mirror, checking to see if I'm tucked in on all sides. I look like a fine girl, just like Zeidy wants me to be, just like teachers always call Chavie, the rabbi's daughter. Fine, like expensive fabric, like good china, like wine.

I hurry back through the empty streets to school. The men shuffle home from their learning sessions to eat the lunch their wives have prepared, dodging me on the sidewalk, making a show of looking the other way. I want to shrink into myself.

Inside the school building I expand in relief. From the safe vantage of my classroom I gaze out the window overlooking Marcy Avenue and marvel anew at the absence of color and life down below, in stark contrast to the buzzing of a thousand girls pent up in this square-block, five-story building. Occasionally a young man, dressed all in black, straggles up Marcy Avenue toward the Satmar shul on Rodney Street, hands swirling through the *payos* dangling near each cheek, keeping them curled into neat spirals. The older men wear their *payos* wound tightly around their ears and use their hands instead to smooth down their prolific beards, even as they are buffeted like flags in the wind. All of them walk quickly, heads down.

In our community, markers of piety are very important. It is imperative that we appear at all times to be pious, to be true agents of God. Appearances are everything; they have the power to affect who we are on the inside, but also they tell the world that we are different, that they must keep away. I think much of the reason Satmar Hasids dress in such a specific, conspicuous manner is so both insiders and outsiders will remember the vast chasm that lies between our two worlds. "Assimilation," my teacher always says, "was the reason for the Holocaust. We try to blend in, and God punishes us for betraying him."

Snap. Mrs. Meizlish flicks her thumb and forefinger loudly under my nose. I start.

"Why aren't you looking in?" she asks sternly.

I shuffle nervously through the loose-leaf binder on my desk, looking for the appropriate stencil. Mrs. Meizlish has the whole class looking at me now, making a show of waiting for me to get myself together. I can feel my cheeks redden. I think we are studying *berachos* now, and I know I have the "Guide to Proper Blessings" somewhere in here. I make a show of finding the right place, and Mrs. Meizlish gives me the barest nod of approval.

"Which blessing for strawberries?" Mrs. Meizlish, still standing in front of my desk, asks in the special Yiddish singsong.

"*Bo-rei pri ha'ad-am-ah,*" the class sings back in unison. I whisper along halfheartedly so that she can hear me, hoping she'll move back to the center of the classroom so I don't have to stare up at her chin, covered in a wash of black baby hairs.

After recess, it's time for the daily modesty lecture. Mrs. Meizlish continues where we left off in the story of Rachel, Rabbi Akiva's saintly wife, and the rest of the class stares raptly at her. She has a good way of telling a story, Mrs. Meizlish, with her thick baritone that she modulates into an erratic rhythm that never quite lets you get comfortable. She always pauses at the best parts of the story to smooth a few stray hairs into her braid or pick an invisible piece of lint off her skirt, while the suspense builds and the girls gape anxiously at her.

Not only was Rachel, wife of Akiva, a truly righteous woman, but she was also an exceptionally modest person, to the point where—and here Mrs. Meizlish pauses for effect—she once stuck pins into her calves to keep her skirt from lifting in the breeze and exposing her kneecaps.

I cringe when I hear that. I can't stop picturing the punctured calves of a woman, and in my mind the pricking takes place over and over again, each time drawing more blood, tearing muscle, gashing skin. Is that really what God wanted of Rachel? For her to mutilate herself so that no one could catch a glimpse of her knees?

Mrs. Meizlish writes the word ERVAH in big block letters on the chalkboard. "*Ervah* refers to any part of a woman's body that must be covered, starting from the collarbone, ending at the wrists and knees. When *ervah* is exposed, men are commanded to leave its presence. Prayers or blessings may not be uttered when *ervah* is in sight."

"Don't you see, girls," Mrs. Meizlish proclaims, "how easy it is to fall into that category of *choteh umachteh es harabim,* the sinner who makes others sin, the worst sinner of all, simply by failing to uphold the highest standards of modesty? Every time a man catches a glimpse of any part of your body that the Torah says should be covered, he is sinning. But worse, you have caused him to sin. It is you who will bear the responsibility of his sin on Judgment Day."

When the bell rings to signal final dismissal, I have my book bag packed and ready, jacket in hand. I hurry out of class the second the teacher gives us the signal, hoping to make it at least to the second floor before the staircases become choked by the crowds. Sure enough, I race down the first two flights but come to a short stop as I round the corner to the second floor, where groups of chattering students squeeze through the doorways, pushing and shoving through the crush on the staircase. I'm forced to take it one slow step at a time, as I wait for the other girls, who are in no rush, to move. It seems to take forever to descend those last two flights, and I feel as if I am holding my breath, until I finally burst out of the stairway on the first floor, zigzagging through clusters of first graders to get to the exit. I cut a straight path through the front yard with its high brick walls topped with loops of barbed wire, gallop down the wide stone steps, and spare only one last glance at the headless gargoyles jutting from the turrets of the crumbling stone building.

The new spring air thrills me as I run, shoes slapping loudly on the pavement, down Marcy Avenue, leaving the slow-moving crowd behind me, racing to be the first one home. The streets are full, swollen with schoolgirls in pleated skirts spilling over into the grimy gutters. Cars honk as they drive slowly past. I feel my shirt collar digging into my neck, and I open the top button and shake the collar loose, inhaling deeply. There are no men to be found, not now, not at this hour, when the street belongs to me, and to me alone.

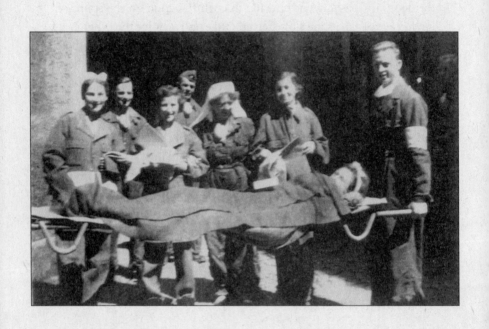

2

The Age of My Innocence

*The Hasidim had great leaders—tzaddikim, they were
called, righteous ones. Each Hasidic community had its
own tzaddik, and his people would go to him with all their
problems, and he would give them advice. They followed
these leaders blindly.*

—From The Chosen, *by Chaim Potok*

Zeidy wakes up at four in the morning to go study Torah at the synagogue
across the street. Just about when I wake up, at eight o'clock, he comes
home for a spartan breakfast of whole wheat toast, American cheese, and
a slice of pale green Italian pepper. He sits across from me at the small
kitchen table and I watch curiously as he eats, ritualizing the process
with precise motions, cutting his food into small pieces and chewing
contemplatively. Often he becomes so immersed in the process of eating
that he doesn't respond when I speak to him.

He says the blessing after meals loudly before retiring to his office
downstairs, ostensibly to work on whatever real estate project or finance
deal he is involved in at the moment. No one knows what Zeidy actually

does for work. *Is he the merchant or the scholar?* I always wonder; where does he fit into the ancient trade-off between the tribes of Issachar and Zebulon?

Of the founders of the twelve tribes, Zebulon was a ship merchant and Issachar was a Torah scholar, and in order for Issachar to support his family and Zebulon to gather merit for the afterlife, they made a trade: Zebulon would support Issachar if he could garner fifty percent of the rewards Issachar accrued with his scholarship. An agreement was reached, one that was carried down for thousands of years, and in present-day Williamsburg, the trade-off still flourishes.

Learning collectives called *kollels* abound in Williamsburg. The collectives are full of earnest young men bent over ancient texts, while they and their families receive a special stipend from the wealthier members of the community. *Benk-kvetshers*, these scholars are called sometimes, literally "bench squeezers," because of their consistent presence on the primitive wooden benches lining the *kollel* buildings.

If you're not rich, you might as well be a Talmud student. You'll have prestige. Every young girl of marriageable age wants to be set up with a brilliant young scholar so she can brag to all her friends about what a catch she got, and so she can gather a luxurious trousseau funded by her wealthy father. Money is always paired with scholarship. So it has been for countless generations.

Zeidy is considered both a scholar and a businessman in this community. Immersed in financial reports by day and the Talmud by night, he is a jack of both trades, but is he a master as well? I don't know much about Zeidy's life. We may have money, but we sure don't spend it. Bubby has been begging to change the worn blue carpet in the dining room for years now, but Zeidy insists that *luxus,* luxury, is not something to be enjoyed in this lifetime. "A broadened mind, not body," says Zeidy, "is the pursuit of life. Luxury will only deaden your perceptions, numb your soul."

Is it a luxury if it spares Bubby the difficulties involved in cleaning challah crumbs and grape juice stains embedded in the fabric? She wants hardwood floors so badly.

I wear hand-me-down clothes, while the rest of the girls at school wear the latest fashions from Friedman's Dry Goods store. Everyone knows pleats are out, argyle is in, but by the time I get to wear it, it will be too late.

Zeidy says to bear my suffering with dignity, like a banner. "You are the chosen one," he says, "and that is a garment more royal than any found in a dry goods store."

Every Jewish girl, Zeidy says, is a *bas melech*, a daughter of a king. If your father was such an important person, Zeidy asks me, as a king, would you go around embarrassing him by wearing torn and dirty clothes? No, he pontificates, slamming his palms on the table excitedly, you would behave in a manner fit only for royalty, because the rest of the world is looking at you to show them what true majesty is all about. In the same way, Zeidy goes on to explain, we are God's chosen people, and we must comport ourselves as would befit the children of an illustrious monarch, so as not to embarrass our true father in heaven.

Our teachers in school repeat this metaphor to us many times over. I feel tempted at times to ask Zeidy if I should run in the streets screaming like a lunatic, as would befit a daughter of my true, biological father, who walks aimlessly in stained shirts, talking to himself, but I never do, because I don't want to see the pained look on Zeidy's face when I remind him of his suffering. To think that Zeidy survived the war so that he could bring more Jewish children into the world, to replace some of those who were lost, and then from his own children should come his suffering!

My father wasn't the first misfortune to befall our family, and he wasn't the last. Only recently my uncle Shulem's son went insane at the age of seventeen. Baruch's nervous collapse hit Zeidy especially hard. He had been the prodigy of his family; his rabbis and teachers praised him for his outstanding Talmudic genius. By the time Baruch was diagnosed with acute paranoid schizophrenia, he had lost the ability to form coherent sentences, speaking in a strange language no one could comprehend. Zeidy kept him locked up in a room in his office for months, slipping trays of food that Bubby had prepared through a little slot in the door. He didn't want to release him, fearing the damage that could be done to our family if we had another raving lunatic roaming around Williamsburg. One night Baruch got out somehow, smashing through the door with his fists, emerging with bloody gashes on his arms. His screams were guttural;

they burst endlessly out of his throat like those of a wild animal in pain. He destroyed everything he could get his hands on. They had to wrestle him down in the hallway, the paramedics, and sedate him. I watched from the upstairs landing, tears streaming down my face.

Later, when Bubby finished cleaning up the mess he had left, she sat white-faced at the kitchen table. I heard her whispering into the phone as I folded dish towels. He had defecated everywhere, leaving neat piles of stool on the carpet. My heart hurt for Bubby, who had never thought it was a good idea to keep Baruch locked up downstairs but had acquiesced like she did every time Zeidy made a unilateral decision.

Still, I understood why Zeidy had acted the way he did; in our community it was unheard of to place a mentally ill person in an institution. How could we trust an asylum run by gentiles to care for a Hasidic Jew and meet his needs? Even the insane are not exempt from the laws and customs of Judaism. In a way, Zeidy was brave to undertake the care of Baruch's soul, even though he was ill equipped to deal with the effects of his psychosis. I felt sorry for Baruch, who would surely be locked up in a strange place that didn't understand him, who would never be able to rejoin the only community he had ever known.

It is from children that you have the most *nachas*, the most pride, Zeidy always says, but also the most pain. *Tzaar gidul bunim*, the agony that comes with raising children, is the ultimate test of faith, he feels. God gives us children so that we may struggle all our lives to provide for them, protect them, and shape them into devout servants of Hashem.

Zeidy comes from a legacy of oppression. His ancestors lived in Eastern Europe for generations, enduring pogroms that were not unlike the persecution during Hitler's reign. I can't comprehend how a person who comes from so much pain and loss can perpetuate his own oppression. In small ways Zeidy cages himself, depriving himself of harmless joys, and yet it seems the very deprivation fulfills him. Is it guilt that drives my grandparents to inflict continuous suffering upon themselves, bear laborious burdens, never once accepting the possibility of easement?

I think pain makes Zeidy feel clean, purified. Every Friday night he places his palms on the east wall of the dining room and prays his own personal prayer to God, and when he prays, the tears cascade down his cheeks like rain, like I've never seen on any other man, and I think it makes him feel better, it allows him to live in his life without feeling repulsed by the abundance that surrounds him. Zeidy believes that souls come into this world to endure and be cleansed for the world to come, and the trials of life give him great comfort. Deprivation doesn't make me feel that way at all. It makes me feel dirty and irritable, and crying chokes up my throat and nostrils until I can't breathe past the pain. Still, I carry it too, just like all of Bubby and Zeidy's children and grandchildren. We too are part of the legacy of loss.

"I survived only so that you could be born," Bubby reminds me every so often. Zeidy agrees. "So many times, I wondered why I was allowed to live," he ruminates. "But with time it became clear to me that all of my children and grandchildren had to be born, and it is my responsibility to make sure they grow up to be good Jews, *ehrliche Yidden*, to give meaning to my survival. I can't possibly imagine wasting this precious gift I was given, not when so many others were deprived of it." He takes the leftovers out of the fridge and stirs them together in one pot for his dinner. He won't let Bubby throw any kind of food away.

Bubby cuts the moldy parts out of the vegetables and puts them back in the fridge. Freshly baked cakes and pies are stored in the freezer for special occasions, and after they have been cut up and enjoyed, Bubby wraps every leftover crumb and stores it again. I long for novelty snacks such as chocolate bars and potato chips, and now that I'm growing, I find myself eternally hungry, the space between mealtimes a yawning gap in my stomach.

The hunger I feel is physical, but it is more than that too; it is a hole that needs to be filled indiscriminately, with food being the convenient option. How to explain my relationship with the food that Bubby puts on my plate? I build elaborate fantasies around each dish, making up stories of how each came into existence, feeding an appetite that feels bigger than the natural bellyache of hunger. There is a yawning chasm in me that threatens to grow wider if I don't stuff the gap with as much as I can manage. Food is a temporary fix, but it's better than staying with that emptiness.

Lately I've found myself doing the strangest things. When Bubby

and Zeidy go away and I am left alone in the house, I can't stop thinking about the cakes in the freezer. Their presence calls to me so loudly
I become distracted by it, unable to focus on even the most exciting
book. Guiltily, I open the freezer, gazing at the stacked, foil-wrapped pans
of apple pie, chocolate brownies, filbert fudge, and marble cake. Only
a sliver, I tell myself, carefully sliding the uppermost pan out from the
shelf. But once the cake is uncovered before me on the kitchen table, I
can't stop myself from cutting slabs of it, stuffing it into my mouth with
my fingers and swallowing as fast as I can, spurred by the fear that I may
be caught red-handed. As I cram hunks of frosting-laced brownie down
my throat, I watch as fat crumbs fall all around me, and when I'm older
I will remember the sense of desperation I felt, seeing myself reduced to
such circumstances. Later I scrub the kitchen floor painstakingly, determined to remove every shred of evidence; I feel as guilty for eating as I do
for reading. I am left with the constant feeling of having done something
awful, and yet I am still hungry.

When I grow up, I'm never going to be stingy when it comes to food,
I resolve. Sometimes I crave the simple pleasure of a fresh tomato, with
firm skin and tender flesh. I pinch quarters from the *pushka*, the box
where Bubby puts the charity money, and buy rosy slabs of watermelon
to eat on the porch, dripping juice and black seeds onto the flowerpots.
Little seedlings push themselves out between the petunias weeks later
and Bubby plucks them curiously, examining them before pronouncing
them weeds.

In the backyard, strawberry plants begin to bud along the limestone
pathway, and the wild roses snake their way up the barbed-wire fence at
the back. The loganberry tree hangs heavily over the porch. Bubby is
worried it will prevent the sunshine from getting to her tulips, but Zeidy
says we can't cut it down because it's a fruit tree and biblical law prohibits
cutting down fruit trees. Even pruning is questionable.

By the time Passover rolls around, the berries will be falling sloppily
onto the porch, mushy splats of dark purple staining the fake grass carpet.
More cleaning for Bubby.

• • •

The Jewish bookstore in Borough Park sells books that Zeidy doesn't approve of. He likes me to read in Yiddish, gaudily illustrated tales of legendary tzaddikim, who perform predictable miracles through prayer and exercises in faith, whose stories spill abruptly out over the length of twenty or so pages of monotonous language. He brings home Yiddish weeklies, periodicals depicting news mined from old journals and encyclopedias, outdated essays on midcentury politics or Jewish cantorial music. I know there are other works written in Yiddish, but they are banned. In fact there is a whole world of Yiddish literature I will never be allowed to read. Sholem Aleichem is forbidden in this house; he was an *apikores*, a so-called liberated Jew. Satmar people do not read anything written by liberated Jews, even if it is written in the holy language of Yiddish.

Still, the Jewish bookstore sells everything that pertains to Jews, and I feel somehow less guilty bringing home a book from there than from the library. If I get caught, I assume it's a lesser offense. I am shocked by the irreverent tone in *Tevye the Milkman*; who knew anything written in Yiddish could sound so crass and offensive? I've always thought of it as a formal language, but apparently there are many Yiddish words that have gone out of fashion, because the Yiddish of today's Williamsburg is nothing like the earthy, naughty Yiddish of the nineteenth century. It makes my cheeks burn just to read it.

By far the most exciting read is *The Chosen*. I opened it to the first page in the bookstore out of mild curiosity. I had assumed from its cover, a depiction of an earlocked Hasid clutching a prayer book, that it would be a boring story about a good Jewish boy. But to hear the familiar streets of Williamsburg described in the opening chapter as "cracked squares of cement . . . softened in the stifling summers," juxtaposed with descriptions of the other ethnic forces that dominate my small, crowded district of Brooklyn, was like an immediate jolt to my literary sensibilities. A book about my home! Terms and references that, finally, felt familiar to me! What a wonderful new sensation, to delve into the pages of a book and realize that the familiar sense of alienation, of confusion, was gone. How easy it was to identify with the characters and story lines in *The*

Chosen, for they were still going on around me right now, to this day. The Williamsburg of Chaim Potok had changed, surely, but its essence, its history, was still the same. I was certain that if Zeidy caught me with this book, it could hardly offend him. After all, this book was about us. If there was a book about us out there, then perhaps we weren't so strange after all.

Although I have heard many times the history of our little Satmar community, I do not know much about the history of the Hasidic movement itself, and *The Chosen* is my first jarring introduction to my past. I begin to understand the link between Sholem Aleichem's bawdy characters and myself. I had once thought myself far removed from tales of the Diaspora, but there is, apparently, something of a connection between Hasidic Jews and a certain provincial naïveté, or even ignorance. It is an innocence that Hasids value, that they refer to as purity and righteousness, and it challenges the native scholar, who must struggle to maintain that innocence while still sharpening his mind over the Talmud. I suddenly see my grandfather through new eyes. I have always thought him to be possessed of a brilliant mind, but it is Talmudic genius that he is known for. Chaya often shakes her head and sighs about this, telling me Zeidy will never be able to apply his scholarly intelligence to practical matters. His street smarts, she says, are nonexistent. Still, what if he wants it this way? What if this is the way of life he has chosen, to follow in the footsteps of his ancestors who walked blindly into the traps the gentiles set for them, turning to God instead of their own wits for survival? Genius can only be put to good use in the study of the Torah. For all else, one must rely on faith.

Because it is the first time I'm reading *The Chosen*, I side with Danny, the Hasidic boy, in almost everything. His father's Talmudic arguments are what feel familiar to me, and Danny's outlook strikes me as innately correct even before I've fully thought it through. For every Zionist and liberated attitude that Reuven's character introduces, I have a counterargument ready. Later, in my adulthood, I will read the book again, even watch the movie, and understand that I wasn't equipped, as a child, to make room for arguments that would undermine every single choice made for me, that would shatter the foundations of my very existence. I would see that I had to believe everything I was taught, if only to survive. For a long time I wouldn't be ready to accept that my worldview could be wrong, but I do not look back with shame at my ignorance. It is that innocence that Zeidy strove to instill in me, the sweet, childlike naïveté of my ancestors that is supposed to last on into adulthood and even old age, and that I would eventually shed almost all of, except the very basic root of it at the heart of my nature. Years later, even when I gazed at the world with eyes wide open, I would still be innocent in my heart.

Thwack. I love the sound the walnut shell makes when it finally gives way under my grip, cracking neatly along its own center. The nutcracker has already forced blisters out of my palm where my hand presses against its two sides, coaxing the hard nutshell into submission. I'm making *charoses* for the Passover seder, and Zeidy says on Passover it's forbidden to use the ready-shelled walnuts, based on the tiniest chance that they might have come into contact with *chametz*, so we crack all the nuts ourselves. Or at least I crack them. Bubby's grating the horseradish for the bitter *marror*, with her face turned away from the bowl to avoid the stinging fumes. Her eyes are red and teary. The bitter herbs will be eaten later to commemorate the slave labor Jews were forced to do in Egypt, but I think Bubby has already had her fair share of that reminder for today.

Bubby wipes away another tear and takes a deep breath before attacking the stubborn tuber with renewed zeal. The horseradish is difficult to grate, and Bubby has only a small pile of shredded *marror* in the bowl. Small in stature, she hunches her shoulders as she puts all her strength into the task. I don't think of Bubby as a physically strong woman, even though she's borne eleven children and been through the worst hell imaginable in the concentration camps. She doesn't sleep very well, and most days it seems as if her chores keep adding up even as she finishes the last of them. The homemade borscht, the pickles she sours on her own, even the nuts have to be cracked before they can be used to make *charoses*.

I can't take it anymore.

"Bubby, stop! I have an idea. Don't move, I'll be right back."

I race to my bedroom and rummage through my bottom dresser

drawer until I've found what I'm looking for. Back in the kitchen, Bubby laughs out loud when she sees me. I'm wearing my swim goggles and nose clip, remnants from last year's summer exploits.

"See?" I say in a high-pitched, nasal voice. "Now I can grate the *marror* without having to worry about the fumes." The goggles are fogged at the edges, but I can see Bubby shaking with laughter as she hands me the grater.

I slip on a pair of rubber gloves and rub the radish vigorously against the serrated plane of the grater. Sure enough, I'm barely affected by the sting. On the other side of the table, Bubby cracks the walnuts efficiently with one hand on the cracker, flicking them out, still whole, into the bowl of *charoses*. She shakes her head in both wonder and amusement as I work my way down to the very root of the horseradish. I'm so proud to prove myself useful in the kitchen, even if it is in a bizarre way.

"See? Now you have all the *marror* you could possibly need."

Everyone starts arriving for the seder just after Bubby has wiped down the plastic-covered kitchen counters. All the food has been prepared in special Passover jars and stacked in the foil-lined fridge. Aunt Rachel arrives first, with her three daughters in tow.

"*Gut yontif, gut yontif,*" Rachel announces loudly to no one in particular. She kisses Bubby on the cheek but her eyes are elsewhere, sweeping critically over the long dining table, which is groaning slightly in the middle where all the leaves have been inserted.

"*Mami,* your *tishtech* isn't long enough for the extension, you have to put a double. See, here, you can see the liner sticking out." Rachel clucks her tongue in dismay.

"I'll get another tablecloth," I volunteer. Rachel is already looking past me to the mirror, adjusting the front of her caramel-colored wig where the bangs dip into her left eye. Her long, slim-knuckled fingers smooth the heavily sprayed section expertly. Rachel is the only one in the family who wears one hundred percent human-hair wigs, not one synthetic hair in them, even though Zeidy is always warning us that one lenience leads to another. He warns us not to go down that treacherous path of *pritzus,* or promiscuity, where one misstep is all Satan needs to pull us into the abyss. Everyone knows Rachel is vain, that she buys her designer clothing at Saks and not at Daffy's discounts, that she styles her wigs in the latest looks and packs on her makeup before Shabbos so that it lasts even to the next day. I even heard her sister Chavie whisper one day that she stopped shaving her head and that she now has about three inches' growth already. Perhaps that is what Zeidy means about the path of *pritzus*: Rachel probably only thought about growing her hair in once she decided to push the leniency with wigs to the very limit. It's hard to stop at just a little bit, I can understand that, but Zeidy's solution to that problem is not exactly amenable to the average woman. He would have us renounce all vanity, but that would be unrealistic.

Roiza and Baila have their hair in fat curls still bouncy from the hot rollers their mother used, held in place by identical velvet headbands. The daughters closest to me in age, they sit primly on the edge of the plastic-slipcovered sofa, arms folded neatly in their laps. I eye their matching houndstooth skirts and soft black cashmere sweaters enviously. I didn't get new clothes for the holidays. I smooth the pleated velvet folds of my empire-waist dress, handed down from one of my aunt Faigy's daughters. The hem is frayed slightly, so that the burgundy velvet looks pink at the edges.

Baila is the pretty one, because she has blond hair. They say blond hair runs in the family, but I can barely coax a few summer highlights from my dishwater strands. Roiza is the dark one, but with big, pale blue eyes and luminous white skin. All of us have Bubby's prominent apple-shaped cheekbones.

I don't look like either of them, really. They look like Weissmans, like their father's side of the family, robust, with sneaky eyes that dart to and fro and a smile that's more of a smirk. I look like Bubby. I'm the only one who looks a lot like her. Most everyone else has my grandfather's genes, the Mendlowitz genes, the big nose, the blue eyes, and the fire-engine hair. I have Bubby's eyes, gray, heavy-lidded, secretive; her hair, not blond, not brown, but thick and strong, like the hair on her passport photo; her smile, close-lipped, frugal. It's just Bubby and me that exhibit the Fisher genes.

As I help Bubby with the second tablecloth, there's a knock at the door, and without waiting for a response, my aunt Chavie enters, with her baby boy nestled against her shoulder. Roiza and Baila run to take the baby from her, cooing excitedly to his sleeping figure, while Chavie and Rachel exchange a sisterly kiss and retreat to the kitchen with Bubby to gossip in Hungarian.

I watch the girls fuss over the baby. His tiny features curl up in annoyance as they stroke his cheek. His name is Shimon. He is a *muzinka*, an only child, born late. Chavie and Mordechai were married seventeen years before they had him. Everyone was so happy when he was born. Bubby cried at the circumcision ceremony. There is no greater curse than the curse of childlessness, Bubby said to me that day we were coming back from visiting Chavie at the hospital. Like with Auntie Sarah, a mercy on her soul, who died without ever having children.

"A curse on that Mengele, son of the devil, who scorched her insides with acid," she says, making a spitting sound and waving her hand to ward off the devil. When Shimon comes home from Maimonides Medical Center there is a thick red thread wrapped around his right wrist. No way the evil eye is touching this one.

I think of wearing a red thread too sometimes, but really, what would the evil eye want with me, in my worn velvet dress, with my hair, straight and limp, that's never seen a curler. I wonder what a velvet headband would look like in my hair.

By 9:30 p.m. the men can be heard clomping up the stairs, the freshly laid taps in their new holiday shoes colliding loudly with the tin sliders fastening the linoleum. I go to open the door, and they all stream past me, first Zeidy, followed by my uncles and cousins.

"*Gut yontif, gut yontif!*" A chorus of holiday greetings is heard all around. Bubby's sons kiss her on the cheek; her sons-in-law merely nod their heads respectfully. I kiss Zeidy's wrinkled hand and wish him a good *yontif*.

Zeidy is already wearing his white *kittel*, and I can see Bubby shaking her head when she notices the deep creases in the fabric. The others slip on their *kittels* in preparation for the seder, buttoning the long white linen coats all the way from the bottom to the top, then cinching them with a belt at the waist. They line up on the right side of the table, leaving the women to sit on the side closest to the kitchen. They are supposed to be angels tonight—that's why they wear the white *kittels*—but to me it just looks like they are wearing dresses.

As Zeidy prepares the kiddush, I fetch the Passover pillows and lay them out over the large armchair at the head of the table so that Zeidy can recline in true Haggadah fashion when eating the matzo. The others gather to the table, adults in the front and children in the back. Bubby has laid out all her best silver and the table is crowded with it, each wine flask and candlestick competing with the next, and the glare from the brass chandelier is so bright, it hurts to keep my eyes open.

We all stand for kiddush, with our own individual silver goblets filled to the brim with wine. We're supposed to drink it all after the blessing, down to the last drop to make room for the next cup, but I can barely manage a sip without grimacing. Bubby makes the Passover wine from scratch, and I've watched it ferment in the fridge for the past two weeks. Roiza laughs at my expression.

"What's the matter?" she asks, leaning close to me. "Too strong for you?"

"*Nu!*" Zeidy calls from the front. His hearing is excellent. "What is this, idle talk? On Pesach?"

I don't answer, but I elbow Roiza sharply in response. We all know there's no talking allowed at least until the eating starts. Until then we have to sit quietly as Zeidy plods through the Haggadah reading. I hope he doesn't spend too much time on his *drashah*, the annual sermon that's always about the same thing, but there's quite the crowd this year and that really gets him going. It's the first night of Passover, and that means that the last bite of matzo has to be eaten before 1:00 a.m. It's already 10:30 p.m. Surely that means Zeidy has no choice but to speed things up.

Sure enough, Zeidy pauses after the *Mah nishtanah* to place a marker in his Haggadah and close the book, pushing it aside. He's getting ready to tell the story.

"Here he goes," Roiza whispers into my ear. "Right on schedule."

"Roiza Miriam!" Zeidy calls out. He insists on calling all of us by our full names. Without him to do that, he claims, some parts of our names would be forgotten, even by us, and our namesakes obliterated. "Devoireh! It would do you both good to pay attention to what I have to say."

Zeidy is going to talk about his time spent in the Hungarian army during World War II. He doesn't usually talk about his experience during the war, but once a year he feels it's appropriate, especially on a night that commemorates all the persecution our ancestors were put through. I think he's trying to tell us that the Passover celebration is still current and real; whether it's freedom from the Egyptians or the Nazis doesn't matter. The point is, we should cherish the freedom we have right now and not take it for granted. Zeidy always warns us that our freedom can disappear at any moment, according to God's decision.

I can hear him start with the funny part, to hook the children in. Yes, yes, I know, it's preposterous, really, assigning Zeidy to be the army cook, when he can barely warm up his own soup. He had to ask the scullery maid how to make *kraut pletzlach*. Hilarious.

"Three meals a day I had to cook, for a whole army. I kept a kosher kitchen and everything, all in secret, of course. When I was at a loss, I asked the kitchen maids to do the cooking and I would do their cleaning. I hardly ever had time for prayer, and when I did, there was rarely a safe place to hide."

I finger the gold-edged pages of my Haggadah, with its luxurious cowhide cover that has Bubby's name inscribed on it in gold letters. Fraida. Only Zeidy calls her that. She doesn't call him by his name, though, only *meyn mahn* or "my husband."

"On Passover there was no flour to make matzo, only potatoes. So we ate potatoes instead of matzo, half a potato for each person, dipped in plenty of saltwater."

I look over at Bubby. I can see she feels the same way I do now. She's covered the side of her face that's facing Zeidy with a calloused hand, and although she's looking down at the table, I can see her shaking her head in exasperation. She's heard this story many more times than I have.

It's Bubby's story that rarely gets heard. Bubby, who lost everyone in the war, whose every relation was brutally murdered in the gas chambers of Auschwitz while she labored in the factories of Bergen-Belsen. Bubby, who was near death from typhus by the time liberation came.

It's Bubby who lights a *yahrzeit* candle for every one of them, from little baby Mindel to fourteen-year-old Chaim. But she almost never talks about it.

Zeidy knows he was lucky to get away with army service, even if he got his beard and *payos* cut off.

When the plate of horseradish is passed around, Bubby takes a generous helping. I pretend to spoon a heap onto my plate, but I purposely end up with only a couple of shreds. It smells awful. I stick my tongue out tentatively, slowly initiating contact with the white threads on my spoon. At the first touch I can almost hear a hissing sound, as the herb burns my tongue. I feel my eyes welling up.

Looking over at Bubby, I can see her chewing dutifully on her portion. I wonder how Bubby is so ready to remember the bitterness of captivity without really being able to celebrate freedom from that bitterness. I don't know if her work will ever really be over. After the Haggadah she'll have to serve the meal, then wait until the men finally finish the ceremony at dawn, at which point she'll have to clean up the entire mess before going to bed.

"*Ow! Ow! Ow!*" Roiza yells suddenly, pointing to her throat. She gasps for water.

"What's the matter?" I ask. "Too strong for you?"

"*Nu!*" Zeidy says. "Enough with the *shtissim* talk already!"

After the eight days of Passover are over and all the regular dishes are back in the unlined cabinets, Zeidy begins marking the *omer*, the special forty-nine-day countdown to Shavuos, the holiday that commemorates the day the Jewish people accepted the Torah at Mount Sinai. During this holy period, called *sefirah*, we are not allowed to listen to music, cut our hair, or wear new clothes. It is a somber time, set ironically against a backdrop of gorgeous spring weather.

Zeidy is especially introspective during this time. After the *havdalah* ceremony that follows the end of Shabbos, he stays at the table for a long time, sniffing the smoking embers of the braided yellow *havdalah* candle, periodically dipping them in the spilled wine so that they make a hissing sound. The dishwasher quivers furiously, hot steam escaping as the load of Shabbos dishes is scrubbed clean, and the roar of the giant vacuum cleaner I use to scour the carpet overwhelms any sound.

Bubby and I are in the bedroom folding linens when we hear Zeidy calling from the kitchen, his voice barely carrying over the hum of the washing machine's rinse cycle.

"Fraida, is there a cake in the oven? I smell burning."

Bubby clucks disapprovingly, scurrying to the kitchen. "What cake? I have time to bake a cake, you think, on *motzei Shabbos*? When did I whip it up, tell me, in the ten minutes since you made *havdalah*? Before or after I put in a load of laundry?"

I follow Bubby into the kitchen and soon see what is causing the smoke detector to go off. On Zeidy's head, his mink hat crackles and smokes energetically; it must have caught fire from the embers. Zeidy rests obliviously in his chair, still sniffing the candle.

Bubby rushes over, muttering in annoyance. "Husband mine, your *shtreimel* is burning, not a cake," she sputters, and before Zeidy can protest, the fur is crackling angrily in the sink, the hiss fading slowly under the rush of water from the faucet.

"See, Zeidy?" I say with a smile. "You're so holy even your *shtreimel* is burning."

Later, the shrunken mess sits sodden and morose on the dining room table, a testament to Zeidy's piety and absentmindedness, two qualities that would be considered interchangeable by many. I delight in retelling the story to all my cousins, who laugh hysterically at the idea of Zeidy sitting innocently at the kitchen table while his *shtreimel* flickers enthusiastically overhead.

Sunday, Zeidy goes shopping for a new model, grumbling bitterly about the cost (two thousand dollars and up), and refuses to let Bubby throw out the burned one just in case it can still be saved. A trim here and there, he says, maybe a good brushing, and I can still wear it on Shabbos. Bubby laughs, because the *shtreimel* is so obviously charred and collapsed, there's no way it can ever be worn, and when Uncle Tovyeh arrives to take Zeidy to the hat shop, she stuffs it into a garbage bag and takes it to the Dumpster in the construction lot across the street.

Zeidy comes home with a new hat, much higher than any of his old ones because that's the new fashion, but the mink is too shiny, and you can tell he was looking for a bargain. The expensive *shtreimels* have a softer, more natural look, but this new one is stiff and haughty and very unsuited to Zeidy's personality.

"Only for weddings I will wear it," he says, and puts the hatbox on the highest shelf of the living room closet, behind his other hats.

Zeidy is one of the most dignified people I know, yet he only dresses in old, shabby clothes. The idea of wearing something new and expensive horrifies him. I crave dignity, but I only feel proud when I am wearing new and neat things. What brand of self-pride is the consciousness that Zeidy has, that he can dress like a pauper and still command respect?

I know Bubby feels the same way I do. Zeidy never let her buy clothes for her daughters when they were young, so she would go to the big department stores in the city and look at the new fashions, inspecting every seam under the guise of testing its quality. She was really memorizing the dress pattern, and later she would re-create more modest versions at her sewing machine, using the finest fabrics available for purchase. If she was sewing the clothes, then Zeidy would let her buy fabric. He approved of her thriftiness; he called her *geshikt*. He was proud to have an efficient wife.

So Bubby's children were always well dressed, and no one knew her secret. Since it was widely known that Zeidy was a wealthy man, who would have dreamed that those lace-trimmed dresses with exquisite details had not been purchased from Saks Fifth Avenue?

In the photos of my grandmother when she was still a young mother, she looks impossibly elegant and feminine. Her T-strap shoes are dainty and slim-heeled, her shapely calves peeking out from underneath a long, graceful skirt. Her waist is still defined even after three children. She would continue to maintain that figure even after she had given birth to the eleventh. They were all born so close together, it's a wonder that she managed it, but even today Bubby is a perfect size six.

After all this time, though, she is tired of fighting for everything. She has given in and no longer nags Zeidy to buy new clothes. And she doesn't use the sewing machine anymore. I wish she would take it out from underneath its wooden table, just once, to sew something for me, but to ask would be presumptuous. If I am truly lucky, one of my aunts

will bring a dress back for me from one of many shopping trips to Daffy's
discount store, dropping it off at Bubby's house like an afterthought.

Spring works its magic here too, in the grimy streets of Williamsburg.
The trees burst into blossom, filling up every available space with lush,
heavy boughs. Strong tree limbs poke insistently into the rib cages of
brownstone homes; their scents pour into windows left open to receive
the breeze. Until the stifling heat of summer sets in, my neighborhood is
suspended in momentary perfection, a fantasy filled with swirling gusts of
pink and white petals that rain down on the sunlit pavement.

In May, Zeidy joins the other men on their way to the anti-Zionist
parade in Manhattan. On every Israeli Independence Day, the Satmar
Hasids make the trip from their various communities to demonstrate
their opposition to the State of Israel. Contrary to what is commonly
believed about Jewish support for Israel, the Satmar Rebbe insisted that
we had to take it upon ourselves to fight for the destruction of Israel,
even if it meant martyring ourselves for the cause. Zionism is a rebellion
such as our history has never seen, said the rebbe. The idea that we could
bring about our own redemption from exile, how preposterous! Faithful
Jews wait for the messiah; they don't take up guns and swords and do the
work themselves.

The parade is a strange sight. No one knows why an obviously Jewish-
looking person would hold a sign that says Destroy Israel. But to me, it
makes sense. I've always known that the State of Israel should not exist.

It is up to us to atone for the deadly sin of Zionism, the Satmar Rebbe
said in his manifesto, the *Vayoel Moshe*. Every Satmar home has a copy
of that anti-Zionist bible. The book relates the history of Zionism, how it
started in the early twentieth century, how a small group of Jews took up
the bizarre idea of carving a Jewish homeland out for themselves. Back
then, everyone thought they were crazy, but the rebbe, he knew what
they would become. He predicted it.

Many times they attempted to bring about their evil goals, he wrote,
but only after the Holocaust did they garner sufficient political and social clout to actually achieve power. To use the Holocaust for sympathy
is an affront to all the souls who perished, Zeidy relates; certainly these

innocent Jews did not martyr themselves so that the Zionists could take control.

Bubby is very bitter about the Zionists too. She tells me of all the Jewish people who tried to escape to Israel to get away from the Nazis, and how the Zionists turned the ships away upon arrival, sending them all back to the camps. They didn't want to populate their new land with ignorant Jews from religious shtetls, she tells me; they wanted a new kind of Jew, educated, enlightened, devoted to the cause. So instead, she says, they took little children, who were still young enough to be molded, and when people heard that, they realized that if there was a chance their children could survive, it was worth separating from them.

In school we learn about how the children were beaten and abused until they had renounced their faith and promised everlasting devotion to Zionism. I understand that Jews and Zionists are two different things; one cannot be both. In fact, I'm pretty sure that the only real Jews are Hasids, because to add even a drop of assimilation to the mix instantly disqualifies anyone from being a real Jew. Although women are not allowed at the protest, I would gladly join, if only for Bubby's sake and the family she lost in the war. Someone has to do the work, and if the "liberated" Jews can't be bothered, then we have to double our efforts, surely.

I've seen the photos, all of them. Black-and-white portraits of Bubby's sisters and brothers, her parents, her grandparents; all of them are dead. I keep them wrapped in a paper towel in my top drawer and pull them out when I'm feeling strong enough. Their faces are so real, I can't make sense of it. The baby, killed when she was two years old. *How can it be?* I ask God. *How can these living, breathing faces be gone? They're my ancestors!* I always cry when I see the photos, and I have to put them back in the paper towel quickly, before my silent heaving sobs turn into wails. Bubby doesn't like to talk about her family, and I don't want to be the one to remind her.

The Zionists used the Holocaust for sympathy, she says. But tell me, what do they know of the Holocaust? Not one true survivor among them, she says. Not one. And I believe her, because there are tears collecting in the wells of her eyelids.

The rabbi has forbidden us from traveling to Israel. Until the messiah comes, the Promised Land is off-limits. In school there are strict rules about it; even if one has family living there, we are not allowed to visit. To do so would warrant permanent expulsion. It strikes me as a particularly unfair rule, to prevent us from glimpsing the country where our roots so firmly lie, the country our teachers talk about when they tell us of our illustrious history. Still, I know there are girls who have broken the rules, whose families have taken circuitous routes and brought their daughters into that forbidden land. In fact, in only two weeks, thousands of American Jews will be making a trip to Israel for the holiday of Lag Ba'Omer, the anniversary of the death of Rabbi Shimon Bar Yochai, the great second-century sage who wrote the Zohar, the chief work of Kabbalah. In fact, I know that my aunt Chavie traveled there a year before her son was born to pray at Rabbi Shimon's grave. It is traditional for infertile women to pray for a son there, promising in exchange to return to the grave site when the child is three years old and perform the first-haircut ceremony on Lag Ba'Omer. Chavie will surely take Shimon when he is old enough, because everyone knows it was a miracle that he was born, and only Rabbi Shimon could be responsible for such a miracle. Even Zeidy approved of Chavie's efforts; for the purpose of reproduction, some rules could be overlooked, even if the Satmar Rebbe created them.

Lag Ba'Omer is a very exciting holiday. On every street in Williamsburg the men build large bonfires and dance around them until dawn, singing traditional tunes while the women peek out of windows or watch from the stone stoops. The flames licking upward send an eerie orange cast over the men's faces, their earlocks catching the light as they swing enthusiastically along to the dancing. I like to stay up as long as I can to watch, because the scene is so powerful and mesmerizing, even if I don't understand exactly what it means.

The fire department sends trucks to every corner to monitor the fires, and the firemen stand outside, leaning casually against the truck sides, watching the goings-on with remote expressions on their faces. They are mostly accustomed to safeguarding our activities, and some seem resentful of being constantly called to service our community. They aren't friendly to us, because we aren't friendly to them. I wish I could talk to one of them, but somebody would see me. It would be considered very inappropriate behavior.

Instead, I watch them. Their uniforms are bulky and sag on their frames, but their faces are clean-shaven, a stark contrast to the faces I'm used to seeing. The eyes that gaze so coolly out on the scene are clear and bright, unhidden by thick glasses or hats. If I stare long enough at one of them, perhaps he will stare back, I think. I do, willing him to meet my eyes, but he doesn't know. He can't see what I'm thinking behind the mask that makes me look like everyone else. For once I blend into the crowd.

Looking at those smooth-cheeked firemen, I feel a strong and desperate longing to bridge the chasm that lies between us. It burns my face and chest, as if the bonfire flames were consuming me from the inside out. If those around me knew how I felt about those goyim that performed our work for us, they would be horrified, and even I am ashamed by my unreasonable attraction. There is nothing more dangerous than a goy, but I am drawn to the mystery of the foreign world so close to my own and yet so far away.

The firemen don't see me the way I see them. The goyim I will meet later in life will not be able to fathom my fascination with them. But still that painful, burning desire will follow me for many years, igniting each time I meet eyes with a man whose jaw is glistening from a fresh shave, whose eyes gaze directly into mine without repugnance or shame, unspoiled by the shadow of a fur hat.

In June the heat comes in early, dewy wet and slipping off the leaves of the overburdened maples lining the street. Zeidy goes down to the garden to cut flowers for Shavuos, because it's a tradition to decorate the house with blooms and ferns in remembrance of how the barren Mount Sinai was adorned with blossoms for the occasion. As Zeidy clips chunky pink roses and delicate irises, Bubby watches from the porch, calling to him to be careful, mourning the loss of color in her garden. Zeidy doesn't really understand how happy flowers make her feel, but only when they are growing from the ground. Within a day or two these beautiful flowers will be drooping limply, their lives cruelly cut short. For what else should we have a garden, says Zeidy, if not to honor the Torah?

On Shavuos we eat creamy cheesecake with a sweet cookie-crumb crust, and triangular kreplach filled with farmer cheese that Bubby takes out of the freezer and fries in a skillet of melted butter. After waiting a half hour, we eat the meat meal, platters of smoked turkey sliced and smothered with red cocktail sauce, chicken legs sautéed in caramelized onions, and chopped liver as well. The purpose of eating separate dairy and meat meals is symbolic; at Mount Sinai the Jews agreed to keep the laws of the Torah, even ones that entailed significant sacrifices, one of which was the commandment to separate milk and meat. "We will do and we will hear," said the Jews at Mount Sinai, instead of the other way around, demonstrating a blind faith that Zeidy says we still have to be proud of. All of us were at Mount Sinai, says Zeidy after the meal is over and everyone is patting their bloated stomachs. The Midrash says that every Jewish soul was present when the Torah was handed down to the chosen people, and that means that even if we don't remember it, we were there, and we chose to accept the responsibility of being a chosen one. Therefore, Zeidy lectures further, for any of us to reject any one of the laws would mean we were hypocrites, as we were present at the time the commitment was made. There is no immunity for a Jewish soul.

I wonder how old my soul has to be to have been present at Mount Sinai. Did I say yes because I wanted to fit in? Because that sounds like me, afraid to think differently out loud.

Yet the contract we made with God so long ago is not the same contract Zeidy made with the rebbe fifty years ago. When the Satmar Rebbe announced his plans for a *kehillah*, a community, in Williamsburg, Zeidy pledged his allegiance before he even knew what it entailed, and in doing so he tied his whole family, and all of its future generations, to this community. Back in Europe, Zeidy's family didn't live like this. They weren't extremists; they were educated people who had homes with wooden floors and Persian carpets, and they traveled freely throughout the Continent.

It was the rebbe who decided I couldn't read English books or wear the color red. He isolated us, made it so we could never blend in on the outside. If I wasn't there when the agreement was made, why am I still obligated to follow all these rules? Can Zeidy really expect me to walk in the rebbe's shadow as blindly as he did, when he was scared and lonely, as all the survivors were, and there was nowhere else to turn that felt safe?

3

The Dawning of Knowledge

"[T]he child will grow up knowing of what is great—
knowing that these tenements of Williamsburg are not the
whole world."
        —From A Tree Grows in Brooklyn, *by Betty Smith*

There are three weeks of nothingness between school and summer camp, three long weeks of unbearable heat. I go out just for a few minutes to sit on the stoop, and even in the shade I feel lethargy set in instantly, my hair flattened limp by the humidity, my spirits deflated. My legs itch underneath thick woolen tights, which, ironically, do not protect me from mosquitoes. I am addicted to the bright pink Italian ices from Mayer's grocery store. They last forever, and my stomach is cherry-sick by the time I scrape out the bottom of the paper container.

Just when I think I will die of boredom, my cousin Moshe comes to stay with us. It's because he got kicked out of yeshiva, I hear Bubby whisper on the telephone when she thinks I'm asleep. Always making trouble, that boy, she says, sighing.

From my bedroom at 5:30 in the morning I hear Zeidy wake Moshe up like a drill sergeant. "Get up. It's time for prayers. Let's go. Get up. Come

on. The sun is rising. We pray at first light. Get up. Get dressed." He
drags the boy out of bed by his ear, and I hear Moshe stumbling blindly in
search of his clothes as Zeidy barks at him. Moshe is here to suffer a dose
of Zeidy's discipline, the cure-all for bad apples. With his twelve siblings
to worry about, Moshe's parents have enough on their plate.

Zeidy wants him to find a good *shidduch*, an arranged match, but fat
chance anyone's going to marry an eighteen-year-old boy who's not in yeshiva. There is no sign of a beard on Moshe's smooth-cheeked face, and
I can't tell if that's because he's tampering with it or just a late bloomer.
If he were trying to stop the growth of facial hair, it would be a serious
offense indeed, and I'm thrilled at the prospect of such mischief.

I tease him about his lack of facial hair.

"Tell me the truth," I say, "do you pull them out by hand? Or do you
use a razor blade? Maybe a tweezers!"

"Shut up, you little snitch," he snarls at me. "You don't know from
nothing. Mind your own business."

Still, he comes by my room in the evenings after prayer, going
through my stuff, teasing me. He knows he shouldn't be talking to me
because I'm a girl, but Bubby won't scold him, and Zeidy is still learning
at the *kollel*. Later I will overhear Zeidy giving him a stern lecture about
the impropriety of fraternizing with females.

"What business do you have talking to girls," Zeidy says in a hushed,
angry voice, after he has pulled Moshe aside, "when you should be spending your every free moment learning the holy Torah and focusing on
your future? Which girl, tell me, will look at a boy like you, who can't sit
through one *shiur*, let alone a full day's learning?"

I glance over in his direction. Moshe doesn't say anything, only looks
at the ground, where his feet shuffle nervously, his face betraying a true,
deep misery that something within me recognizes.

The disapproving lectures don't help much. Moshe still abandons
his *seforim* to come talk to me, and feeling a mixture of pity and curiosity, I let him. When Bubby goes to visit her friends in the evenings,
I show Moshe how to roast marshmallows over the stovetop. We im-
pale the kosher marshmallows on the metal skewers Bubby uses to make

shish kebab, so of course they are fleishig. We can't eat them with our chocolate-syrup-and-milk concoction.

Moshe teaches me how to make prank calls.

"Hello? Yes, this is Con Edison calling. We've been having some problems in your area and we need you to go check if your fridge is running. Oh, it is? Well, then, go get your sneakers and run after it!" I bang the receiver onto the base and we dissolve into hysterical giggles. My ribs ache in the best way.

One night Moshe says to me, let's dial random toll-free numbers with funny words, like 1-800-BOGEYMAN. Sometimes we end up actually calling the right number; 1-800-TOILETS offers to fix our pipes for us.

"Hey, listen to this," he says, and he dials 1-800-FATLADY and puts the phone on speaker. A woman's voice comes on, but it's a machine, I can tell. She sounds breathy and weird. "Thick . . . fat . . . juicy . . . ," she breathes, and I press the Off button quickly. Moshe laughs loudly at my reaction and I feel as if I have been tricked. The air in the room changes.

"How old are you, Devoiri?" he asks.

"Thirteen, why?"

"Really? You're thirteen? I can't believe it. I thought for sure you were seventeen. You look so much older!"

"Nope. I'm thirteen." I scrape the last of the marshmallow off the metal skewer with my teeth. Moshe watches me lick my lips and shakes his head in wonder.

"What?"

"Nothing. I just can't believe you're that young."

Zeidy pulls me aside in the morning and asks me if I learned the laws of *yichud* in school this past year. We learned some of them, sure. I know a girl can't be on her own in a room with a man, even if there are other women there too. She can be on her own with two or more men. You have to leave the doors unlocked if you ever end up in a situation with a man. No touching. No singing aloud, of course. But Zeidy and Bubby leave Moshe and me alone at night, without a concern, and I leave the door open like I'm supposed to anyway. Besides, Moshe is my cousin. I mean, we're related. Those rules are just for show.

• • •

When Bubby goes to Aishel, the old-age home, to feed the patients, I run down the street to Mayer's grocery to get an Italian ice. Cherry or lemon flavor, I can't decide. Lemon is tart and clear, cherry a cloying sweetness that lingers afterward in the dark pink stain on my tongue and teeth.

As I'm standing over the sliding door of the box freezer, Rodrigo, the Mexican boy who works for Mr. Mayer, accidentally brushes past me on his way to the back. The aisles are narrow, and without thinking about it, I jerk away. Cherry, I decide, and grab the red one from the freezer. Before I can close the sliding door, I feel a hand on my butt. There is a distinct pinching sensation but for a split second only, so I can't be sure, but then I whip around and see Rodrigo disappearing into the mildewed darkness of the back room.

I am frozen for a moment, one hand on the Italian ice, my back turned to the freezer to protect myself. My face is hot red. The indignity of it burns in my throat. The Mexican! On my own street!

Fury fueling my steps, I walk quickly to the front, the heels of my shoes tapping self-righteously on the hollow wooden floor. At the counter, old Mr. Mayer is leaning over his account books, both his hands shaking from Parkinson's, the tips of his yellow-white beard brushing the frayed pages of his ledger.

I plunk two quarters down on the butcher-block counter. I know better than to give it to the shopkeeper directly: that's not allowed. Mr. Mayer doesn't even look up. I pause for a moment, unable to decide if I should tell him something about what happened or just let it slide. It's so embarrassing.

"Mr. Mayer."

He doesn't look up. I think he may be slightly deaf from old age. More determined to get his attention now, I raise my voice.

"Mr. Mayer!"

He lifts his head slightly and peers through his bifocals at me.

"Tell your Mexican boy not to lay a hand on the customers."

Mr. Mayer stares at me blankly, his large eyes peering at me from yellowed sockets. I think perhaps he hasn't heard me, but then I see his lips quiver with intended speech, only nothing comes out. For a moment, shock has frozen his hands, withered claws that seem suspended above the counter until he reaches out and scoops up my two quarters in one palm, the other hand pushing toward me a wooden scraper wrapped in white tissue paper. He's not going to say anything. Reluctantly, I take the scraper and walk out the front door, the bell ringing frantically as I make my exit.

Back at the house, I crouch on the front stoop and watch the pigeons fight over the crumbs Bubby left in the front yard. The Italian ice rests, still wrapped, in the cradle of my two palms, the paper container growing softer as the ice melts. Cherry-pink liquid drips out the bottom and runs through my fingers, staining them with rivulets of red. I feel nauseated.

I should tell someone. Maybe if I tell Zeidy, he will go down to the grocery himself and yell at Mr. Mayer, and this time the grocer will listen, and he will know that he can't just let his workers get away with whatever they want. There should be justice. I'm a Jewish girl; at least in my own community, I should be safe.

But how can I bring myself to tell Zeidy? What words will I use to describe the experience? It's too embarrassing to even contemplate. And if I were to tell him, what if he thought it was somehow my fault? Wasn't I somehow implicated in the story? I don't want to see the look of disappointment on his face.

My hands are becoming numb from the cold container in my palm, and the chill spreads up my arms and into my shoulders and chest. I shiver violently, as if shaking off an invisible demon. Just imagining the taste of the sickeningly sweet cherry-flavored ice brings bile to my throat now. I drop the still unopened sodden container in the metal trash bin. As I get up to go inside, I notice the slate underneath my feet is stained dark by the mess I made.

Shabbos lasts the longest in June, and this week I spend the afternoon on the couch because of mysterious abdominal pain that won't respond to Bubby's usual dose of antacids. Zeidy doesn't say the *havdalah* blessing until 10:30 on Saturday night, but at 11:00 p.m. Rachel and Tovyeh come all the way from Borough Park with their kids for the Melaveh

Malkah, the post-Shabbos meal. I take a few Tylenol and the pain dulls into a faint throb, and I join my cousins at the dining room table for scrambled eggs and vegetable salad, while Moshe is dispatched to the kosher pizza store on Marcy Avenue, where the line usually extends into the street on a Saturday night.

When Moshe gets back with the large, oil-stained cardboard box in his hands, Zeidy and Tovyeh are already deep in some Talmudic debate, and after I've finished doling the pizza out to the kids, Zeidy gestures for me to come closer. He wants me to bring up a burgundy from the cellar, Kedem brand, with the yellow label. I hesitate. I'm scared to go alone downstairs in the dark. I know there are rats in the cellar; sometimes even the stray cats get in and play killing games with them.

"I don't want to go alone," I say.

"All right, then, Moshe will go with you. But make sure you get the right one. Moshe! Go with Devoireh to the cellar and turn on the lights for her so she can see. Here are the keys." And he hands us his key ring, heavy with keys to every lock in the house.

Moshe and I traipse down three flights to the cellar, the last flight shrouded in darkness and what I think are cobwebs. I can smell the deodorant he uses, sharp and strong, even though he's supposed to use unscented products. His footfalls are heavier than mine. I wonder why Zeidy lets us go down to the cellar alone. I'm sure it's against the rules, but Zeidy would never allow it if it were, so I guess it's okay.

Moshe fumbles with the fuse boxes, trying to find the right switch in the dark. Finally a weak orange light emanates from bulbs strung across the ceiling pipes and illuminates the dank cellar. The piles of junk loom more clearly now—old suitcases stacked upon each other, an ancient pram with one wheel missing, old mattresses—and at the back, the wine crate.

Even with the makeshift lighting I can't see very well, and I pull out bottle after bottle, looking for the elusive burgundy, while Moshe makes no move to help, instead pacing behind me.

I think I've found the right one, Kedem burgundy, yellow label. I squint to make sure, then hand it to Moshe.

"Here. Take that upstairs. I'll shut off the lights and lock up behind us."

Moshe takes the bottle from me and sets it down on the floor.

"What are you doing? That floor is cement! You could break the bottle! Zeidy will be furious." I reach to grab the bottle, but Moshe grabs me by both wrists. "Wha—What are you doing?" My voice cracks.

I feel him guiding me to the wall, and I'm not struggling, my arms paralyzed by shock. One finger still grips the heavy key ring. Standing this close to me, his tomato-sauce breath on my forehead, Moshe's body feels unexpectedly large and solid. His grip on my wrists is tight and painful, and my forearms feel brittle, like twigs. Me, who can lift an air-conditioning unit up a whole flight of stairs.

I giggle nervously. I scan his face to see if this is just a silly game he is playing, this bad boy who got kicked out of yeshiva and wants to scare me in the cellar. But his face isn't relaxed into his usual pose of disinterested amusement. His jaw is tense, his eyes narrowed.

I lift my knee up to kick him, but he fixes my legs against the wall with his own thick thighs, crushing me with his weight. One hand lifts my wrists up over my head and the other reaches for the zipper to my housedress. He yanks it down in one quick motion, and I bend over re-flexively to hide myself, screaming this time.

"Stop! Please stop! What are you doing—? This is crazy—"

Moshe puts his hand over my mouth and I taste the salt of his sweat. I can feel him pushing me to the floor, one hand on my shoulder, the other hand on my waist. I remember the key ring and use it now, slamming the keys into Moshe's pelvis, shoving blindly against him.

The sharp edge of a key finds purchase in the soft flab of his abdomen and I dig and twist, my wrist the only part of me with a little freedom of movement, and I use it all, even as I hear him mutter epithets in my ear. His body squirms above me, moving away slightly as he searches for the weapon in my hand. I grunt quietly as I shove the key quickly and deeply into his pelvis, and now he jumps off me, hands clasped to him, groaning.

I pull my zipper back up as I make my escape, weaving through the piles of junk, bounding loudly up the creaky wooden stairs and into the bright light of the parlor floor. I've forgotten the wine.

Upstairs I pass the dining room and try to sneak off to my room, but Zeidy notices me and calls my name. "*Nu*, Devoireh!" He looks expectantly at me. "Do you have the wine?"

I nod quietly. "I gave it to Moshe," I say.

Sure enough, Moshe comes panting through the door, burgundy in hand, setting it down on the table with his signature smirk as if nothing happened. He turns to look at me, authority in his gaze, something proud and powerful behind his eyes, and I turn on my heels away from him, hands pressed to my hot cheeks.

In my room I don't turn on the light, lying instead in the almost-blackness marred only by the weak peach-colored light filtering in from the streetlamp outside my window, the shadow of maple branches creating patterns on the walls of my narrow room. With my hands I trace the outlines of my body, fingers trailing down my neck, past the space between my breasts and settling on my stomach, trying to see if the tingling sensation burning from there can be felt in my skin, like the heat from a fever. My skin feels cool and smooth and quiet. I lie on my bed for a while, even as the noises from the dining room begin to fade, and I hear people clunking heavily down the stairs and out through the pair of front doors and into the street. I can hear Tovyeh get into his car, and in a moment the big blue Dodge Durango purrs off into the night.

I hear Bubby getting ready for bed, Zeidy learning by himself in the dining room, and finally Moshe coming into his bedroom at two a.m. I stay awake for a very long time, hands resting on my stomach, still in my clothes, listening for something, but no sound comes from my throat. At dawn I fall asleep.

When I'm sitting at the Shabbos table on Friday night, listening to Zeidy sing the traditional hymns, I burst into loud, gulping sobs, stopping him in midrhyme. No one can understand my sudden penchant for hysterical tantrums; Zeidy tells me I should pray for *menuchas hanefesh*, peace in my soul. "What could you possibly have to cry about?" he asks gently, looking up from his holy books. It's true, I want to shout, I have nothing to cry about, nothing when it compares to you, and the pain you can claim as your own.

For me to tell him why I'm crying would seem ungrateful. Is it Zeidy's fault that God sent me into a world that had no place to put me? How do I explain to him about the giant hole that threatens to swallow me up if I don't fill it with *things*; how do I tell him about pride and desire, and about the misery that comes with not *having*?

Everything in this world that you think you own is not really yours, Zeidy says. It can be taken from you at any moment. Small comfort, to think that my few possessions can be stolen in the night. A parent, a sibling, a house, a dress—all of those things are possessions; in the long run, they don't matter. Zeidy says he knows this because he knows what it is like to lose everything. He says that the only thing of value one can achieve in this life is *menuchas hanefesh*, the deep, inner serenity that prevails even in the face of persecution. Our ancestors were so strong, they could maintain complete calm even under the gravest of circumstances; grievous bodily torture and unspeakable anguish did nothing to sway them from their tranquil position. When you have faith, Zeidy says, you can grasp how meaningless life is, in terms of the bigger picture. From the perspective of heaven, our suffering is minuscule, but if your soul is so weighed down that you cannot see beyond what's in front of you, then you can never be happy.

How to find such inner peace that nothing can sway it? The world around me is so real and tangible, I cannot resist; heaven seems hardly as wonderful a prospect.

Moshe was finally suggested a match this week. Zeidy is thrilled that someone might be interested in the grandson he had almost given up on. But when I get a call on the girl's behalf asking for more information about the boy's character, I don't praise him as the custom entails. Instead, I brazenly defy tradition, I call him a bad apple, a crazy, a *shlechter*. And when my *zeide* finds out what I did, he sits me down to yell at me, but before he can finish, I beat my two palms down on the table and cry out.

"What? What is it?"

"He tried to . . . He tried to . . ." But I don't know what he tried to do. I give up and leave the table, even as I hear him calling after me to come back, but now I don't have to talk if I don't want to. Now I have the right to go away.

Zeidy asks my aunt Chaya to talk to me, and she uses soft words to get me to open up, and I tell her, not all of it, just enough so that her face twists with rage and she mutters softly, "Animals. They're just animals."

"Who?"

"Boys. Young boys. I don't know what Zeidy was thinking, bringing him here with you in the same house."

In the end, Moshe got engaged to an Israeli girl. Everyone knows that an Israeli *shidduch* is a last resort. Fathers in Israel are so poor, they will give their daughters to anyone who can pay. Moshe will have to move to Israel to live near his wife's family, and I will never have to see him again.

Bubby is on the phone with one of her daughters when I discover the thick, viscous blood in my underwear, and I can hear her voice through the bathroom door, full of lamenting sighs. I want to wait until she puts the phone down before I break the news of my impending death to her, but I'm too terrified to control myself, so I open the door a crack and motion for her to get off the phone. She asks the person on the other end to hold on and comes toward me with a slightly irritated look on her face.

"*Nu*, what is it, *mamaleh?*" she asks hurriedly, pulling her turban back over her ear.

"I'm bleeding," I say, in my most quiet voice, waiting for her to spring into shocked action, maybe to call Hatzolah, the volunteer EMS team, to take me to the hospital.

"Here, *mamaleh*," she says briskly, opening the bottom drawer of the bathroom vanity. She takes out what looks like a long, narrow swath of cotton and hands it to me. "Put this in your underwear," she says, "and I will go to the pharmacy soon to get you some pads."

I don't understand how she can be so calm. She tells me it's no big deal that there is a gallon of blood gushing out of me, because apparently it happens to everyone, and it's healthy. Think of it as your body cleaning itself out, she says. It will go away in a few days.

When she brings a box of Kotex home from the pharmacy, she tells me to keep it hidden at the back of my closet so no one should see it. Such things don't need to be talked about, she says. It doesn't do anyone any good.

It's hard to make a secret out of the process of changing the pads, like bandages, every few hours. I have to wrap them in paper and a plastic bag, like Bubby showed me, before putting them in the garbage can nonchalantly, so that no one suspects. I feel strangely depressed, as if I have somehow switched bodies and the new one isn't to my liking. I can't wait for the bleeding to go away, like Bubby promised it would. I hope it never comes back.

Soon I can no longer count on my body being the same every day, bony and sleek like it used to be. Now it seems as if every day my clothes fit me differently, and the mirror never shows the same reflection. I become frustrated with my inability to control what my body does or looks like.

My friends have become obsessed with diets, bringing plastic containers of iceberg lettuce for lunch instead of the usual bagel with cream cheese. Try as hard as I want, I can't resist the silky taste of peanut butter on white bread, or the way the chocolate shell breaks delicately off a vanilla ice cream bar.

Some girls take the diets too far. Chani Reich spends her recess time jogging up and down the hallways to burn calories she doesn't appear to be consuming. Bruchy Hirsch is hospitalized for weeks because she collapsed during classes once. Even her parents couldn't get her to eat.

Modesty is the highest attainment for a young woman. Indeed, the modest girls are the skinniest, hiding their natural bodies from curious view, maintaining the innocence and purity of childhood. How long, I wonder, can girls turn their backs on impending womanhood?

After all, it won't be long before we all become mothers. These years form the twilight of our childhoods, our last carefree moments before real life begins.

I go off to summer camp with my new underwear and a stash of maxi pads, feeling like one of the older girls now, like I'm on the verge of something huge and important. The sprawling campgrounds are located in the farthest corner of a moist, sweltering valley in the Catskills, miles off the main highway. Satmars like to be as far away as possible from the gentiles who live in the Catskills year-round, and they don't want us to be able to walk into town or interact with anyone on the outside, so we spend our summers deep in a property that can only be reached by a primitive, hard-to-find dirt road that stretches for miles.

The grounds are springy with moisture, with mushrooms popping up under the shade, as the rains settle into the concave areas and the resulting pondlike puddles trickle down hillocks for weeks before finally thinning out and evaporating in the humid air. Only the large, raised field areas are kept dry for camp activities.

I choose a lower bunk underneath Layala, a husky girl with blond hair and blue eyes who's always stirring up trouble. When the night supervisor steps out on the porch for fresh air and conversation with the other girls on duty, I lift my legs and pound the bottom of her mattress as hard as I can, and the metal bed frame vibrates with movement. Layala inevitably bursts out yelling, and that brings all the ODs (what we called those doing "overnight duty," like a night watch) running in, shining their flashlights between the beds, trying to determine the source of the commotion. I lie still beneath my thin summer quilt, eyes closed, breathing measured and slow, a portrait of innocence.

Summer is a time for mischief. I do everything I'm told not to do. I stay in the bunk during swim hours and hide in the bathroom when they come check the bunks for stragglers. I hate swimming in my long blue swimdress with the palm tree emblazoned on it to remind me that I am a Satmar girl. That is the meaning of the rabbi's last name: *Teitelbaum* is German for "palm tree," and the symbol is everywhere—on the cabins, the buses, the stationery, and the swimclothes. The minute my swimdress gets wet, it bags heavily around my knees, slapping my calves with each step.

Some girls roll up the legs and arms of the swim costume and lie on a towel they have spread over the hot concrete, trying to catch the few rays that penetrate the swimming area's high enclosure. The looming brick walls throw a deep shadow over most of the pool area. Almost everyone is tan by the second week of camp—everyone, it seems, but me, who can't coax the faintest glimmer from my pasty-white skin. While Layala turns dark brown and limber, all I have to show for myself are scabby knees and a sprinkling of freckles on my nose.

I run up demerits quickly, as I fail to show up for *shiur*, the daily sermon, and get reprimanded for nodding off during prayer. The only building on the campgrounds that isn't simmering with heat is the humongous dining room, in which the entire camp eats their meals in shifts. The dining room fits about fifteen hundred people at once, and its ceiling is striped with whirring air-conditioning units that keep blessedly cool air circulating throughout the cavernous space.

We say prayers out loud before and after each meal, with one girl chosen to lead on the microphone. I wait all summer to be picked, but only the good girls get to go up front. I try out for a part in the major play, and I dazzle the counselors with my loud, clear diction, but I am given only a small part, while the big parts go to Faigy and Miriam-Malka, well-behaved girls whose fathers have clout. Perhaps if Zeidy were to involve himself more, then people would feel they had someone to answer to about their treatment of me, but Zeidy doesn't know about such things, and because the counselors know that they won't be held accountable, they don't really care about my happiness. Occasionally, if I ask for it, Bubby will send a package with the bus that comes up to the Catskills on Fridays, but they are never like the packages other girls get, the ones that are stuffed with sweets. She sends foil-wrapped sponge cake and fresh plums. Still, it is better than nothing. It is a way to show that I am cared for, like everyone else.

This is the summer that Milky and Faigy shower together, and the rest of the class whispers about them behind judging palms. Layala tells me lurid tales of the two girls in their bathing suits splashing themselves in the bathtub with the door closed. She crawls into my bed one night while the OD is chatting outside and everyone else is sleeping, putting her hands on my breasts and asking me to feel hers to see if they are bigger. Of course they are bigger, and she lords it over me like it's something to be proud of, like she won a competition. I change bunks for second half. I choose a bunk above Frimet, who's quiet as a mouse except for when she cries into her pillow; then she makes tiny squeaky sounds like the rubber tires of a toy truck.

There are two summer camps now, one for people like me who come from families that support Zalman Leib, the Satmar Rebbe's youngest son, and one for people who come from families that support Aaron, the eldest son. Both sons are competing to inherit the dynasty when the current rabbi passes away, and the prolonged battle has turned ugly.

Golda is in the camp for the Aroinies, as we call them, so even though we spend the school year together, I don't get to see her all summer. She comes to visit me on my birthday, and when she gets off the big air-conditioned coach bus that stops at all the Hasidic colonies and camps in the Catskills, we walk as far as we can away from the sound of the foot stamping and hand clapping in the main cabins so we can have privacy.

We wade into the *gan yehudah*, the large field area at the front of the camp where they let the grass grow tall to obscure the view, even though we're in Kerhonkson, New York, and the nearest neighbors are twenty miles away. Golda and I sit pretzel-legged in the grass and make daisy chains out of the weeds, our fingertips stained green from splitting grass shoots. We both hate camp. We hate yelling our guts out for no reason. We hate playing on the hot concrete all day the games counselors invent for us. Golda writes songs. I write in my journals. I wish I could sing like her, or at least look like her, with her deep olive skin and warm, beautiful smile that lifts up her cheekbones, turning them into glowing mounds, her teeth like diamonds in the sun. Golda is pretty, even with the beginnings of acne on her forehead. I think she will have a dream of a life, that fantastic things will happen to her, because she has that face, the face of a woman to whom earthshaking things are bestowed.

In the field, I doze off at one point, and Golda's words scroll down like Chinese calligraphy in the background of my dreams, then fade. The sun burns the fabric of my clothes, and my clothes burn me. The metal zipper on my skirt turns white hot. Golda too dozes off beside me. Through half-closed eyes I can see her black hair glint in the sun, tangled with weeds. I feel an ant bite my leg, and it hurts, not like a mosquito bite, but like the pinch of a minuscule tweezers, and I scratch. I feel blood trickle down my leg, seep through my stocking, and the fabric dries instantly into stiffness.

Golda and I are both startled by the sound of the siren. The field is empty, as well as the parking lot beyond it. Everyone is in the main cabin watching the *machanayim* game, Hebrew for a more modest version of dodgeball. The wailing sound rolls closer and farther away, its volume erratic, the sound scratchy. It's coming from a megaphone. Golda and I peer through the grass and see Mr. Rosenberg, one of the few male residents on the campgrounds, as well as Mrs. Halberstam, the grossly overweight camp director in her housecoat and turban, wading into the field, Mrs. Halberstam holding the megaphone in one hand.

Golda and I look at each other in puzzlement. Should we get up? Should we lie low? Why are they here?

"*Maidlach!*" Mrs. Halberstam's voice cracks through the old megaphone. She's talking to us!

"Come out of the field, girls. You need to come out right now." I can see her now, cheeks splotchy from the heat, eyes squinted almost shut. She won't go any further, but it's clear she sees us. We are probably in trouble for not being where we're supposed to be. Or maybe they're afraid of ticks. The grass here hardly ever gets cut.

Golda and I scuffle out of the field. We try to mold our faces into innocence, even as our teeth clench to contain our giggles. Mrs. Halberstam looks panicked, and it's not pretty. Mr. Rosenberg looks extra stern, his eyes open wide and staring, his scraggly orange beard seeming to stand straight out. They escort us out of the field in silence.

I wonder why the two most important people in the camp staff were sent to discipline us for such a minor infraction.

At the edge of the field they stop, Mrs. Halberstam turning to address us, Mr. Rosenberg standing behind her in a show of tacit support, his manic gaze focused on us, both hands twirling his burnt-orange *payos* in superfast motions, betraying his fury.

"What were you doing in there?" Mrs. Halberstam asks.

"Nothing. Just schmoozing," Golda answers flippantly. She's never afraid of authority, especially since they're not her authorities. She goes back to the other camp at the end of the day, and she has different superiors to answer to there.

Mrs. Halberstam grows angrier. "Do you know what that looked like out there? What's wrong with you? What do you want people to think about you? Do you want to be sent home?"

I'm completely confused. Golda looks like she just got slapped in the face. What on earth can she mean?

"Look, we really were just talking. We're friends. We haven't seen each other all summer. She's from the other camp," I say, trying to placate her.

The director pauses to look at Golda. Mr. Rosenberg steps in. They whisper to each other. "Is that true?" she asks of Golda, and Golda nods in response.

"Well, if you wanted to talk, why would you go all the way into the field? Why can't you just sit at one of the picnic tables? Or even one of the field areas where the grass does get cut? This proves you didn't just come here to talk!" Mrs. Halberstam pontificates triumphantly.

What else does she think we could possibly have done? I wonder. I rack my brain trying to figure out what she is accusing us of.

Golda looks just as perplexed. We're both scared.

I start to cry, forcing tears out of my eyes, which is a mean feat in this weather. I'm very good at crying on demand, and I progress to wailing very soon. Both their faces soften visibly as my sincere regret becomes obvious.

"Look," Mrs. Halberstam says, "if you want to talk, go sit by the picnic tables near the dining room. What's wrong with talking there? Go like good girls and don't let us catch you alone in the *gan yehudah* again."

Golda and I leave as fast as we can and sit down at one of the picnic tables, looking back to see if they are still watching us. When they turn up a different path, we breathe a simultaneous sigh of relief. I sit across from Golda, wringing my hands in my lap. We don't talk. Our friendship seems tainted now. We both know we have been accused of something, but we aren't sure what. We know it's something truly awful, but how can we defend ourselves against a charge we don't understand? The joyful mood we were in earlier has disappeared.

Golda goes home that afternoon with the rest of the girls, and I don't hear from her all summer. But the next time someone asks me to go to the *gan yehudah* with her, I politely decline, and I start to wonder if there are girls who go there for other reasons than simply wanting peace and quiet. After all, it *is* the only place on the campgrounds that offers privacy.

Layala begs me to switch back to my old bunk. We can be special friends, she says, and she will look out for me, because she is a big girl and everyone is afraid of her brute strength. Even her voice is hoarse with power, thick with threats.

Two weeks before camp is over, upstate New York becomes infested with clouds of tiny flies, a result of the heavy rains accumulating in the valleys. The grounds are besieged; the swarms of tiny flies descend upon us like a plague. They are in our mouths, our noses; we breathe them. One flies into my eye, and then I get an infection. I wake up with my eyes glued shut and have to wipe green matter with a warm washcloth to get them open again. In the mirror my eye stares back at me, swollen and red, wanting to slink away into its socket to sulk.

I think of the ten plagues that Moses brought upon the Egyptians. In school we learned that even though Pharaoh was willing to let the Jews go after the first plague, the plague of blood, God hardened his heart on purpose each time. This way, Moses would bring down ten plagues, each more miraculous and brutal than the last, to show the true extent of Hashem's might.

I can't decide if this is more like the third or the eighth plague: lice or locusts. The flies are everywhere, just like they were in Egypt. Girls stumble blindly around the campus, eyes squeezed shut and lips pursed to avoid an invasion. The flies crawl up our noses anyway, like the gnat in Titus's brain, and I am terrified that they will bore holes through my skull and descend upon my brain like maggots, until all the matter is devoured and I am left a hollow body, devoid of meaning.

Is my soul in my brain? If my brain is gone, does that mean my soul disappears too? What am I if I can't think or speak? But what about gentiles, who have no souls? How are they different? My teacher says Jews have a spark, a *tzelem Elokim*, that makes us irreversibly special. We all carry a tiny piece of the light that is God. That's why Satan is always trying to seduce us; he wants to get at that light.

I wonder, did he bring these flies, this eerie supernatural swarm? Or is it a punishment from God? I look at my white face in the mirror, the face of a Jewish girl, of a chosen one, and wonder just where it was that I went so wrong as to deserve such grand retribution.

Camp is ruined. We are let out a week earlier than expected. The coach bus glides silently off the expressway and into Williamsburg, and I can see that the streets are choked by Hasids returning early from the Catskills. There are buses standing all along Lee Avenue, discharging dazed passengers and worn luggage. The young boys smooth their wrin-

kled black suit jackets and brush their hats with dampened fingertips before heading in the direction of home. The girls are met by their fathers,
who help them load cardboard boxes wrapped in packing tape into the
trunks of their minivans.

The Catskills have expelled us, sent us prematurely back to the
swollen, humid bowels of the state. Here the air is thick with dust and
exhaust, blowing hotly around us like the breath of an angry animal.
Standing on the overpass of the highway with my luggage tucked between my legs, I look up at the flimsy gray sky, just to see if it's the same
one that stared back at me in camp, indifferent and unassuming. Perhaps
there are no plagues, only the fickleness of nature. Perhaps there are no
consequences, just ugliness. Maybe punishment is something that only
comes from people, not from God.

In the week before school starts, I have time to pursue my own interests.
In between shopping trips with Bubby to buy new shoes and stockings for
the coming year, I board the bus to Borough Park, determined to sneak
a few books home. I have not read anything all summer; bringing books
to camp with me would have been too dangerous. It feels nice to have
time to myself again, and enough privacy that I don't have to be afraid
my thoughts are being overheard.

The library still has the school reading lists on display, and the carts
are groaning with the weight of new paperbacks, their spines sparkling
on the shelf. I grab the most recent Harry Potter book as well as the
first in the popular Philip Pullman trilogy, and for good measure, a book
recommended by the library: *A Tree Grows in Brooklyn*. I still remember
the warm, cozy feeling I had when I read *The Chosen*, like slurping down
Bubby's chicken soup on a cold winter day. After all, am I not a girl growing up in Brooklyn, just like the heroine of this book claims to be? How
different can she and I be, when we live on the same dust-choked streets?

Literature was just as incongruous in Francie's Williamsburg as it is
in mine. Elegant words skip reluctantly off the page to join the impoverished heroine in her crowded, teeming environment. Her world was
almost too full of suffering to make room for the innocent, flirtatious
beauty of classic poetry and literature. I watch dreamily as Francie is

elevated to positions of greater material comfort throughout the book, as she takes minuscule but steady steps away from the extreme poverty she starts out in, but always with a sinking feeling in my stomach that the happy ending I'm hoping for may very likely never come. And as I become more deeply entangled in Francie's prospects, I take it more personally when she fails or is disappointed, because I feel somehow that if she can come out of it, then so can I, in some way—come out of this grimy world in which I'm stuck, seemingly, for good.

In the end, Francie goes off to college, and I do not know if I must make of this a triumph. Is it a given, then, that all her dreams will come true? I can never go to college, I know. They censor the word out of our textbooks. Education, they say, leads to nothing good. This is because education—and college—is the first step out of Williamsburg, the first on the path to promiscuity that Zeidy always promised me was an endless loop of missteps that distanced a Jew so far from God as to put the soul into a spiritual coma. Yes, education could kill my soul, I know that, but where did Francie go, I wonder, after college, and did she ever come back? Can you ever really leave the place you come from? Isn't it best to stay where you belong, rather than risk trying to insert yourself somewhere else and failing?

High school starts on Monday. I have three more years left of school, of childhood. I resolve to leave Brooklyn one day. I cannot be one of those girls who fritters away her entire life in this small, stifling square of tenements, when there is an entire world out there waiting to be explored. I don't know how, but maybe my escape will be accomplished in small, steady steps, like Francie's. Maybe it will take years. But I know, with great certainty, that it will be.

4

The Inferiority of
My Connections

*"Could you expect me to rejoice in the inferiority of your
connections? To congratulate myself on the hope of relations,
whose condition in life is so decidedly beneath my own?"*
—From Pride and Prejudice, *by Jane Austen*

My right hand gripping an exposed ceiling beam, the left one leaning on
the shoulder of the woman balanced precariously beside me, I struggle to
maintain my high-heeled footing on the slender back of the synagogue
pew. I have snagged a front-row spot in the Satmar synagogue on the
night of Simchas Torah, and like everyone else in the shul, I am waiting for the Satmar Rebbe to make his entrance fifty feet below me. In
the women's section, a narrow gallery that surrounds the synagogue, I
peer through tiny holes in the tightly slatted wooden partition to get a
glimpse of the men dancing downstairs. I wonder what would happen
if the flimsy panel gave way and all the women leaning on it were to
tumble down into the abyss. What a scandal, for men and women to
mingle in such a holy place, on such a holy night. I can't stifle a giggle

at the image, and the dour middle-aged woman crouching in front of me turns around to glare.

It's my first time attending the festivities, and I'm not sure I have a taste for it. The crush in the shallow gallery is overwhelming. Thousands of women have come from all over town, dressed in their holiday best, the married ones decked out in white silk kerchiefs, the young girls in freshly starched suits and perfectly styled bobs. All of them scramble madly over each other in an attempt to catch a glimpse of the rabbi's dance. Being only fourteen, my friends and I have a hard time competing with the older married women for the best view, but dignity is less important to us, and so we don't mind assuming the most awkward positions to seize a prime space.

Only two minutes to midnight.

How senseless it seems, as I watch my friends contort their limbs, craning their necks to get a better view; how utterly ridiculous to expend so much effort for a tiny peephole's view of an old man swaying back and forth with a scroll. I am bored, and my neck hurts, and the rabbi hasn't even arrived yet. Downstairs I see the men milling about in a sea of prayer shawls; they move in slow streams, their dance a side-to-side sway. The synagogue has long since exceeded its legal capacity, but the cops parked outside, perhaps greased into silence, sit comfortably behind their wheels in a show of security. Every ten minutes someone else faints from the heat, and a cry for Hatzolah is heard. I watch one of the men throw off his prayer shawl and call for a stretcher, and the victim is removed to one of the side rooms. Around me the women shift impatiently, still waiting for the rabbi. All this is just foreplay to them, a prelude to the exquisite moment when our rabbi will dance with his divine bride, the Torah.

Even if I can't muster the fervor of the crowd, I know I must appear to be engrossed in the proceedings; how else can I justify my pushing and shoving to get to the front if it's not to soak up some measure of divine ecstasy? I need to be seen here. There isn't a woman in Williamsburg who would pass up the chance to see the Satmar Rebbe's annual dance.

The men sing wordless songs. There are seven Simchas Torah tunes, and they are all primitive melodies strung together by meaningless syllables. But these sounds are classic Jewish sounds, expressions of pure, animal emotion that transcend any language. On this night, words aren't needed. Thousands of men lift their hands to the heavens and stamp their feet rhythmically on the stone floor, singing, "*Oy yoy yoy yoy, yei ti ri rei ti ri rei ti ri rei oy yoy!*" and "*Ay yay yay yay, ay di ri ra ra ay di ri ra ra . . .*" I am almost swept away myself, by the power of all those voices blending together; for a moment it seems as if these men can blur the lines between heaven and earth with their rapturous singing. I can no longer see people; instead I am surrounded by saints; all sin is temporarily wiped clean. Only I remain mortal, fallible. Perhaps I am beginning to understand the glory of this event after all; maybe the only reason I scorned it is because I am truly ignorant, overlooked by the divine light that seems to shine on everyone else. I feel as if tonight may be the night when I finally understand my role, my common destiny, and shake off the cold threads of doubt that separate me from my people.

I've come here with five friends, the most exclusive clique in our ninth-grade class. The queen bee is here as well, with her perfect two-name combination that ripples enviably off my tongue: Miriam-Malka, of the shiny auburn flip and deep dimples. I am convinced her regal status is a result of that wonderful name alone, that inimitable combination with the rare advantage of not being shared by hundreds of other girls in Williamsburg. (I am one of five girls named Devoiri in my ninth-grade class, and one of perhaps a hundred in my school; my ordinary name is hardly the stuff of nobility.) Watching her dangling effortlessly from the ceiling beams with one foot on the arm of a chair and the other leaning against the partition, peering through the highest peephole in the screen, I desire her certainty. Miriam-Malka belongs here; this is her natural habitat.

Miriam-Malka, the big shot who kills with kindness, the girl everyone wants as an ally, is fickle when it comes to selecting her company, and I am lucky to be in her dazzling entourage, but to stay inside her circle I must constantly prove myself worthy. I'm here tonight not to see the rabbi but to show Miriam-Malka that I'm just like the other girls in our group, that I can think of nothing more exciting than a trip to the jam-packed synagogue on the night of Simchas Torah.

"Shh, the rebbe is here," a woman whispers excitedly, elbowing me in
the ribs to quiet me down, even though I haven't been talking. The wom-
en's section hushes immediately. I try to peer through the partition again,
but ten other women are pushing me to get to the same peephole, and so
eventually I have to use my knee to insert myself back into the throng at
the front. Downstairs, the sea of men has parted to make a path for the
rabbi, and a little clearing has been created for him, with the whole crowd
pushing and shoving behind the front row of *gabbaim,* the strong young
yeshiva students who serve as the rabbi's constant escort. The *gabbaim* link
arms, creating a human fence around the rabbi to keep the crowd from surg-
ing forward. Everyone wants to touch Reb Moshe, shake his hand, kiss the
fringes of the ivory prayer shawl that is draped over his head and body, or
simply look into his holy eyes, glazed over with age. I can see him, frail and
bent, holding the scroll close to his chest, swaying ever so slightly in the
midst of the small clearing. From my vantage point, he is as tiny as an ant
in the quivering mass of men, his stature bent, his aura so feeble as to seem
almost insignificant. It is the tangible reverence vibrating throughout the
synagogue that projects a halo of ethereal grace on this dainty, fragile old
man. With the unquestioning faith of so many people focused directly on
him, he can't help but take on a divine quality, yet I am awed not so much
by the rabbi himself as by the jubilant crowd he commands, and the magni-
tude of their devotion. It makes me almost want to worship with them, just
so I can be one of them and feel what they feel, but that man down there is
too ordinary-looking to stir in me that absolute, unquestioning zeal.

I leave after the third dance, even though there are four more before
the celebration ends at dawn. It is already 3:30 a.m., and I've never been
good at functioning at this late hour. I'm tired of wrestling with the other
women for a spot I don't really want. I still need to find my way back home
in the dark. I say good-bye to my friends, murmuring an excuse about
meeting my grandmother outside, but they can't hear me in all that noise
anyway. I walk down the very stairs on which they say the first rabbi's only
daughter was pushed to her death, and in her womb the child who stood to
inherit the coveted Satmar dynasty, which others already had their eye on,
was killed only weeks before he was expected to be born. I hate taking those
steps on my own. I can feel her, Roize, the rabbi's only, precious daughter,

standing there with her large pregnant stomach, watching me with those trademark Teitelbaum eyes. Her pain lives within me. Unlike the others, I cannot forget. That was when Satmar was still a young community, hardly worth fighting over. Now the current rabbi's sons are squabbling like children over a plastic throne. Where, I wonder, is the brotherly love that God commanded Jews to feel for each other, now, in this community that calls itself holy? Back in Europe, Zeidy says, no one would dream of fighting to be called a rabbi. In fact, they often turned down the position when it was offered to them. A man truly worthy of being a rabbi is a humble one. He is not in search of power or recognition. But in this day and age, rabbis are chauffeured in black Cadillacs and have private ritual baths built into their opulent homes. They are the celebrities of Hasidic culture. Children trade rabbi cards and boast of having rabbinical connections. On Purim, the holiday of masquerades, they Scotch-tape long beards made of white cotton balls to their chins, drape themselves in faux-fur coats, and walk with the aid of a shiny wooden cane. What more does every child dream of than to grow up to be a rabbi, or at least a rabbi's wife?

I walk home quickly through the dark streets of Williamsburg, and aside from the occasional straggling Lubavitcher Hasid visiting from Crown Heights, I am alone, and by the time I reach my corner, the magic has faded, and the whole night seems to be just a temporary blip in what has become a pattern of disenchantment. My moment of ambivalence is but a triviality in the face of the hard grid of cynicism that has already mapped out my consciousness.

I never want to be a rabbi's wife. Not if it means being like my *bubbe* and always having to submit to my husband's will. I am hungry for power, but not to lord over others; only to own myself.

In school on Monday, everyone seems to have forgotten about Simchas Torah. We won't catch a glimpse of the rebbe again for another year; neither will we visit the synagogue. Girls don't go to shul. We pray at home, or in school; it doesn't matter where or how. Only the men's prayers are regimented; only theirs count. We begin the school day as usual, our first hour spent reciting the morning prayers from our siddurim, our Hebrew prayer books. For some reason I never learned to read or speak Hebrew fast enough to keep up with the class's furious chant, so I move my lips and make sounds occasionally to look like I'm praying. When we were younger, we had special tunes for each prayer, and that would help me remember the words. Now that we are past the age of twelve, singing is forbidden to us at all times. The absence of melody drains all the joy out of prayer for me, and although I go through the motions for the sake of the watchful overseer, I have no feeling for it anymore.

The academic year has now begun in earnest. Although school officially started in September, the last month has been so riddled with holidays, including Rosh Hashanah, Yom Kippur, and Sukkot, that the academic calendar only consisted of a couple of days crammed between them. It is now mid-October, and the next long holiday is Passover, in early spring. Although a long, uninterrupted season of school days stretches before us, my friends and I take sufficient comfort in that we are finally in high school, a rank that comes with a significant amount of power and privilege.

Our new classroom is large, and its walls have white-tiled patches all over them; the others say it used to be a bathroom before it was con-verted into a classroom. The plumbing features are still there, cut-off pipes extending from various points on the walls. This building used to be PS 16, the Eastern District public school, before the neighborhood was completely overrun by Satmar families and the zoning collapsed as a result. The empty building was appropriated by the United Talmudical Academy of Satmar and turned into a private school for girls.

This massive Gothic structure, whose gargoyles were pronounced idols by the rabbi and summarily chopped off, encompasses a full square block and boasts over eighty classrooms. Nearly half a century has passed since it was first purchased, and it has become severely overcrowded, with many of the classrooms subdivided by pressurized walls and class sizes numbering between thirty and forty students each. As one of the biggest classes in the grade (thirty-seven students), we get one of the larger class-rooms, with room at the back to play *kugelech*, a game similar to jacks, where five gold-metal dice are juggled in various permutations. I am not very adept at such games; I usually don't last more than three rounds.

While my classmates prepare the necessary books and supplies for the upcoming lesson, I inspect the view; I've never been on this side of the building before. From the window of my classroom, I can see the overpass of the Brooklyn-Queens Expressway, and the tiny triangular block situated in the middle of the overpass that houses the public library. The stately redbrick building stands alone, draped and encircled by thick strands of ivy and surrounded by a high wrought-iron fence. The entrance is on Division Avenue, overlooking the highway, with three tiers of wide stone steps leading up to its looming Gothic doorway. I know that Satmar students who must pass the library on their way to school take care to walk behind it, and the block on which its entrance is located is rarely trespassed. We are forbidden to enter the library.

Zeidy says the English language acts like a slow poison to the soul. If I speak and read it too much, my soul will become tarnished to the point where it is no longer responsive to divine stimulation. Zeidy always insists I speak Yiddish, the language of my ancestors that God approves of. However, Yiddish is nothing but a hodgepodge of German, Polish, Russian, Hebrew, and other random dialects. Many of them were once considered as secular as English. How is it that Yiddish is suddenly the language of purity and righteousness?

Zeidy doesn't know it, but I don't even think in Yiddish anymore. The books he claims are treacherous serpents have become my close friends. I've already been corrupted; I'm just good at hiding it. Now, looking at the library from my classroom window, I wonder if perhaps what Zeidy predicted came true, that the books slowly dulled my soul until I was no longer receptive to the godliness right in front of me. That would explain my inability to be moved by the rabbi's dance on Simchas Torah; everyone else around me is still pure and unsullied, but I have been defiled by words and rendered blind and dumb to anything holy.

I was ten years old when I last snuck into the forbidden building, although even at that age I understood how important it was to avoid being seen. The library was largely empty. The silence made the massive rooms seem cavernous. I explored tentatively, unable to escape a crippling feeling of self-consciousness that comes with the absolute knowledge of being watched by God. I'm too afraid to go back there now, because I have so much to lose. My carefully cultivated social status could collapse. If Miriam-Malka were to find out, I'd never live it down.

I don't want to suffer through my next three years of schooling because of one careless mistake. Surely, I think, I can have my cake and eat it too.

These days I ride the city bus to the Mapleton branch of the library, thirty minutes away. It is unlikely that anyone will catch me there, and so I feel safer, taking the time to browse the back shelves before heading to the front desk. My new library card is shiny white plastic with the library logo, and at home I slip it between the box spring and the mattress to keep it securely out of sight. Thin paperbacks can be hidden there too; hardcovers are shoved behind the dresser.

I am jolted out of my reverie by the sudden hush that befalls the classroom. Mrs. Friedman, who teaches second period, is standing at the door, waiting for the routine respectful overture; all the students stand ramrod straight beside their desks until the teacher enters. I am at the window, not at my desk where I belong, and the teacher clears her throat, looking expectantly at me. I stumble quickly back to my seat, my face flushed. Already I am singled out.

Mrs. Friedman is Satmar royalty; her maiden name is Teitelbaum and she is a second cousin of the rabbi himself. *Rebbish*, they call the lucky ones who can claim some connection with rabbinical ancestry. With her tightly bound headscarf, stooped shoulders, and makeup-free face, Mrs. Friedman exudes saintliness. The rest of the class is poised at their desks with pen and paper ready for the lecture, their total obedience inspired by the teacher's imperial presence.

Derech eretz, Mrs. Friedman writes in large Hebrew script on the chalkboard. We will be learning about honor codes in second period. By the time we graduate, Mrs. Friedman assures us, we will know the proper behavior expected of us in any form of interaction in Hasidic society.

"The first and most basic rule of *derech eretz* is to always address an elder in the third person. For example, never use the word *you*, only say *the teacher* or *the principal*."

Zeidy is my elder. Do I need to start addressing him in the third person? How will that work? I wonder. "Does Zeidy want his tea with lemon?" What about Bubby? I can't refer to her in the third person: it's so impersonal. I feel as if the honor codes work to distance us from the people we love; by referring to them in the third person, I am ensuring that the age order comes before blood and personal ties. I don't like that idea at all. I can't bear to push away the few people to whom I feel close.

Like clockwork, I zone out after five minutes, the teacher's face a blur, her lips moving but no sound emerging. When the bell rings, it feels like only seconds have passed, seconds in which I have decorated my future castle in luxuriant velvets and oak-paneled libraries, with wardrobes that are all entrances to Narnia-like kingdoms. I lose myself within the opulent labyrinth of my mind.

Although I have given up on the possibility that I too might one day fall through the false back of a closet into dreamworld, I have retained the hope that a great future still awaits me, if not in a magical universe, then at least in a world outside this one.

I climb the four flights of stairs back to the classroom after a dry lunch in the bleak, windowless school cafeteria. My favorite period is next: English. The word is only a euphemism for the brief time each day when we receive our government-mandated dose of secular education. It is the only period in which I shine.

My new English teachers are "modern girls" imported from Borough Park. They aren't college graduates, God forbid, but they have real high school diplomas. More educated than any Satmar graduate could ever hope to be, these modern girls have grown up in a less restrictive Hasidic environment that we Satmars don't recognize as quite authentic. As Satmar girls, we don't owe these teachers any real respect, as they are poisoned by an excessively secular education and a negligent attitude toward religion. Misbehavior during English is never punished as severely as it is when it occurs during Yiddish period.

Miss Mandelbaum is tall, with bright yellow hair that she wears in a high ponytail. Shockingly, she's wearing lip gloss (that's too pink to be ChapStick, I can tell). Her smile shows two rows of teeth and an indecent portion of upper gum. She has a hoarse voice, as if she hasn't slept in days, and I can see in her jerky movements her nervous eagerness to please. She teaches us literature and reading comprehension. Today Miss Mandelbaum distributes a five-page short story with most of its contents blacked out by the school censor.

The story takes forever to get through, since the girls are all poor readers. They receive no other reading practice besides these weekly stories, many of which are on a fourth-grade level. Although I love to read, I can't stand the literature sessions, because I finish the story on my own in two minutes, and then I have to sit still for the rest of the hour as the class struggles through it. After ten minutes of my uninterrupted daydreaming, Miss Mandelbaum notices me looking out the window, my chin resting on my arm and my legs swinging idly. As Frimet stumbles over the words, breaking them into awkward syllables that, when strung together, sound nothing like the original word, the teacher motions to me with her finger pointed at the story in her hand, reminding me to "look in." With improvised sign language, I show her I've already read the whole story. I can see from the disdainful look on her face that she thinks I'm lying, that she assumes I'm a dumb girl who can't read and I'm pretending to be finished. She asks Frimet to pause.

"Devoiri, you read now."

"Okay," I say, "where are we up to?"

Ruchy, who is sitting in front of me, turns around to show me the place, and I begin reading a passage from the badly maimed piece on a little boy and his pet dog. After two sentences, I glance upward to catch the shocked glimpse on Miss Mandelbaum's face. Coming from Borough Park, she isn't expecting to find a student here who can read decently, let alone quickly, easily, and with excellent inflection. I can tell she is wondering how I could possibly have come by such perfect English.

The rest of the class already knows I'm a good reader and relishes the teacher's comeuppance. They love it when I read, because my loud, lively reading and expressive interpretation of the story actually make the session fun. Miss Mandelbaum, however, is annoyed.

"Well, clearly you don't need any reading practice, but the other girls do. We need to give everyone a turn."

The class groans as Esty begins her usual barely audible rendition. She whispers so that her mistakes can't be heard. Miss Mandelbaum commands her to speak louder, but we all smirk, knowing it will never work. Esty pretends she is very shy, hunching her shoulders and blushing furiously so that the teacher will give up. I smile a small, secret smile. The game is on.

Miss Mandelbaum switches from student to student, asking each of them to read loudly and clearly, but they all repeat Esty's routine. Eventually she has no choice but to ask me to read, which I gladly do, with delightful ostentation. The rest of the class cups their palms around their faces to hide their amusement.

This is how I have achieved my own unique niche of popularity. I have no intention of being a docile student in English period this year. While acting out during Yiddish period will only make me an outcast, audacity during English lessons will make me something of a hero, if a notorious one. There is nothing I could be learning that is not worth missing out on for a bit of fun and an admiring audience.

When the bell rings for dismissal, I grab my bag and fly down the four flights of stairs, jumping them three at a time, until I am finally outside the custody of the voluminous building. Marcy Avenue streams with clusters of students walking home from school, whispering quietly, stepping off the curb when men pass. Most men, however, know not to be on the street at this hour, when all the girls in Williamsburg are set free, sent home to help their mothers with dinner and care for their younger siblings.

I come home to an empty house, as usual. Bubby has gone to the old-age home to help feed the patients, so I retreat to my room for an uninterrupted hour of reading. *Little Women* is under my mattress this week—the thin paperback edition, which is convenient for hiding. I still cannot decide if Jo is a boy and Laurie a girl, or the other way around, or if they are both boys. I like Jo.

It seems as if only minutes have passed when I hear my grandfather's heavy footfalls up the stairs, and I quickly stash my book under the mattress again, tucking the sheet in so it doesn't look disturbed.

I am a good girl, I am a good girl, I am a good girl.

I rearrange my facial expression into one I think a good girl would wear—meek, blank, unassuming. Sometimes I am afraid Zeidy, with his piercing blue eyes and luminous white beard, can see through my performance, his God-given intuition penetrating my carefully constructed mask. My heart would break if he knew the truth about me. I'm not the *aidel maidel,* the modest girl, he worked so hard to create.

• • •

My new stockings have thick brown seams running up the back. Now when I walk the streets, it's obvious I'm a high school girl, as only they get to wear seams. It used to be you started wearing them in tenth grade, but then the rabbi decided that the ninth graders were too mature to be wearing plain dark-colored tights. My teacher says the seam is there so that people won't mistake the flesh-colored stocking for my leg, a reminder that it's just fabric and not the horror of exposed skin. I don't understand how anyone could mistake the stocking for my leg, seeing as how the skin on my leg is so white and the stocking a murky coffee color.

I think my ankles look slim and pretty, though, in the new stockings, with my new brown leather penny loafers just like what the other girls are wearing. I can't believe I'm already in high school. Only three more years of school. I could be married in four years.

All the teachers in high school seem to know me or know about me, even though I've never met them before. They pay special attention to me because I don't live with my parents.

I'm the only girl in my class who doesn't live with her parents. The only girl in the grade aside from Raiza Ruchy Halpern, who lives with her aunt because her parents died when she was younger. Everyone calls her "nebach" or "rachmanus" behind her back, and sometimes I'm terrified that that's what they call me too. A pity, a charity case, a nothing.

"Please don't make me the charity case," I tell my teacher when she approaches me after class, asking me if I need someone to talk to. My differentness surrounds me like a halo. It's sickening.

My friends are older now. Their older sisters are getting engaged. They know that my lack of parents means I will have a harder time getting married, and that means I am different from them. The difference is like a new, full-grown elephant in the room, and it makes everyone uncomfortable.

Esty Oberlander has a sister at home who is twenty-two, my friends whisper. She got stuck waiting for her brother to get married, and by the time she was up for consideration, she was already twenty-one, three years too old. Even if you come from a fine family like the Oberlanders and you have more money than you can ever spend, a twenty-one-year-old girl does not go easy.

I won't go easy, not with two renegade parents blocking my path. I have to pass my father on the street and pretend not to recognize him, even when he waves energetically from across the road, his coffee-splattered shirt stretched awkwardly over his belly, his skinny legs shuffling eagerly toward me. My mother openly lives her life as a goy, and who could guarantee that the same insanity won't enter my head like it did hers? Only complete lunacy could explain why someone would reject God and the ways of his people, like she did.

At least I have no sisters in front of me to keep me waiting. I know Zeidy will start looking into matches when I turn sixteen, and he won't wait long.

If you have no roots, you have no legacy. All our worth is defined by the worth of our ancestors. We make the name for our children. Who would want me, with no name to pass on?

My mother has been gone for as long as I can remember. Her mysterious disappearance, her surprising deviation from the path, is the subject of much scandal. I carry the burden of that disgrace.

"Why do bad things happen?" I ask Bubby. "Do they come from Hashem?"

"No, not Hashem. Only Satan," Bubby answers, drying the dishes with a red-checkered tea towel while I load them into the cabinets. "All bad things are because of him."

Did Satan make my father slow, with a mind like that of a petulant child, unable to care for himself or for me? Did Satan dump me, an unloved foundling of fate, into the hands of my grandparents, already exhausted from raising their own children?

I don't understand. Isn't Hashem the one in control? How can Satan operate so freely under his jurisdiction? Surely Hashem created Satan, if he created everything. Why would he make something so terrible? Why won't he stop it?

"Hitler had chicken feet, you know," Bubby remarks. "That's why he never took off his shoes. So they wouldn't see he was a *sheid*, a ghost." She scrubs at the burned remains of chicken fricassee on the bottom of a cast-iron skillet, her calloused fingers marked by years of housework. I don't think this world is such a simple place, in which bad people have deformities that mark them as evil. That's not how it works. Evil people look just like us. You can't take off their shoes and know the truth.

We learn in school that God sent Hitler to punish the Jews for enlightening themselves. He came to clean us up, eliminate all the assimilated Jews, all the *frei Yidden* who thought they could free themselves from the yoke of the chosen ones. Now we atone for their sins.

The first and greatest Satmar Rebbe said that if we became model Jews, just like in the olden days, then something like the Holocaust wouldn't happen again, because God would be pleased with us. But how are we pleasing him with our little efforts, the thicker stocking, the longer skirt? Is that really all it takes to make God happy?

Bubby says it can happen again anyway. She says people don't realize it, but stuff like the Holocaust has been happening to Jews for centuries, every fifty or so years. We are right on schedule for another event, she says. Pogroms, Crusades, the Inquisition, it's all the same. To think that we are in control is ridiculous, she says. But she doesn't say this in front of Zeidy, who believes the Satmar Rebbe can save us from anything. After all, the Rebbe himself was miraculously rescued from the concentration camps, and now we celebrate that day as a holiday every year.

Bubby says everyone hates Jews, even the ones who pretend not to. It's the way God made the world, she says, they can't help it. She warns me never to trust a goy, no matter how kind he appears to be.

It's strange to imagine a whole world of people I've never met hating me already, when I'm so young and I haven't even done anything yet. My mother is a goy now. Does that mean she's one of them? Does she hate me too?

Bubby scoffs at my question. A Jew can never be a goy, she says, even if they try their hardest to become one. They may dress like one, speak like one, live like one, but Jewishness is something that can never be erased. Even Hitler knew that.

At night I lie awake after the street traffic quiets down and I fold my pillow in half and press the tense edge into my stomach, bending my body around its crease. I ask God if he loves me. Will he send another *sheid,* another Hitler, to kill me too? Did he put the gnawing pain in my belly or did Satan?

I feel unloved. By my parents, yes, and by the people who reject me for being their offspring, and by my aunts and cousins who look down at me because I'm evidence of a familial scandal, but mostly I feel unloved by God, who surely put me here and forgot about me. Without God's love, what chance do I have at happiness?

I fall asleep against a pillow damp with tears, the clatter of the elevated train punctuating fitful dreams. As hooded officers in SS uniforms race through Williamsburg on black stallions, I become swept up in the crowds of people trying to escape, but suddenly I hear the distinct whir of a helicopter, and looking up I can see a woman I know to be my mother, waiting to rescue me. As we zoom off into the nearing dawn, I look down at the panicked masses below us and feel, finally, safe from it all.

I am awakened by the sound of shouting coming from the street. My alarm clock reads three a.m. Frightened, I tumble out of bed and race to the window. Bubby and Zeidy are awake in the next room as well, and my head turns in the window grate to see both of them looking out the window next to mine. On the street, men clad in white pajamas and bedroom slippers run madly through the road, screaming, *"Chaptz'em! Chaptz'em!"*

Catch him, they are screaming, catch the interloper who invaded us in the night. As they scream to all the neighboring homes, more and more men bound down the stairs of brownstones in their pajamas to join the chase.

"What happened?" I ask, looking toward Bubby in the next window over.

"They broke into Mrs. Deutsch's apartment next door, took all her silver," she says, shaking her head in dismay. *"Shvartzes,* a group of young ones, they were; from Broadway they came."

She is referring to the African-American neighborhood on the other side of the tracks, where we are never allowed to wander. The el train has always acted as a barrier between us and the variety of ethnic people that populate this part of Brooklyn, like indigenous weeds springing up among the abandoned factories and warehouses. Williamsburg is so ugly, who else would want to live here, says Bubby, except the lower classes?

Jews do well among the lower class, though. Bubby says it's convenient for us to be presumed poor and unintelligent, so as not to spark the jealousy and resentment of the gentiles. In Europe, she says, the goyim were angry at Jews who forgot their place and became richer and more educated than their gentile peers.

I see the *shomrim,* the community guardians, pull up at the house next door in their armored jackets with the neon logo on the back, stepping off motorized bikes. Three bearded men drag a young black teenager by his hands, and I can see he hangs heavily between them.

"That boy can't be older than fourteen!" says Bubby, looking down at the captured culprit. "For what does he have to steal, so he can be in a gang? Ach, so sad, from so young they are already trouble."

The *shomrim* members crowd around the quivering boy. I watch them kick him mercilessly until he is sobbing and wailing, "I din't do nuttin', I swear! I din't do nuttin'!" He cries out his one defense, over and over, begging for mercy.

The men beat him for what seems like forever. "You think you can come in here and do what you want? Impress your friends? Where are your friends now, huh?" they ask mockingly. "You think you can bring your filthy kind into this neighborhood? Oh no, not here. No, we won't call the police, but we'll take care of you like no one else can, you understand?"

"Yes, yes, I understand . . .," the boy wails. "Let me go, please, I din't do nuttin'!"

"If we catch one of you here ever again, we'll kill you, you hear? We'll kill you! You tell your little friends that, you tell them never to come near us again or we will rain hell down on their black souls."

They step back, and the young man lifts himself up and flees into the night. The *shomrim* get back on their bikes, brushing off their shiny jackets. Within fifteen minutes, the street is as silent as death again. I feel sick.

Bubby pulls her head back in from the window. "Ah *mazel,*" she says, "so lucky we are to have our own police force, when the real police can't catch a nut when it falls from a tree. We have no one to depend on, Devoraleh," she says, looking at me, "except our own. Don't forget that."

I chastise myself once again for feeling compassion at the inappropriate time. For the teenager I should not feel pity, because he is the enemy. I should feel bad for poor Mrs. Deutsch, who got the fright of her life and lost all her precious silver heirlooms. I know this, and yet I wipe shameful tears from my cheek. Luckily no one can see them in the dark.

My father comes pounding up the steps and knocks loudly on the front door. "Mommy!" he calls, his voice breathy with excitement. "Did you see? Did you see what happened?"

When Bubby opens the door, I can see my father standing in his creased, dirty pajamas, his body quivering strangely as he bounces on the balls of his naked feet.

"I chased them!" he announces triumphantly. "I was there when they caught him."

Bubby sighs. "What were you doing running with no shoes, Shia?"

Blood seeps from his toes onto the doormat, and my father is oblivious, his face alight with idiotic exuberance.

"Go home, Shia," Zeidy says sadly. "Go home and go to sleep." He closes the door on my father's face, gently, almost reverently, his palms lingering on the knob even after my father's footsteps can be heard retreating down the hall.

I try to avoid my father. Somehow I understand that the more I distance myself from him, the more I avoid the shame that is associated with his retardation and strange behavior. It's hard for me when I walk on the street with my friends on Shabbos and we pass the cupcake lady on Hooper Street, who has hairs growing out of the warts on her chin, or Golly the Meshuggener, who smokes stinky cigarettes on the corner of Keap Street and Lee Avenue, a glazed look in his eye and confusion in his movements. The girls make a fuss about crossing the street to avoid them, and I wonder what they would do if they were to encounter my father rambling down Lee Avenue toward them. Perhaps they already have, without knowing who he was.

I am mostly angry at how everything seems to be working against me in this life. Enough that I have to deal with divorced parents, with a mother who is a goy, but a crazy father too? It just feels hopeless, because no matter how hard I try to be perfect, no matter how much I fit in, I can never shake my ties to him.

I don't understand how I can be related to this man, whom I look nothing like, but mostly I don't understand why no one in my family ever tries to help him, to get him treatment. They just let him wander around and fend for himself, embarrassing me in the process.

Bubby says that a problem child is a punishment; Zeidy says it's a test from God. To treat a problem is to evade the suffering that God felt you deserved. Also, Bubby says, when you start figuring out why a problem is a problem, and you start putting terrifying labels on it, then suddenly everyone knows there's a problem, and tell me, says Bubby, tell me, who will then marry all your other children, when you have a son with a medically diagnosed problem? Better not to know, she says. Better just to accept God's plan.

They tried to make the best of the situation, in their own way. When my father turned twenty-four and still no matchmaker had been successful in finding him a wife, Bubby and Zeidy started looking overseas, hoping to find a young girl in unfortunate circumstances who would be willing to come to America for the promise of a life of comfort. An entire seven-room apartment they prepared, on the third floor of their brownstone home, with brand-new parquet floors and elegant wallpapers, outfitted with comfortable furnishings and luxurious rugs. Money was no obstacle; they would pay for the wedding, the travel expenses, anything the girl should desire. And it was my mother they found, child of an impoverished divorcée, living off the charity of her London benefactor as she attended the Jewish girls' seminary. She jumped at the chance to leave, to go to a new country where all sorts of possibilities awaited.

Bubby and Zeidy thought they were done raising their children before they took me in, but when my parents' marriage began to fall apart soon after I was born, and my mother disappeared to follow her dreams of higher education in America, I was left in their care. Also a punishment, perhaps? I wonder if I am but another figment of the suffering that Zeidy takes such spiritual relish in, if to my grandparents I am but a test from God, one to be borne humbly, without complaint.

In books I pick the perfect parents and imagine what it would be like to be born to them, living in a pink-walled room with a canopy bed, with a window overlooking a lush suburban lawn.

My imaginary parents would get me braces to straighten my teeth and buy me nice clothes. I'd go to real schools and maybe even to college. I'd play tennis and ride a bike. They wouldn't tell me to keep my head down and speak quietly.

On Shabbos my lack of family stands out more sharply than it does during the week. After all, I have no younger siblings to take care of and no older ones to visit. Shabbos is a time meant to be spent with family, and I have no one to spend it with but my grandparents. Which is why I look forward especially to visitors; sometimes one of my married cousins will come by to pay their respects to Bubby and Zeidy, and I will get some respite from my boredom.

However, as soon as my cousins start having babies, they can no longer visit, because it is forbidden to carry on Shabbos. Unable to use a stroller, they are stuck at home until Shabbos is over.

This has been a heated topic at the Shabbos table these past few weeks, because recently a rabbi in Williamsburg decided it's lawful to carry on Shabbos because of the new *eiruv*. Halacha, or Jewish law, forbids carrying anything on one's person in public domain, but with an *eiruv*, a symbolic fence surrounding public property, the area is considered private, and carrying children, house keys, and other necessary items becomes legal.

All the other rabbis say the new *eiruv* isn't kosher. There's no way, they claim, to create a "private domain" in a place like Brooklyn. The main issue, they say, is Bedford Avenue, which runs through Williamsburg and continues on for miles through different Brooklyn neighborhoods. I don't understand the legal implications of the debate, but I do know that it's all anyone is talking about these days.

In the beginning no one was actually using the *eiruv*, because people were skeptical about its ability to remain intact in a neighborhood where graffiti pops up on freshly painted walls before they have a chance to dry. But slowly, as more rabbis are giving the *eiruv* their own personal stamp of approval, women have started showing up on the streets with their baby carriages on Shabbos afternoons, and every time there is a sighting, Zeidy comes home after shul with more reports of people using the *eiruv*. Groups of incensed young Hasids have taken to lying in wait on the main avenues to shout at these women as they walk past—women who, in their sincere opinion, are clearly flouting Shabbos law. Some are even throwing rocks, Zeidy says angrily. Again, he laments, these kids don't care for halacha; all they care about is that they have something to shout about.

Zeidy actually believes the *eiruv* is kosher, having studied the issue extensively on his own, and there's no religious opinion I respect more than my grandfather's. I admire his unique combination of Talmudic intelligence and open-mindedness. Zeidy never says no just for the sake of saying no, like some rabbis. A good rabbi, Zeidy says, is one who can find the *heter*, the loophole in the law that allows for flexibility. A rabbi who lacks sufficient knowledge of the Talmud will always lean toward the stricter side, because he is unsure of his own ability to find the loopholes.

However, Zeidy warns me not to use the *eiruv*, even though he considers it perfectly kosher. If other people consider it an *aveirah*, a sin, then I could possibly violate the law of *ma'aras eyin*, where one appears to sin and so misleads others into judging them as having sinned. He worries about the crowds that gather to shout angrily at perceived violators, screaming "Shabbos, Shabbos, holy Shabbos!" over and over in furious tones. He doesn't want to attract that kind of righteous anger to his family.

I don't mind much, since I don't have a baby to carry around anyway.

On Tuesday the eleventh of September, 2001, I am late to school. At a quarter past ten in the morning, I walk the three blocks to the high school building at a fast clip, but as I round the corner to Harrison Avenue, I notice something is different. The sky is an ominous shade of gray, hanging heavy and low on the rooftops. It doesn't feel like the onset of rain, but the air is murky somehow, like it has too much construction dust floating in it. In school, the windows are open because there is no air-conditioning in the building and fall hasn't really arrived yet. Normally the noise from the street overwhelms the sound of the teacher's voice and we have to close the windows for sessions, but today the street is eerily quiet. No drilling, no honking, no sound of trucks bumping along the metal plates on the wide two-way street outside. All I can hear are the faint chirping sounds of sparrows.

At one o'clock the PA system crackles faintly as the secretary struggles to work the ancient intercom. It is almost never used.

"All girls are dismissed." The voice is muffled but loud. There is a small shriek of feedback that makes us cover our ears, but then the secretary's voice is back, clearer this time. "Please pack your things and file out the exits in a neat, organized line. There are buses waiting outside to transport those of you who live far away. We will notify you when school is back in session."

I look around at my classmates in confusion. The only time they ever cancel school is if there is a fire or some other emergency. It is in nobody's interest to have a community full of idle young girls lolling around the streets. But there are no alarms going off. Why are they sending us home? Most of the girls are too grateful to be released to inquire. They zip up their briefcases and line up in the hallways, giggling excitedly. Only I am curious, it seems.

I walk home pensively. Zeidy might not even believe me when I get home. He might think I'm just trying to skip school. What will I tell him, that we were suddenly dismissed? It sounds ridiculous.

Zeidy is not in his office when I tiptoe quietly through the front hall. His door is wide open, but his desk is unoccupied. Upstairs, Bubby is kneading challah dough in the kitchen, her apron coated in sticky dough residue. The phone is cradled under her ear and she doesn't say anything when I come in noisily, dropping my book bag on the chair. I listen to her conversation, but she's not saying much, only nodding here and there and asking vague questions like "Why?" and "How?"

Finally I hear Zeidy's heavy footsteps climb the stairs. He's holding a folded newspaper in his hand. Zeidy never brings secular newspapers into his home, but sometimes he goes across Broadway to the Mexican bodega to read the business section of *The Wall Street Journal*, if he needs to know something about the stock market. I wonder why he's bringing it into the house.

He motions to Bubby to put down the phone. "Look at this," he says, spreading the newspaper out on the floury tabletop. On the cover is a photo of the Twin Towers burning, it seems. I don't understand why Zeidy is showing this to us.

"What is this?" I ask.

"It's a terrorist attack. Happened this morning, would you believe it? A plane flew into the Twin Towers."

"This morning?" I ask in disbelief. "What time this morning?" It's a quarter past two in the afternoon right now. If a plane crashed into a building in the morning, wouldn't we have heard something before now?

"Eight-something. I'm going to go buy a radio so we can listen to the news."

I'm shocked. Zeidy never lets us listen to the radio. This must be serious; this must be why we were dismissed early. We spend the rest of the afternoon huddled next to the tiny radio in the kitchen, listening to the same broadcast over and over again. "At eight forty-six this morning, a plane crashed into the first tower . . ."

"They'll blame it on the Jews," Zeidy says, shaking his head. "They always do."

"Not the Jews," says Bubby. "Israel, but not the Jews."

"No, Fraida, don't you understand?" Zeidy says slowly. "They think it's the same thing."

Bubby thinks there will be another Holocaust. She thinks there will be riots and Americans will want to kick out all the Jews. She says she always knew it would happen again.

"Do *teshuvah*," she begs me. "Repent in time for Yom Kippur. The world can turn upside down in the space of a moment."

They say a fish talked in the village of New Square, which is a small Hasidic compound in upstate New York. The still-writhing carp opened its mouth and spat out a warning to the Jews to atone for their sins or there would be hell to pay. There's a whole panic about it. Apparently Moshe the fishmonger was busy killing and cleaning carp to meet the holiday demands, and just as he was about to bring the heavy cleaver down on the fish's head, it opened its mouth and a voice sounded from it. There were witnesses to the event; both Jewish and gentile workers in the fish market claim they heard the fish speak. It announced itself by name and declared it had been sent to remind the Jewish people that God was still watching, that he would punish them for their misdeeds. "Seek forgiveness," the fish announced, "or destruction will rain down on you."

Since this occurred just after the Twin Towers were attacked and right before Yom Kippur, the annual day of atonement, the story was especially juicy. What else could this be but a reminder to us all? True repentance was in order. There was proof of reincarnation in our very midst.

The details of the story spread quickly and changed constantly. Every day someone was stopping by the house to bring a fresh report of the supposed true version. But the truth didn't matter; the bottom line remained the same. If the fish talked, then it was all real. It was frightening to contemplate. One could no longer expect to go through the motions of atonement on Yom Kippur, mouthing prayers out of a sense of obligation. Everyone around me was truly galvanized now; they were taking it seriously.

I too want to believe the fish talked, but not for that reason. I don't want to think about my sins and the pack of punishments God has in store for me. I want to focus on the magic of it, the miraculous testimony of a fish before he gasped his last breath. They say it was served at the fishmonger's pre-fast meal, coated in the gelatin that formed around its own skin.

Zeidy doesn't believe in the talking fish. He says that God doesn't perform miracles anymore, not in this day and age. He prefers to work according to the natural order of things, so his interference won't draw attention. I understand why one would be skeptical of such a story, but I don't concur with Zeidy's reasoning. Why would God suddenly stop performing miracles? Surely the same God who split the Red Sea and delivered manna in the desert didn't suddenly lose his appetite for drama. I'd rather believe in reincarnation than hell. The idea of an afterlife is so much more tolerable when returning is an option.

Zeidy will go to New Square for Yom Kippur just like he does every year, even with the fuss about the talking fish. He and the Skverer Rebbe go way back, and at one point he even wanted to move there, but Bubby resisted. She said she had a bad feeling about the village, back when it was just two rows of suburban homes on the northwestern edge of Rockland County. She was right. Now they have separate sidewalks for men and women up there, labeled clearly in color-coded signs. I would be mortified if I had to live in a place where I was banned from walking on certain sidewalks.

Bubby and I stay in Williamsburg and go to shul together, on the only day of the year when the women's section is actually used. Everyone will spend the entire fast day praying for mercy. I am not a good faster, and standing in the shul all day hardly distracts me from my gnawing hunger. Around me everyone is genuinely penitent, frightened by the prospect of their future being decided in heaven today.

In school I was taught that if we don't atone for our sins before the last call of the ram's horn on Yom Kippur, Hashem will exact his own justice. There is nothing in this world that is undeserved, my teachers state emphatically; every ounce of suffering is counted and measured out by God. I begin to understand the logic behind thinking of ourselves as inherently evil; it follows that the more we suffer, the more evil we must be. But Bubby and Zeidy are two of the most devout people I know, and their lives are riddled with suffering. What could they have possibly done to deserve it?

Suffering today is different than it used to be, Bubby explains to me. Nowadays if someone doesn't have nice clothes or a nice car, they complain. "When I was a child, if there was a scrap of food to be found in the house, we were happy," she remembers. "We had each other, and that was all that mattered."

Although Bubby doesn't like to talk about the past, sometimes she can be convinced to tell the story of her mother. Her name was Chana Rachel, and a lot of my cousins are named after her. Chana Rachel was the fifth child in a family of seven, but by the time she got married, she only had two siblings left. A diphtheria epidemic had passed through their small Hungarian town when she was younger, and Bubby's grandmother had watched one and then another of her children die, as their throats closed up and oxygen no longer reached their lungs. When four of her children were already dead, and little Chana Rachel developed the same high fever and mottled skin, my great-great-grandmother wailed loudly in desperation and with the rage of a lunatic rammed her fist down her daughter's throat, tearing the skinlike growth that was preventing her from breathing properly. The fever broke, and Chana Rachel recovered. She would tell that story to her children many times, but only Bubby lived on to tell it to me.

This story moves me in a way I can't quite articulate. I imagine this mother of seven as a *tzadekes*, a saint, so desperate to save her children that she would do anything. Bubby says it was her prayer to God that helped her daughter recover, not the breaking of the skin in her throat. But I don't see it that way at all. I see a woman who took life into her own hands, who took action! The idea of her being fearless instead of passive thrills me.

I too want to be such a woman, who works her own miracles instead of waiting for God to perform them. Although I mumble the words of the Yom Kippur prayers along with everyone else, I don't think about what they mean, and I certainly don't want to ask for mercy.

If God thinks I'm so evil, then let him punish me, I think spitefully, wondering what kind of response my provocative claim might elicit in heaven. Bring it on, I think, angry now. Show me what you've got.

With a world that suffers so indiscriminately, God cannot possibly be a rational being. What use is there appealing to a madman? Better to play his game, dare him to mess with me.

A sudden feeling of peaceful resolution washes over me, that traditional Yom Kippur revelation that supposedly comes when one's penance has been accepted. I know instinctively that I am not as helpless as some would like me to think. In the conversation between God and myself, I am not necessarily powerless. With my charm and persuasiveness, I might even get him to cooperate with me.

In school, I hear hushed rumors about a Jewish library in Williamsburg, hosted once a week in someone's apartment, where you can take out two kosher, censored books, all written by Jewish authors. I convince Zeidy to let me go. If I can get books from a kosher library, I won't have to hide them under my mattress. My heart won't pound every time I hear a noise outside my room.

When I arrive at the designated address, the building's shabby lobby is empty, and I take the rickety elevator up to the fifth floor. In the hallway I can see that the door to 5N is open slightly, light from the apartment bursting out into the dank corridor.

Inside, a couple of high school girls peruse the wall of bookshelves. I recognize one of them, the girl with the straight black hair and the wide jaw, with eyebrows that arch into dark points above pale green eyes. Mindy is in the same class as Raizy's older sister, a grade above me, and they say she's the smartest kid in the school. A writer, she calls herself. She carries a journal with her everywhere, I've seen it. In the cafeteria she scribbles while biting into the sandwich she holds in her left hand.

She probably won't recognize me if I say hello. And she's a year older than I am. Why would she even want to talk to me?

She checks out two fat books and leaves with a friend. I wish there were someone like that in my class, someone who loved to read, even if it was just kosher books.

Zeidy comes home carrying one of the *pashkevilin* the street is littered with, angry flyers targeting the new "artists" who have recently become enamored of Williamsburg. Williamsburg was never supposed to attract this kind of crowd, drugged to a stupor, playing loud music, and wandering through the streets looking for inspiration. No one dreamed others would want to live in such an ugly, crowded place, with rancid odors rising from the gutters.

Now they are taking our land, the rabbis cry. They issue a ruling for a real-estate embargo. No one is allowed to rent or sell to the *artisten*, or hipsters, as they call themselves. But suddenly there are people willing to pay triple the money to live in raw, unrenovated hovels. Who can say no to that?

Hasids take to the streets in protest. They line up in front of the large homes of the wealthy real-estate magnates on Bedford Avenue, shaking their fists and throwing rocks at the windows. "Traitors!" they call them. *"Nisht besser fun a goy!"* You are no better than a gentile.

Curious about our new neighbors, these so-called artists, I venture over to the north side of Williamsburg, toward the waterfront where they all seem to gravitate.

At the Brooklyn Navy Yard, the full Manhattan skyline comes into view, painfully bright in the clear day, shimmering like jewels against the neckline of the river. My breath catches in my throat when I see it, this magical city that lies so close to my home, yet so far away. *Why would anyone want to leave that magnificent place to come here?* I wonder. *What does this dirty neighborhood have to offer besides the freedom to disappear into a self-imposed ghetto?*

I resolve to venture into the city on my own. I look at maps in the library—subway maps, bus maps, and regular maps—and try to memorize them. I'm afraid of getting lost; no, I'm afraid of sinking into the city as in a quicksand, afraid of getting sucked into something I can never escape.

As the J train makes its slow, swaying start across the rickety elevated tracks leading to the Williamsburg Bridge, I look down at the dirty, sludge-colored rooftops of Williamsburg and feel finally tall enough to overcome its flat, indifferent demeanor. I didn't expect to feel this good getting out. So good, I want to prance around the subway car, leaping from pole to pole in exhilaration.

On the F train I don't feel hardly as serene. Perhaps it's because I'm underground, but most likely it's because of the two middle-aged Hasidic women sitting opposite me. Although their round, sagging faces are devoid of any expression, I just know they are judging me, wondering what I'm doing going to the city on my own. I panic suddenly: what if they recognize me? Worse, what if they know someone who knows me? I couldn't bear to be found out.

I get off at the next stop and emerge on Fourteenth Street near Union Square, a thoroughfare choked with traffic and pedestrians, alive with the sound of honking cabs and braking buses, the smell of street meat wafting from the vendor carts. The noise, the sights, the smells are so overwhelming that for a moment I don't know where to turn. Then I glimpse a Barnes & Noble sign and head toward it desperately, knowing somehow that once I am inside and among the books, I will be safe.

In the bookstore there are attractive display tables everywhere, telling me what I want to read so that I don't have to figure it out for myself, which is reassuring. The new books do not appeal to me. Their covers seem too colorful and tawdry. I like reading stories that took place a long time ago, with photos of slender-nosed women on the covers, dressed in silk and lace. I feel I have more in common with the characters in older novels than I do with modern-day heroines.

I decide to purchase a cheap paperback edition of *Pride and Prejudice*. The first sentence is what draws me in. "It is a truth universally acknowledged, that a single man in possession of a good fortune must be in want of a wife." It is immediately apparent to me what this book will be about, and there is nothing my curiosity is greater about than marriage and, more important, the machinations involved in arranging such a circumstance. No one I know will talk about marriage, or anything concerning it, in front of a young, unattached woman. I cannot wait until my time comes to discover all the pertinent facts; perhaps this book may help to enlighten me.

Pride and Prejudice turns out to be a particularly delicious reading experience. For one thing, I have never come across a book with such unusually formal language and elegant tone. Still, I find it very thrilling; the deliberate and pointed phrases add tension and suspense to the narrative. This is my first introduction to pre-Victorian England; although my mother was born in the United Kingdom, this book is about a country in a vastly different era, and although at first I find much unfamiliar, I soon begin to draw strong comparisons between the world of the Bennet sisters and my own. For one thing, the incessant gossip and conniving ways of the female characters are hardly new to me. Is that not how women amuse themselves in my world as well, with persistent chatter about others, which is instantly replaced with unfailing politeness when confronted with the subject of such gossip? How thrilling to be able to identify with Elizabeth so easily, and to feel along with her the infuriating injustices meted out in her society. I laugh along with her at the hypocrisy and narrow-mindedness clearly displayed by characters that suppose themselves to be superior.

Really, I am not far off from a character in *Pride and Prejudice*. My entire future will also depend upon the advantageousness of my marriage. Status and reputation are just as important in my community, and based on equally trivial terms; while financial standing seems to be the primary concern of the exquisitely civilized Brits, my world emphasizes a more spiritual form of currency. What is most obvious to me about Elizabeth's thoughts and expressions is her innate frustration; perhaps she too is furious at being put in the humiliating position that women are always falling into, that inevitable role of the object to be chosen by the male, in whom all power rests. For a woman of such intelligence and wit, surely it is beneath her dignity to parade herself in front of the most distinguished of men, in hopes of a few morsels of attention. It is clear that Elizabeth hardly desires to lure a wealthy man into her clutches; unlike the other female characters in the book, she exhibits an independence of spirit that makes me love her. I am so anxious to discover what happens to her because, strangely, her fate feels strongly intertwined with my own.

I return to the pages of *Pride and Prejudice* as often as time will allow, sneaking in chapters whenever I can. In school I pretend to be scribbling notes diligently, but my thoughts wander far. The country town of Netherfield comes to vibrant life in my imagination, and the faces of its inhabitants appear rosily in my mind's eye.

What story could be more relevant to me than a young girl of marriageable age rejecting the choices others make for her and exerting her own independence? To think that once upon a time the whole world was like this, and I wouldn't have been the only one dissatisfied with my circumstances. If only Elizabeth were here to give me advice, to explain to me how the rebellion that comes off so gracefully in the book could be pulled off in real life.

This is my third and last year of high school. We graduate early because there's no point wasting another year in pursuit of an education we don't need. We won't get New York State diplomas, only a pompous-looking piece of parchment signed by the principal and the rabbi. Truthfully, I'll have no use for a diploma anyway, for I will never be allowed to find work beyond the few positions available for women in our society. The message is loud and clear: any effort invested in my education after this point would be a complete waste.

Still, for our last year we get to take an English class with Mrs. Berger, the most educated teacher in the school, who comes in from Queens every day, her hair crammed into a giant floppy hat. Mrs. Berger has two master's degrees and an air of superiority that no one can stand. Mostly, she is notorious among the students for being a grouch. I've watched her push and shove her way through the crowded school hallways before, knocking her heavy heels on the tile floors. Her face reflects disgust and annoyance. If she thinks this job is so beneath her, I wonder, why does she keep coming back every year?

When Mrs. Berger walks into our classroom at the beginning of the school year, she gazes at us with a look of bored disdain.

"Well, then," she says, "none of you are going to write the next Great American Novel, that's for sure." Her voice is thick with contempt, but underneath it I can hear exhaustion and disillusionment too.

Immediately, I want to challenge her statement. Who is she to say none of us will ever write anything of substance? Are we not great Americans, because we don't write books? Is reading any less than writing? Are Hebrew books worth less than English ones? Who is she to judge us? I'm surprised at my own hot indignation, when normally I am the one to criticize the lack of academic ambition around me. If only she could look at me and see that I was the exception, instead of lumping me in with the group as every outsider does.

She passes out a booklet, copies made from the grammar books we can't have, censored for forbidden words.

"My first rule," she says, turning to the blackboard with a fresh piece of chalk. "No colloquialisms, no idioms, no euphemisms." And she underscores each word with a thick white line.

I've never heard of these words before, but suddenly I love this hard, scowling woman who looks at us with such bitter dismissal in her eyes. I love her for continuing to come here year after year, offering students a curriculum they are ill-prepared to learn and disinclined to use, because I have been waiting my entire academic life for someone to tell me something I don't know.

I worship this woman, who enters our classroom each day hurling fresh insults at our indifferent group, for giving me the gift of motivation, because I have set out to prove to her that I am worthy of her efforts. Of the three hundred students she teaches a year, of the thousands she's taught in the past decade, if there's just one student who takes her seriously, maybe she will realize that she is more important here, more appreciated than she can ever know.

"No one has ever gotten an A in my class, and no one ever will," Mrs. Berger announces with finality. "The closest anyone came was an A minus, and that was last year, the first time since I came here fifteen years ago." Everyone knows it was Mindy. She was the first girl to get that grade with Mrs. Berger.

Now I am determined to get that coveted A. Around me I can hear the students shifting in interest. A challenge, no matter what kind, is something exciting, something to break up our routine. We're all delighted at the prospect.

I do get an A that year, after a few months of hard work. When I finally see the scarlet letter stamped on the paper Mrs. Berger returns to me, I look up at her triumphantly.

"See? I did it! You said no one could do it and I did it!" There is a hint of condescension in my tone, because a part of me is thrilled to be able to give her a taste of her own medicine.

Mrs. Berger looks at me blankly, no reaction in her face. After a moment she sighs suddenly, dropping her shoulders in defeat, and I mistake this for surrender.

"And so?" she retorts, looking me in the eye. "What are you going to do with that A, now that you have it?"

I don't understand the sadness on her face when she keeps giving me my perfect grades back, A after A, because I think she should be proud, that my good work is a reflection of her teaching skills.

This has been an excellent academic year for me in general, in both English and Yiddish. Knowing it was my last chance, I finally buckled down and got the perfect report card Zeidy always wanted me to get. Understandably, I'm nervous about next year; only good grades and references can help me get the job I want, teaching the English program in elementary school. I have this idea that if I could have had myself as a teacher when I was younger, it would have made all the difference, and that maybe somewhere out there is a girl like me, who wants to know more than she is allowed.

Mindy, the girl who also loved to read and write, has a job teaching seventh-grade secular studies. Everyone is talking about it. It's shocking, really; you would've thought, if she'd teach, that she'd teach religious studies, considering her background. I wonder how she got away with it, how her family allowed her to pursue such a vocation. Her mother wears a *shpitzel* wrapped around her head with only a thin band of synthetic hair sticking out the front. Even Zeidy wouldn't have ever asked Bubby to wear something like that. A wig was good enough for him.

In order to be considered for a teaching position, I have to give a model lesson in late spring, for an eighth-grade classroom. Mrs. Newman, the curriculum adviser, is observing, as is Chaya, my aunt, the English principal. Everyone thinks I am guaranteed a job because my aunt is the elementary school principal, but I think they overestimate her power. She is a puppet in the hands of the male authorities who control the school, in a position of false power that comes with a kind of shame. Being an expert in secular studies is not exactly something to be proud of. She started out supervising grades 1–8, then, slowly, they took it away from her, and now she is reduced to grades 6–8. Of all the English principals in the school, she is the best, and therefore the worst. She's the only one who wears a wig and nothing else on top, no hat, no scarf. It's not like it passes for real hair, but they are worried it makes a statement. They don't want the Satmar girls to wear their wigs frankly like that, with no sign that their hair is fake.

In late August I get the notice. I have a job, teaching sixth grade. I will earn $128 a week. I buy a straight skirt and a blazer in navy blue wool, with a light blue oxford shirt to match. I choose navy blue leather loafers with chunky square heels that make deep tapping sounds on the freshly waxed tile floor of the school hallways. I remember this building, the time when I feared the powerful people patrolling the hallways, the ones with the key to the creaky elevator, the staff who could get us in trouble on a whim. Now *I* have the key to the elevator and no longer have to climb the crowded stairwells.

The students look at me with awe. I'm barely seventeen, but to them I am looming on the cusp of adulthood, basking in that twilight moment between childhood innocence and the shackles of womanhood.

Mindy and I become instant friends, just like I always hoped we would. Finally, we are on equal footing. After we finish teaching, we walk to Lee Avenue Pizza and sit at the small table behind the counter nursing foam cups of hot coffee between our palms and talking about our jobs and the politics that go on in the office. Gradually it comes out that Mindy used to sneak books too, wherever she could find them, and we've read many of the same titles. Shockingly, she even listens to FM radio on headphones, and she shows me how to turn the dial on my stereo.

On Radio Disney at 1560 on the AM dial, Lizzie McGuire is singing "What Dreams Are Made Of" and I'm hooked. "Last Christmas" by Wham! seems to play on repeat at every station, and a lot of sugary Britney Spears and Backstreet Boys and Shania Twain. I lie awake for hours at night with my headphones on, listening to foreign, promiscuous tunes I never knew existed. I like electronic and trance music. Mindy likes teen pop.

I think I am in love with Mindy. I write her poems. I dream about giving her the world. We buy popcorn and slushies and sit on one of those benches behind the projects where no one ventures because the hooligans buy drugs there. We huddle on benches under scaffolding and shiver with cold until four a.m., unwilling to retreat to our respective homes.

One Shabbos in January, the snow comes down thick and powdery and Mindy doesn't come over to visit as usual, and I am lonely all afternoon. Sunday morning I call her and say, "Let's spend the day in the city. Let's sneak onto the J train and get lost on Broadway. Let's go see an IMAX. What if someone sees us? I don't care. We'll wrap scarves around our faces. No one will recognize us."

I love that, like me, Mindy is impulsive. Even reckless, perhaps. We take the subway to Manhattan and keep our heads lowered in the train car for fear of being recognized.

To get to Lincoln Center we have to wade through piles of blackened slush and tall snowbanks, but it feels like a revolutionary trek. The woman behind the desk at the Sony theater must think us strange: long skirts and thick beige stockings, matching bob haircuts tucked behind headbands. I look for auditorium 2. I think I see it, at the very top of the glass building, and we enter a small theater with a balcony and red curtains and red velvet seats. When the movie starts, I can see it is not an IMAX at all, and the characters aren't animated like they looked in the poster. Mindy is frightened suddenly because this feels like a bigger sin, seeing real live people in a movie. I'm scared, too, by my own boldness, I think, but it would feel silly walking out now.

The movie is called *Mystic River*. A child gets kidnapped in front of his friends, and I think something bad happens to him. Then a girl gets murdered. A lot of people get killed, and everyone seems angry and full of secrets. It's my first movie and I don't quite understand what movies are for yet: if they are representations of things, if they are true narratives, or if they are mere amusements. I feel both violated and guilty; doesn't this prove that I was wrong all along, that my independence and rebelliousness will only lead me to grief?

When we get outside, the sun is blinding and the glare reflects off the snow on the ground. I blink repeatedly in the light, standing there on the corner of Sixty-eighth Street and Broadway with Mindy's gloved hand resting in mine. Neither of us says a word.

We don't go back to the theater after that. Later when I try to remember the movie, I cannot recall the faces of the adult actors, only their bodies, laced with foreboding. Even when I am older and have watched many films and can recognize celebrities' faces, I will never be able to recall Sean Penn's appearance in that movie, or the faces of other famous members of the cast. The people in that movie seemed frighteningly real to me. Having no frame of reference for their voices, their expressions, I believed that those characters were as alive as Mindy and me, trapped in a frightening tableau.

Perhaps they are right about the outside world, I thought at the time. What a nightmarish existence it must be, to live in the shadow of such violence. When I grew older, I would realize that the dangers that movie presented existed in my own community as well, only they were shrouded in secrecy and allowed to fester there. And I would come to the conclusion that a society that was honest about its perils was better than one that denied its citizens the knowledge and preparation needed to fend off their approach.

If you are forced to confront your fears on a daily basis, they disintegrate, like illusions when viewed up close. Maybe being always protected made me more fearful, and I would later dip cautiously into the outside world, never allowing myself to be submerged completely, and always jerking back into the familiarity of my own life when my senses were overwhelmed. For years I would stand with a foot in each sphere, drawn to the exotic universe that lay on the other side of the portal, wrenched back by the warnings that sounded like alarm bells in my mind.

5

Possessed of a Purpose

The purpose which now took possession of her was a natural one to a poor and ambitious girl, but the means she took to gain her end were not the best.
—From Little Women, *by Louisa May Alcott*

The matchmaker calls almost every night now. I know because when Zeidy takes the call, he goes downstairs to the privacy of his office, and every time I pick up the upstairs phone, he gets quiet and says *hello, hello,* in his quivery, tired voice and I'm forced to replace the receiver gently so that he doesn't hear the clicking noise. Bubby stretches the wire of the phone all the way to the bathroom, where she closes the door and lets the water run as she speaks, pretending it's one of her daughters calling to talk.

Do they think I don't know what's going on? I'm seventeen. I know how it works. At night Bubby and Zeidy have hushed conversations in the kitchen, and I know they are talking about matches.

Zeidy will want someone pious, someone with a strong Satmar family background, someone he can be proud to be associated with. After all, marriage is about reputation. The better the match, the better the family name. Bubby wants a boy who won't look down at the floor when he talks to her, like the *farfrumteh* boy that my cousin Kaila married, a boy so religious that he won't even talk to his own grandmother because she's a woman. I want someone who will let me read books and write stories and take the subway to Union Square so I can watch the street musicians play. Mindy still has a twenty-four-year-old brother ahead of her and knows she has time, at least two years, but I have nothing to stop me. She thinks I will marry someone more modern, maybe someone who listens to secular music in secret too, who watches movies and goes bowling like the modern Orthodox Jews in Borough Park.

I have more freedom now than I did when I was in school. I'm a working girl, which means I have earned the right to spend time unsupervised without having to account for it. I can meet other teachers for lesson-planning sessions; I can shop for school supplies. But it seems to me that what I've really earned is a sort of precarious trust. I did well in my last year of school, I landed a prestigious job, and ostensibly I am everything Zeidy and Chaya ever wished me to be. To their credit, they think, I turned out perfectly. Apparently my chances for an advantageous marriage have much improved as a result of my positive outcome, and although I am not apprised of any of the goings-on, the excitement suddenly swirling around me is palpable. All the hushed conversations, the looks—they make it clear that I am somehow ripe for a fortunate happening. I have never been so conscious of myself. Looking in the mirror at my newly grown-up face framed by a mature layered haircut, I am flushed with my own sense of importance. Is this not the best time in a girl's life, when the whole universe is pregnant with mysterious possibilities? The most miraculous happenings are possible when things are still unknown. It is only when all has been decided that the excitement fades.

I do not concern myself with the details of the heated talks between my grandparents and my extended family about my marriage. I understand that knowledge cannot possibly matter anyway; all it can do is drive me crazy with suspense and anxiety. What is meant to happen will happen regardless; what my family wants will come to pass. The best thing I can do is enjoy this time as much as possible.

Zeidy doesn't inspect my room anymore, not like he used to. I can read books more freely without fear of being discovered. Now I go to Barnes & Noble and buy hardcovers with my own hard-earned money. The first books I purchased were ones I had already read in the library but remembered fondly. The recent edition of *Little Women* lies between two slips in my bottom dresser drawer, a stark contrast to the tattered copy I held in my hands a few years ago. When I was younger, I delighted in the shenanigans of the spirited sisters, but now, in my second go-round, I feel delicate pangs as I see Jo's struggles for what they really are. She's a woman who can't fit comfortably in her time, whose very life and destiny are unnatural to her. How cursed are these characters who appear in all the books of my childhood. They are burdened with the constant ache of absurdity; the pressure of society's desire for the reformation of their character is like the binding feeling of an ill-fitting dress they attempt to thrash their way out of. Surely I will also be softened and tamed by society in the way Jo is presumed to be. If there is any promise in the reading of this book, it is that somehow they will all find a way to fit comfortably in their world, even if both participants must give a little in the struggle. Perhaps I too can carve a place for myself in this world I have always been at odds with. Now that I'm grown up and changed, like Jo, I can be myself and still be a proper young woman. In the end, the winds of love and marriage made Jo into the lady she resisted becoming for so long. Perhaps my temperament will be magically calmed as well.

Tuesday I come home from work at a quarter after four and it's already darkening outside, the sky streaked with purplish-gray clouds, a pink halo outlining the tops of the bare branches. Bubby's waiting for me at the door, ushering me into the house with a sense of urgency in her movements, her voice distracted and jittery.

"Where were you so long, *mamaleh*? It's late, we have to go soon, *schnell* take a shower, *mamaleh*, and make your hair nice. Put your navy suit on."

I'm confused. Did we have a special occasion tonight that I forgot about? Maybe a cousin's wedding or a bar mitzvah?

"*Nu, nu, mamaleh*, make fast, make a shower, let's go." When Bubby gets distracted, she translates from her original Hungarian and the phrases sound odd.

I wait for her to explain, but she doesn't say anything else. I do as I'm told.

When I come out of the shower in my blue zippered bathrobe with a towel wrapped around my wet hair like a turban, the phone rings, and Bubby puts her lips close to the mouthpiece on the receiver and covers it with her hand so I won't hear. She murmurs like that for a few moments, then hangs up and makes a face like it's nothing, and I pretend I believe her.

As I'm getting dressed in my room, she knocks and says through the closed door, "Devoireh, we're going to go meet someone at six o'clock. Blow-dry your hair and wear your navy suit, with the pearl earrings. You have makeup? Put on a little bit of makeup. Not too much, just a little foundation and some blush."

She knows I have makeup, she's seen me wearing it, even though I try to make it barely noticeable.

"Who are we meeting?" I call from inside my room, buttoning my shirt quickly.

"We're looking into a match for you, and you are going to see the boy's mother and sister. Your aunt Chaya and uncle Tovyeh are taking you; they will be here in an hour."

I stop in the middle of tucking my shirt into the waistband of my skirt, my hand frozen at my side. My first "meeting." This is the first step in every *shidduch*, I know. You meet the potential mother-in-law, maybe a sister too, then the same thing happens to the boy. Then, if both sides like what they see, they introduce the boy and the girl.

They want to make sure I'm pretty, that I'm not fat or horribly short or disfigured. That's all the meeting is really for. Every ounce of information about me has already been gathered at this point. Now they want to see how I dress, if I'm a good girl. I know this; I know how to play the game. When my hair is dry, I part it in the middle and tuck both sides behind my ears, an *aidel* hairstyle that all the really good girls wear. I smear a dab of foundation over my face and it gives my skin an orangey tint. It's drugstore stuff; I don't know where to get the better products. I sweep CoverGirl blush over my cheeks with the small, flat brush that comes in the case, a motion that leaves a stripe of pink along each cheekbone that I have to blend furiously with my fingers to make believable. But in the

end you can barely tell I have makeup on; my face looks suitably blank,
lit only by the faint glow of the pearls in my ears.

We meet in Landau's Supermarket, the one with the fluorescent
white lighting that makes my skin look ghostly pale, and I twiddle my
hands in my black leather gloves as we go inside. Chaya tries to reassure
me. "We'll only talk for a few minutes. You don't have to say much, they
just want to see what you look like and get the general idea that you have
a pleasant manner, and then we'll go. We don't want to make a scene in
the grocery or have people notice what's going on."

I bet people will notice anyway. I'm so nervous. Luckily it's a Tuesday
and not a pre-Shabbos shopping day, when the stores are packed. Fewer
people to worry about. For a while we patrol the aisles but I don't see
anyone, let alone a mother-daughter pair that could be the ones. The
frozen food aisle gleams; the row of metal-trimmed freezers have glass
doors frosted by condensation and I can see my reflection in them, and I
don't recognize the girl with the pale, pinched mouth and expressionless
eyes. The freshly waxed vinyl floor feels dangerously slippery under my
shoes. I pick a piece of lint off the front of my coat, smooth flyaway hairs,
knead my cheeks to make them pinker.

My future mother-in-law lies in wait in the paper goods aisle. She is
a short, scrawny woman, with a shriveled face and lips so thin they look
like a pencil mark smudged into her skin. My heart sinks a bit when I see
she's wearing a *shpitzel*, wrapped flat and tight around her skull. A shiny
gray satin kerchief with pink flowers embroidered all over it, folded gen-
erously at the base of her neck into a neat bow, ends trailing down her
back. The headpiece is twice the size of her real head and seems to totter
precariously on top of her minute frame. Her daughter—brown-skinned,
mousy-haired—is even shorter than she is, with a square face and small,
squinty eyes. Her canine teeth hook over her lip so that the tips are visible even when her mouth is closed. She stares at me without blinking.
What is she thinking? I wonder. If I'm pretty enough for her brother?
What about you? I think. *Who's going to marry you, looking like that?* I feel a
faint sense of triumph in that thought and gaze back at her calmly.

Chaya exchanges words with the *shpitzel* woman, but I don't hear
them. I think, with such an ugly sister, and such a homely mother, what

can I possibly expect from a boy related to these people? It's not like I'm gorgeous, but these people, to me, are like peasants. I'm not meant for this. Doesn't Chaya understand me at all?

The battered Town Car is waiting for us outside the supermarket and I slip in and scooch all the way to the end, turning my face toward the row of warehouses lining the East River and the lights of the Williamsburg Bridge twinkling above them. My breath creates a patch of fog on the window and I wipe it with my leather glove. Chaya gives the driver the address and I can hear her straightening her skirt, adjusting the front of her wig. She always has to look perfect, even when no one is watching. Even without looking at her, I know her back is perfectly straight, her chin jutting forward and the tendons in her neck trembling with tension.

She won't tell me what I'm so curious to hear and I'm too proud to ask. Over the years, Chaya has made me ashamed of showing any weakness. Emotion, to her, is weakness. I must not feel anything at all; I must not care what happens to me. Only when the taxi turns the corner to Penn Street does she murmur quietly, "I will let you know if there is any news."

I don't bother to answer. Upstairs, Bubby is already in bed and Zeidy is still at the synagogue, studying. I undress carefully, laying my things out on top of the trunk at the foot of my bed. For a while I kneel there, knees scraping against the rough rose-colored carpet, fingering the checkered scarf at the top of the pile, the scarf that Chaya purchased for me to go with my new coat. A *kallah maidel* must have elegant clothes, she told me. It is a sign that you are eligible for marriage. I have never been spoiled with so many new and beautiful things in my entire life. I have a sleek black handbag and Italian leather shoes. Pearl studs for my ears and a silver necklace with my Hebrew name as a pendant. Throughout my entire childhood and adolescence I longed for the trinkets that my friends continually displayed, but I never even dared to ask, and certainly no one would have bothered to answer. Yet in the last six months, I have suddenly been gifted with all the items any young girl could dream of, and for what? To suddenly render me presentable, I suppose. Or perhaps to sweeten me up. If it is the latter reason, I can hardly bring myself to contemplate it, for I know deep down that I am being swayed, like a child, to leap for the candy being dangled in front of me. I acknowledge the thrill that comes with finally being lavished with care and attention. I think I may become too distracted to think of anything else.

The next day no one is home when I get back from work. The lights are off and the fridge is desolately empty. I eat sour pickles with bread for dinner, and I'm too stirred up to read. I lie in bed and marvel at how quickly this moment has arrived, how it always felt so far away and now it is here, and every breath brings me closer to a cusp, a cliff from which I will surely plummet. I fall asleep early, dreaming of horses galloping over ravines, the flashing shadows of passing street traffic and the clatter of the elevated train waking me sporadically likes hooves rattling in and out of my head.

The sound of the creaky front door opening downstairs jerks me awake. It clangs shut after I hear Zeidy and Bubby's footsteps, and I hear all the locks being shut, first the dead bolt, then the doorknob, then the chain. It's past midnight. I hear Bubby speaking but I can't make out what she is saying. I fall back asleep before they come upstairs.

Thursday morning no one will tell me anything, and I'm too proud to ask straight out. But at work Chaya calls and tells me I'm going to have a *b'show* tonight. "Wear your best dress," she says, "and don't worry. Everything will be fine. I met the boy last night," she says, "with Bubby and Zeidy. We went to Monroe to meet him. He's very sweet. You think we would let you meet just anyone?"

I want to ask what he looks like, but of course I don't say anything. I leave work early, and on my walk home I step elegantly like a *kallah maidel* and wonder if anyone can tell. If they knew I was going to my first *b'show* tonight, they'd think differently of me; the passersby would look me over twice, maybe give me some advice, spit away the evil eye.

I remember the *shpitzel* woman from the grocery store, and my heart sinks again. I try to imagine what a son of that woman could look like, and in my mind I picture someone heavyset, with a rounded beard, chestnut brown with reddish accents, perhaps. I see wide nostrils, small, close-set eyes, and a bowlegged walk. Someone paternal, but how can a young boy be paternal? Still, I can't get it out of my head, the image, and it comes with me in the shower and I soap myself self-consciously, as if the bearded man were watching me.

I try coaxing my straight, shoulder-length brown hair into a curl. I am struck by how ordinary my face looks in the mirror. Truly a harsh punishment for me, far from ordinary on the inside, to have this face, this flat white face with a small mouth and heavy eyelids, a face consumed by a length of cheek on either side. Will he be able to tell, when he sees me, how truly wonderful I am? Will he want me? I am resolved to charm him.

Bubby comes home from Aishel and sees me ready and nods in approval. "You look so *elegante,*" she says, in her Hungarian pronunciation of the word. "Such *chinush laba.*" Bubby always speaks Hungarian when she gets emotional. *Chinush laba,* or slim calves, are a treasure in a woman, she always says. She takes out a gold choker from her bureau and hands it to me. "I wore that to my wedding. Your *tante* gave that to me, the woman you were named after. You should wear it tonight."

I've never had real gold jewelry before. I clasp the choker gently around my neck and shift it so that the place where it meets in a point at the center lies where the hollow of my collarbone would be, hidden chastely beneath my pale blue wool turtleneck.

Zeidy comes upstairs to get dressed, and Bubby has already laid out his best gabardine suit jacket on the sofa. He puts on his freshly shined Shabbos shoes and his new *shtreimel.* I'm glad he is wearing the new one tonight. I've only ever seen him wear it for weddings. He must think this is an important occasion, to be so uncharacteristically focused on his image.

Chaya and Tovyeh come by at 6:30, Chaya wrapped in her best fur-trimmed Shabbos cape, cheeks pinched into red circles and wearing her blondest wig. The hair on it is sprayed and teased into a high stiff peak over her forehead. I smooth my hair down worriedly. Maybe I should've used hair spray.

"You ready to go?" she asks cheerfully.

"Where are we going? I thought the *b'show* was going to be here, in the dining room."

"No, *mamaleh,* we're going to Chavie's house. She has more room." Bubby shrugs into her shearling coat. "We're all ready."

Aunt Chavie's house is only a five-block walk away, so we don't take Tovyeh's car. What a sight we must be, the five of us walking abreast; we consume the entire width of the sidewalk. I push the sleeves of my coat together so that they create a muff to warm my hands, my shoulders braced stiffly against the January cold. Everyone walks so purposefully and I have to keep up, trying to make my footsteps sound as certain, *tap, tap, tap*, but somewhere down Marcy Avenue I lose my courage and begin to shiver against the chill, and I can hear the faint clicking as my heels fall out of rhythm.

Only one block to go. What if they are already there? What if my knees buckle as I walk into the living room? I can see Chavie's house already, light pouring out from the front windows. I'm sure my legs are shaking, but when I glance down they seem perfectly sturdy. I admire my slim ankles for a moment before the bitter taste rises back into my throat.

I resolve not to look directly at him, my future *chassan*, but since I don't know where he will be when I get there, I must never look up or meet anyone's eyes, but look down at the floor in pretend modesty.

Chavie's house is warm and lit bright yellow from the sconces on the walls. "They aren't here yet," she says from the window, standing folded in the lace curtain to hide her face from passersby. Still she creates an inevitable shadow, her outline visible through the sheer panel, and I want to tell her to get away because I wouldn't want to give them this impression, that we are so excited we can hardly sit still.

I perch on the edge of the leather sofa next to Chaya to wait. I haven't spoken a word since we left the house and I know my words are not needed, but still I turn to my aunt and ask her in almost a whisper if she will stay with me for a few minutes after they get here and not leave me alone with him right away, because I just need to get my bearings and can't bear to be banished immediately. My voice cracks a bit and gives away my nervousness.

There is a brief, sharp knock at the door, and Chavie runs to open it, smoothing the back of her wig as she goes, quivering with excitement. Her brown eyes glisten, her smile is real; mine is nervous and shaky and retreats into the corners of my mouth when I don't remember to put it out.

I can't see into the exterior hallway but I can hear the heavy footsteps of a group, murmured whispers, and the quick swiping of shoes against a doormat before voices fill the house.

I recognize *shpitzel* woman first, the woman I will call *shviger*, mother-in-law, and the man who must be her husband, equally short with a dangling gray beard and hard marble eyes shadowed by a tightly creased forehead. No sign of the daughter now, I register briefly with some calm. I catch a glimpse of a flat black velvet hat peek out between the man and his wife, the wide rim of the *plotchik* hat concealing the face I want to see without appearing to do so.

A *plotchik*, I think suddenly, in shock. Not a tall beaver hat like my uncle's, not a *krach-hit* like Zeidy even, but a *plotchik*! How is no one noticing this? The panicked question races through the forefront of my mind, filling it completely. A *plotchik* hat, a wide, flat velvet one with a barely noticeable rim, is a sign of an Aroiny, a follower of the rabbi's eldest son, Aaron. Zeidy would never marry me to an Aroiny! Our family are Zollies through and through. We believe the rabbi's third son, Zalman Leib, is the true successor to the Satmar dynasty. I should have suspected something, considering this family is from the village of Kiryas Joel, and ninety percent of the people who live there support Aaron. But I never even considered the possibility. Even though Zeidy never let politics enter his house, and talk of the dispute between the two sons was never allowed at his table, it was always an unspoken fact that Zeidy did not approve of Aaron and his extreme ways. Now he is marrying me off to an Aroiny?

I am completely flustered, but I can't say anything, not when everyone is here, watching me. The boy has his hands folded into the opposite arms of his black satin *rekel*, shoulders bent and face pointed downward, as any modest yeshiva boy should. I notice his blond earlocks, cut neatly at chin length and curled into fat, shiny loops. They swing ever so gently to and fro with his movements.

I see the tip of a tongue sweep out hesitantly and run discreetly across a pair of pale pink lips, then retreat back in a flash, as if it were never there. I can see golden fuzz lining a bony jaw, the fuzz of a teenager on the face of a man I know to be twenty-two. It's unlikely that he trims, so he must be naturally bare. Eli is his name, I know, same name as all the other boys his age, the name of the first and most glorious Satmar Rebbe, now deceased, his throne quarreled over by a family divided in lust and greed.

They are battling it out in the secular courts now, and Zeidy says it's a *shanda*, a *chillul Hashem*, an embarrassment to God. (His voice rises when he gets upset and he rattles his fists on the table, and the china dishes shake and the goblets whinny from the vibration.) He hates it when they take our dirty laundry and hang it out in public for everyone to see. When the case is over and a winner chosen, he says, there will be nothing left to rule. Satmar will be an embarrassment to all. Perhaps he is right but I don't care. I don't feel like Satmar. Satmar is not in my blood, it's not a marker in my DNA. Surely I can remove that label from my identity if I choose to do so.

I wonder if Eli feels like he is Satmar, like it's in his blood and can never be washed away. I make a note to ask him that, when we are alone. A bold question, but I can disguise it in innocent words. I need to feel him out, see if he has his own opinions about this world we live in, or if he just parrots the views of those around him. I may not have a real say in the matter of my own marriage, but at the very least I would like to enter into the arrangement armed with as much knowledge and power as possible.

We all squeeze into Chavie's small dining room, positioning ourselves so that I am directly across from Eli, Chaya at my right and Bubby at my left, with Zeidy commanding the head of the table, my future father-in-law, Shlomeh, at his right side, along with his wife, and Chavie hovering at the foot, trying to serve everyone seltzer and linzer cake. The stiff velvet-covered seat cushion feels hard underneath me.

Zeidy and my future father-in-law exchange *dvar Torah* as is the custom, bantering mildly back and forth about the weekly Torah portion. Watching as they engage, I feel a distinct, prickling pride at how clearly Zeidy has the spiritual upper hand in this situation. After all, has there ever been a man more learned than my grandfather? Even the Satmar Rebbe said he was a Talmudic genius. My future father-in-law is a small man, both in stature and intelligence, I notice carefully, watching his bland face, his beady eyes moving back and forth. He should feel privileged to be talking to my grandfather. Zeidy would have liked to arrange a match with a more prestigious person, I'm sure, but unfortunately, despite my recent run of success I still don't quite merit a superior arrangement, not with my background.

After the perfunctory discussion is over, the adults get up and shuffle congenially out into the kitchen, leaving me at the table with Eli. I keep my head down and finger the fringed edges of the lace tablecloth, running my fingers along the pattern obsessively. The boy is supposed to start talking, that much I know. If he doesn't start, I'm just supposed to wait in silence. I look past him for a moment to the door, left slightly ajar so as not to break the rules, and wonder if they are all listening. I know they are sitting in the next room.

He breaks the silence finally, shifting first in his seat and readjusting his coat.

"So my sister tells me you're a teacher?"

I nod my head yes.

"Very nice, very nice."

"What about you?" I ask, having been given the smallest of go-aheads. "You're still in yeshiva? What's it like at twenty-two? Are there people there who are your age?" I know that will hit a sore point, talking about his age. Most boys are married off at age twenty, the latest. Because Eli is older and still single, his younger siblings have been made to wait for him to get engaged before they can be matched up as well, and anyone in his position would feel guilty about that.

"I guess I had to wait for you to grow up." He smiles pleasantly.

Touché. I'm going to ask about his hat.

"So your family, are they Aroinies? Because I see you wear a *plotchik*."

"My family is neutral," he says, after a careful moment, and he licks his lips again after, as if cleaning his mouth each time he speaks is a spiritual achievement. A purification ritual of sorts.

I get the distinct impression he has carefully rehearsed a script, that he'll say whatever it takes to make me believe what I want to believe. Each time I ask him a question, I get careful, bland answers. He swirls his fingers through his shiny, golden *payos* when he speaks, as if he is still in yeshiva, studying.

"You want some seltzer?" I ask, not knowing in which direction to take the conversation.

"No, it's okay, I'm not thirsty."

We talk some more; mostly I ask questions and he answers. He tells me of his travels: his father took him on extensive tours of Europe to visit the grave sites of famed rabbis. Eli and his nine brothers made their way through Europe crouching on the floor of a commercial van, stopping only to pray at tombstones.

"You went to Europe and all you saw were graves?" I ask, trying not to convey any contempt in my tone. "You didn't see anything else?"

"I tried," he says. "Mostly my father wouldn't allow it. But one day I want to go back on my own and really see it."

I feel instant sympathy for him. Of course his father is at fault, a narrow-minded man obsessed with the spiritual but ignorant of the true importance of anything. Zeidy would never take his sons to Europe and deny them any sightseeing. He always says the world was created for us to admire in all its glory. Perhaps Eli and I might return to Europe together; I've always wanted to see the world. To think that marriage might be my plane ticket to freedom is suddenly enticing.

Any moment now we will be interrupted, but before we are I want to make one attempt at genuine conversation with Eli. I lean forward intimately, hands tucked under the table and resting on my knees.

"You know I'm not a regular girl. I mean I'm normal, but I'm different."

"I can see that by now," he says, smiling slightly.

"Well, I just thought I should tell you, you know. Warn you, maybe. I'm not easy to handle."

Eli relaxes suddenly in his seat, spreading his hands out on the table in front of him. I notice the knotted veins protruding beneath thick calloused knuckles, the lines in his open palms thick and red. They are the hands of a workman, masculine yet graceful.

"That's what I'm good at, you know," he says, giving me an earnest look. "I'm the kind of person that can handle anyone. I'm not worried. You shouldn't be either."

"What do you mean, you can handle anyone?"

"Well, I'm friends with some difficult people. I find them interesting, you know. They spice things up. There are too many boring people in the world. I'd rather end up with someone who has a personality."

It is as if he is auditioning to be my groom, when we both know it is decided anyway. But his manner is pleading; it is as if he wants there to be some grand romance where there is no room for one. Still, I am relieved by his claims, because I feel as if I have fulfilled some sort of obligation. Whatever happens in the future, I cannot be held responsible. I warned him. I told him I wasn't easy to handle.

When Chaya opens the sliding door to the dining room and looks at me questioningly to see if I'm finished, I nod my head. I realize I know only a little more about him than I did thirty minutes ago, but at least I have seen that he is blond and blue-eyed, with a wide sloppy smile that shows all his teeth. Our children will surely be beautiful.

In the hallway Chaya looks at me for confirmation, waiting for my perfunctory acquiescence before we join the rest of the family. Her eyes are shining with anticipation, but that's the only part of her face that's different. The rest of her is as dignified as always. Standing in the narrow, dark hallway, I have nowhere to go but forward, into the light of the kitchen and the celebration waiting for me. There is no room into which I can go if I say no; there are no other doors to choose from. It is a nod and a smile that I must give, and I do it. It does not feel as monumental as I thought it would.

In the kitchen the liquor is already prepared in silver goblets, laid out in front of the men so that they can drink *l'chaim* and pronounce us engaged. Chaya starts calling everyone in our family, and I call a few classmates and let them know, and pretty soon the house is overflowing with people kissing and congratulating me and my future husband.

My *shviger* presents me with an ugly silver bangle with a flower design that I pretend to like, and my friends come by bearing helium balloons and cheeks flushed bright red from the cold night air. Chaya takes pictures with her Kodak disposable camera.

We set a date in August, seven months from now. I won't see him more than once or twice until the wedding, and Zeidy doesn't approve of a *chassan* and *kallah* talking on the phone. I say good-bye after everyone leaves and try to imprint his face on my mind, because it's the one thing about him I know for certain. But the image fades quickly, and two weeks later, it's like I never met him.

My *chassan*'s younger sister Shprintza gets engaged a week after we do. She's twenty-one, and the only reason she couldn't get engaged earlier is that she had an older brother who was still single. I don't understand how anyone could want the girl I met in the grocery store, with the toothy smile and hard eyes, her rough voice and masculine manner. It turns out she is marrying her brother's best friend, and it seems to me she could only be doing that to get as close to her brother as possible apart from marrying him herself.

She and Eli are very close, she told me that night I got engaged, after she had pulled me aside to pose for pictures with her. Closer than any brother and sister ever found. She said it with a hard glint in her eye that made me think she was threatening me, as if to say, "My brother will never love you like he loves me."

But of course he will. He will always put me first. I'm prettier than she is, more upbeat and fun, and how could anyone put her before me?

Eli and I are having a *t'noyim* next week, a party where we sign the engagement contract. Once the *t'noyim* is signed, there's no breaking it off. The rabbis say it's better to divorce than to break an engagement contract. At the party I will get my diamond ring (I hope it's dainty, the way I like it), and I will give Eli his *chassan* watch. I go to the jewelry store to pick one out with Aunt Chaya, and I choose a two-thousand-dollar Baume & Mercier with a flat gold face and a fine gold mesh band. Chaya writes out the blank check that Zeidy gave her without so much as a shiver of hesitation. I have never watched anyone spend that much money around me, and I can hardly believe it. Suddenly, money is no issue. There are unlimited funds available for anything in relation to my engagement. In the dress shop Chaya picks a rich bronzed-velvet dress with copper satin trim and has the seamstress alter it so that it fits me perfectly. (Chaya says good tailoring is a woman's best friend.) Aunt Rachel comes to cut my hair into a short bob so you can see my neck above the high collar of my dress. She says it will grow out again in time for the wedding.

The morning of the party I wake up with pinkeye. It's inescapable; no matter how much foundation I pile on around my eye, the swelling makes my face lopsided. Frantic, I race to the clinic on Heyward Street to get drops, but the pinkeye is still visible in the evening. I have to put on my brave face and pretend it's not there. Although I'm smiling all the way to the party, I feel as if I am in a daze. I can hardly see, and there is a faint throbbing sensation in my forehead. All I can do is pray that no one notices. There would be nothing more mortifying than Chaya taking me to task about looking unhappy at my own engagement celebration.

The professional photographer we've hired arrives early to take pictures just of me and Eli, where we stand three feet apart from each other with a vase of dark, unattractive tropical blooms posed between us. My future mother-in-law ordered the bouquet for the occasion. I already know I hate her taste. I had longed for an airy, Japanese-style arrangement such as some of the local florists are doing these days, filled with pastel orchids and hydrangeas. Instead I have to inhale the sharp odors of eucalyptus. It doesn't feel very bridal to me.

As the photographer tries to get different poses from us, I make sure my good eye is facing the camera. He moves us to the dessert table and has me lift a petit four from the tray and pretend to feed it to Eli. Behind him I can see Eli's mother's shocked expression. She purses her lips together in disapproval at our unseemly display. I bet she's glad none of the guests have arrived yet, to see what's going on.

I think I like him, through the haze of the drops in my eyes; at least I like his smile, his bright blue eyes, the lightness around his shoulders, his masculine hands, his careful movements. I like what I see. I wonder if he likes what he sees too.

When people start straggling into the hall, which is basically the cafeteria of a boys' school transformed by a few strategic wall hangings and some lace tablecloths, my *chassan* and his father go off to the men's section, disappearing behind the metal divider that separates the two sexes. I hope the photographer gets lots of photos from the men's side so I can see later what was going on there, while all the girls from my school come up to me to wish me mazel tov, the traditional congratulatory wish for brides.

When I sign the engagement contract, with all its conditions spelled out in ancient Hebrew that I barely understand, we gather at the end of the divider, where I can see into the men's section, and Zeidy breaks the *t'noyim* plate, specially purchased for the occasion, a fine china dish with a rose-patterned trim. It shatters neatly on the floor, a symbol of commitment, and Bubby gathers up the shards to be put away. Some girls make a ring out of the plate; you can have a jeweler carve out a piece with a flower on it and set it into a simple gold ring. Or you can turn it into a pendant. I don't think I will do that.

My mother-in-law gives me the diamond ring now, and everyone crowds around me to get a glimpse of it, and I'm glad it's simple, although the band is too thick and the diamond small and plain. I know my *chassan* will like his watch, because at least I picked it, and I have excellent taste; Bubby always says so.

The gold looks nice on his tanned wrist, furred with blond hairs. I can see my friends think I have snagged a *batampte*, a tasty one. I am very proud to at least have a handsome future husband. I look at him and think, *What a pretty thing this is to have, a beautiful thing to acquire, to display for the rest of my life like a trophy.* I love how crisp his white shirt collar looks against his golden neck.

Mindy and I spend our free moments after school going over the photos from the engagement party in our usual spot at Lee Avenue Pizza, scooping our soft ice cream into the hot coffee, where it dissolves in syrupy streams as we hurry to catch it at that perfect moment before it's completely melted. Mindy tells me her brother had a match suggested for him, finally, and she's pretty sure he will be engaged soon. Mindy will be free to be set up as soon as he is accounted for.

A part of her is wistful, afraid of losing me to that first-year honeymoon bliss she claims comes to all her friends after they are married. Another part of her is a little envious of what she sees as my pending independence, she confesses candidly. Pretty soon, I tell her, you'll be married off too. It's only a matter of time.

"Who do you think your parents will set you up with?" I ask, but what I really mean is, will you have to wear a *shpitzel*, like your mother, or will you rebel a little bit and fight to be matched with someone who will let you wear a wig and go to the library? For Mindy, marriage may not necessarily mean the independence she craves.

She's never said anything, but I wonder if she's jealous of me, seventeen and about to receive the key to freedom and independence. Mindy

is older than I am, and even if she does get married soon, there's no guarantee her life will be any different. I'm grateful I'm not getting married
to someone who is extremely religious or controlling. I couldn't imagine
having to leave the tight grip of my family only to end up in an even
more restrictive situation.

"Do you think you'll get to choose?" I ask, wondering if Mindy can
plead with her father to pick someone more likely to be understanding
of her nature. "Maybe someone in your family can intervene for you?"

"I don't know," she says pensively, running her fingers through her
shiny black hair and letting it fall back around her high, square forehead.
"I don't want to think about it yet, not before I have to."

I nod understandingly, stirring the lukewarm coffee mixture aimlessly with my plastic spoon, watching as the Mexican kitchen workers slap the pizza dough around on the counter. Most of the women I
know who have gotten married lead the same lives they did before. They
spend their days shuttling back and forth between their parents' home
and their new apartment, busying themselves with daughterly and wifely
duties. But perhaps they don't want anything else; perhaps that is the
life they desire. But for women like Mindy and me, that life will never
suffice. Especially for Mindy. She will never settle down and just be a
housewife.

Mindy shakes her head vigorously as if banishing unpleasant
thoughts, and a familiar, mischievous smile spreads on her face, crin-
kling her eyes. "Promise you'll tell me everything you learn in *kallah*
classes?"

"Of course." I giggle. "I'm going to my first one on Sunday. I'll call
you after."

My gut feeling turned out to be right. Mindy's marriage was arranged
only a year later, and like all her sisters, she married a deeply religious
man. He disapproved of secular books, and it was harder to hide them
from him than it had been to hide them from her family. She stopped
reading and busied herself with having children. The last time I saw her
before we drifted apart, she had already given birth to three and was
pregnant with her fourth. She smiled at me from her doorway, juggling a
toddler on her hip. "It's what God wants," she said, nodding sheepishly.

I turned away from her and walked down the stairs of her apartment building with a sick feeling in my stomach. That woman in the doorway was not the Mindy I knew. The woman I knew would have asserted her independence. She would not have given up and accepted her fate.

That phrase, *what God wants*, infuriated me. There is no desire outside human desire. God was not the one who wanted Mindy to have children. Couldn't she see that? Her fate was being decided by the people around her, not by some divine intervention. There was nothing I could say. Already her husband had decided I was a bad influence. I would not make her life difficult by insisting on seeing her. But I always remembered her.

6

Not Worth Fighting For

"I don't want to fight for anything. I want to just be and do,
with no one saying they're letting me."
—From The Romance Reader, *by Pearl Abraham*

Niddah, says my marriage teacher, literally translates as "kicked aside," but it doesn't really mean that, she rushes to assure me. It's just the word used to refer to a woman's "time," the two weeks out of the month when she is considered impure according to Judaic law. That's what I'm learning now in marriage classes, the laws of *niddah.*

I asked her to translate the term for me. She didn't want to answer me at first, but I pressed her, and as she hurried to explain to me the benefits that the laws of *niddah* offer to a marriage, I felt the blood rise to my head. The term *kicked aside,* even because of impurity, is humiliating. I'm not dirty.

She says in times of the Temple women weren't allowed inside the actual building because of the danger that they might begin to menstruate and thus defile the entire Temple. You never know when a woman will menstruate, really. Women, says my *kallah* teacher, have very unpredictable cycles. Which is why it's important, she says, to rush and inspect yourself if you think you might be getting your period.

A woman becomes *niddah* or "kicked aside" as soon as one drop of blood exits her womb. When a woman is *niddah*, her husband cannot touch her, not even to hand her a plate of food. He cannot see any part of her body. He cannot hear her sing. She is forbidden to him.

These are some of the things I learn in marriage classes. Every time I exit the mud-colored projects building where my *kallah* teacher lives, I am compelled to divide the women on the street into two categories—the ones who know all this, and the ones who don't. I am in the middle, beginning to learn about the pulse that really beats through this world I live in, but still in the dark about many things. I can't help but stare accusingly at the pious married women pushing double strollers down Lee Avenue. "Is this okay with you?" I want to ask. "Agreeing that you are dirty because you are a woman?" I feel betrayed by all the women in my life.

I didn't expect things to be this complicated. Marriage was supposed to be simple, about me finally making a home for myself. I was going to be the best housekeeper, the best cook, the best wife.

After a woman stops menstruating, my *kallah* teacher says, she must count seven clean days, doing twice-daily inspections with cotton cloths to make sure there is no sign of blood. After seven consecutive "white" days, she immerses in the *mikvah*, the ritual bath, and becomes pure again. So my *kallah* teacher says. I cannot imagine all my married cousins doing this.

When you're pure, usually for two weeks out of the month, everything is okay. There are very few rules when a woman is "clean." Which is why, the *kallah* teacher says, a Jewish marriage outlasts all. There is always a renewal of the bond between a husband and wife this way, she assures me. It never gets boring. (Does she mean to say it never gets boring for the man? I shouldn't ask that question.)

Men only want what they can't have, she explains to me. They need the consistent pattern of denial and release. I don't know if I like thinking of myself that way, as an object made available and then unavailable for a man to enjoy.

"You want to get married, don't you?" she asks, irritated, after I voice my unease. I squirm uncomfortably, because what can I say? If I say anything but yes, she'll raise a fuss. Everyone will know.

"Of course. Of course I want to get married. I just don't know if I can remember all these rules."

She shows me the white cloths used for the inspections. They are small cotton squares with jagged zigzag edges, and they all have little cloth tails at one corner. "What are those for?" I ask. "That's just to pull on if it gets stuck," she says. The cloths rest lightly on the greasy vinyl tablecloth, fluttering slightly with each light summer breeze coming through the kitchen window.

You have to inspect yourself twice a day, once in the morning when you wake up, and once before the *shkiyah*, the sunset. If you miss one, you have to call a rabbi and ask if it's okay or if you have to start over from the beginning. If you inspect yourself one day and there's no blood but there's a stain, you have to take it to the rabbi so he can say whether it's kosher or not. If your underwear is dirty, you have to take that to him too. Or you can send your husband.

At the end, when you have fourteen clean cloths to show for your efforts, then you can go to the *mikvah* and get all clean and pure and fresh for your husband. Every time you come home from the *mikvah*, it's like you are a bride all over again. My *kallah* teacher beams when she says this, her eyes widening in exaggerated joy.

I've passed the *mikvah* many times before, without knowing what it was. It's in a discreet brick building occupying most of Williamsburg Street, overlooking the Brooklyn-Queens Expressway. At night men know to avoid that street, but it's not a direct route to anything anyway, so it's quiet during the day as well. Women only go to the *mikvah* under the cover of dark, I learn, so as not to arouse attention. At the *mikvah* there are attendants, all of them older, menopausal women. The rule is you have to have someone certify that you are ritually pure.

I will go to the *mikvah* for the first time as a bride five days before the wedding. I already have a birth control prescription to control my cycle so that I don't end up getting my period before the wedding. If that happens, the *kallah* teacher says, you will be impure, and the marriage won't be consummated. It will be a disaster, she claims; a girl who isn't clean on her wedding day can't hold hands with her *chassan* after the wedding ceremony, and then everyone in town knows she's not clean. It's an embarrassment you never live down. And you can't sleep in the same apartment afterward either, and you have to have a *shomer*, a guardian, the entire time that you are unclean, until you are ritually purified.

I am uncomfortable with the idea of undressing in front of another woman, a strange *mikvah* attendant. I tell my teacher this. She assures me that during the inspection process I can remain in a bathrobe, and that when you immerse in the bath, the women don't look at you until you are in the water, and they hold your robe up in front of them like a curtain when you walk up the stairs.

Still, I've lived my life knowing that even the furniture shouldn't see my naked body. I've never bothered to clear the fog on the bathroom mirror. I've never even looked down there. This isn't right.

The birth control, prescribed by a local midwife, makes me wake up in the middle of the night and clutch my stomach, nausea coming over me in waves. I try crackers and toast and vomit up a neat pile of soggy whole-grain crumbs. The midwife says it will get better with time, and I can go off it as soon as I'm married.

I spend each morning in the weeks before my wedding struggling to overcome the incessant nausea so I can summon the strength to do all my trousseau shopping.

Bubby and Zeidy are too old to have the energy to plan my wedding, so Chaya does most of it. We shop for linens at Brach's Bed and Bath on Division Avenue and buy china and kitchenware at Wilhelm's housewares nearby. I choose a beautiful Villeroy & Boch tablecloth to go on the miniature Formica table we bought, custom designed to fit into the tiny kitchen of the apartment we've rented. I'm going to be living on the fifth floor of a giant apartment building on Wallabout Street, in what used to be the commercial district of Williamsburg. The neighborhood is littered with run-down warehouses and abandoned lofts; double-wide trailers still growl through the streets at all hours.

The apartment is six hundred square feet, with an alcove kitchen, a living/dining room, and a tiny master bedroom. We buy two forty-four-inch beds because the forty-eight-inch ones won't fit, and Shaindy still wants me to have wider beds. She says it's easier for nursing babies. Regal Furniture in Borough Park has the mattresses custom made. There is a little porch off the living room facing Lee Avenue, and if I step out, I can see a long line of porches on either side of me, leading off of identical apartments, all inhabited by newly married couples. On my left a young man smokes a cigarette, his tzitzis fringes dangling over his black pants, his white shirt untucked and stained yellow. Ash dribbles down onto his beard. He sees me looking at him and stamps out his cigarette quickly and goes inside.

Some days I go to the apartment, supposedly to organize the closets and get it ready, but I just sit in the living room and play Hilary Duff on the stereo, keeping the volume low so the neighbors won't hear me listening to gentile music. I trace my fingers over the grain in the hardwood floor and think about what it will be like to be able to live here all the time and never have to go back to the house on Penn Street.

I bring my books here now and hide them in the bathroom cabinet. Bubby wonders what I do for so long in my new apartment, when most of the furniture hasn't even been delivered yet. I'm curled up on the bare floor reading, and this time it's a bad book, a book I wouldn't want to be caught reading at home. Mindy told me about it; she lent it to me after she was finished. *The Romance Reader*, it's called. It's about a religious Jewish girl just like us, who wants to read books and wear bathing suits. But even better, the author was an Orthodox girl too, and she went "off the *derech*," as they say, or off the path. She became secular. Mindy knows the author's mother, she says, who runs a little needlepoint shop in the center of town. She wears a scarf on her head and everything. They say she doesn't talk to her daughter anymore.

Even if the book claims it's a novel, I read it like a breathtaking piece of raw journalism, because the stories detailed within are so current and real, they could be happening to me, and I know that the author must have at least based the book on her intimate life experiences. Like me, the heroine enters an arranged marriage. She is horrified to discover that her new husband is weak-willed and dim-witted. In the end she divorces him but finds herself back at her family's table. In my world, that is the ultimate defeat. Why would she go back to the world she was trying to escape in the first place? She thought marriage would bring her independence; then she thought divorce would truly set her free. But maybe there was never a path to freedom, not for her, not for anyone like us.

I brush away my discontent. My future husband will not turn out to be weak-willed or dim-witted. He will be brave and strong, and we will do everything we were always told not to do, together. We will leave all the craziness behind.

In addition to my *kallah* lessons, Chaya has also signed me up for *hashkafah* classes. Those are also lessons in preparation for marriage, but they don't really deal with the legal aspects. Rather they are supposed to prepare us emotionally for being in a successful relationship. These are group sessions, attended by over a dozen soon-to-be brides, and before the classes start, the girls pile onto the sofas in giggly heaps, comparing jewelry and relating the details of their shopping excursions.

The woman who teaches the class is a *rebbetzin*, a rabbi's wife. She instructs us all to find a seat around the large oak table in her dining room as she stands before the hastily erected whiteboard in the front of the room. In her lessons she outlines scenarios and has us guess solutions to various challenges presented to marital bliss. The girl who guesses right wins her glance of approval. But as she reiterates different versions of what appear to be the same problem, it becomes clear to me that there is only ever one answer. She calls it compromise, but it feels the same as giving in.

The characters in her scenarios are unfailingly formal, and I find it hard to believe that there are couples out there who really interact with each other that way, with all the familiarity of strangers. Surely, even for those who have trouble overcoming shyness, the sense of newness can't last forever? I find it hard to believe that the *rebbetzin* and her husband still approach each other like appliances that need an instruction manual after all these years. The girls around the table seem to take her instructions for granted. I want to shake them all out of their automaton states. Can't you see, I want to shout, how blinded you are by the jewelry and the new linens? You are missing the point! In the end all you will be left with are your closets full of new things and a husband that comes with a remote control!

I feel smug. Certainly I won't talk to my husband in that way, cold and deferential like the teacher advises. Eli and I will treat each other like human beings. We won't have to tiptoe on eggshells. They make it out so that the genders are like different species, doomed to forever misunderstand each other. But really, the only differences that exist between men and women in our community are the ones that are imposed on us. Underneath it all, we are the same.

Chaya asks me about my progress constantly. She is suddenly enthusiastic about the minute events of my life, always calling Bubby's house and asking to speak with me. She chose these two teachers especially for me, she remarks; she knew they would be the perfect fit. My mouth curls into a sneer when I hear her say that, although I only utter a vague affirmative sound in return. A perfect fit? Why would an old, decrepit lady be a perfect fit, when she could have chosen someone younger, more vibrant, and more realistic instead? It never ceases to amaze me how little Chaya really knows about me, after all this time spent controlling my life.

For every special occasion, every holiday, a gift arrives for me from my future husband's family. It is always wrapped in pretty paper and accompanied by bonbons or flowers. First there was a string of fat, shiny pearls resting in a small arrangement of fake fruit for Tu B'Shvat, the new year of the trees. I had already sent my future husband an ornate silver case for the *etrog* he would take to the synagogue with him on future Sukkot holidays. I placed it in a wooden crate that I spray-painted gold and stuffed with ferns and lemons, as well as with some small gifts for his sisters and brothers. The gift giving is a long-standing tradition, and every engagement is marked by the flurry of the exchange, as brides and mothers-in-law compete with each other to see who can send the most prestigious gifts, along with the most elaborate presentations.

On Purim I send my mother-in-law a silver tray with twenty miniature chocolate trifle cups arranged in a row, along with an expensive bottle of wine and two crystal goblets stuffed with layers of milk chocolate and white chocolate mousse. I wrap it in clear cellophane and tie it with a giant silver bow. One of my cousins will drive it up to Kiryas Joel, wedged firmly between the front and backseat so that it doesn't topple. I also send my future husband his own megillah, the scripture that is read aloud twice on the holiday, the ancient account of the story of Queen Esther. It cost Zeidy sixteen hundred dollars to purchase it from the scribe, and the parchment was rolled up and placed in a luxurious leather case made especially for such a document. I slipped it into a glass ice bucket with a bottle of champagne and some rock candy to look like ice. I'm glad I get to send my fiancé nice gifts; I know the boys compare the megillahs and *etrog* cases they receive, showing them off in the synagogue, and it's nice to know that Eli will be able to feel pride in the way he is being showered with such valuable pieces. Zeidy is very generous when it comes to his future grandson-in-law. I have never seen him part with his money so joyfully. It's like he was saving every penny for this occasion.

Zeidy says he will let me call my *chassan* on Purim to wish him a happy holiday. He lets me use the telephone in the kitchen with the short wire, and I know I only have a few minutes to exchange pleasantries, but I'm excited to hear Eli's voice nonetheless. His sister sent me a photo of him a few weeks ago where he is perched next to the gift I sent him, smiling sweetly, and I have not been able to stop looking at the length of tanned arm and his collarbone in the photo. I have tried to imagine what he could look like under that loose white shirt, but to no avail. I can't even remember the sound of his voice, so I'm excited to hear it again. I will try to record it so I can hear his voice replay in my mind over and over after the holiday.

Zeidy calls my in-laws first to relay his greetings, then hands me the phone to speak to my mother-in-law. "We received your lovely gift," she says formally. "It was beautifully arranged." Mine is on the way, but I won't ask about it. Will I get a watch or a brooch? I wonder.

She asks me to hold on while she calls Eli to the phone.

"A *guten Purim*," he says cheerfully, and I can hear his impish smile through the receiver.

Purim is his favorite holiday, he tells me. The costumes, the music, the drinking—what's not to love about it? It's the one day when everyone gets to let loose.

"Did you get my gift to you?" I ask. "Did you like the wine I sent? I picked it especially for you."

"Yes, I got it, thank you, it's beautiful. My father took the wine though; he won't let me drink it. He says it's not kosher enough for him. You know my father, he only buys wine with the Satmar rabbinical seal. Nothing else is good enough for him."

I'm horrified. My grandfather was with me when we purchased that wine. Zeidy is a holy man, much holier than Eli's father. How dare my future father-in-law imply that Zeidy is less vigilant than he is! I'm ticked off.

Eli breaks the awkward silence. "I sent you something too," he says. "It will get there soon. I helped put it together, but mostly my sisters did everything. Still, I hope you like it."

I feign cool indifference. It is unseemly to express too much excitement over gifts. At Zeidy's impatient signal I say my good-byes, suddenly aware that everyone in the room is listening.

"Happy Purim, Eli," I say, rolling the smooth syllables of his name carelessly before I realize that it's the first time I've said his name out loud to him. It feels suddenly, strangely intimate, but before I can say anything else, the clicking sound at the other end of the line abruptly dispels the sensation.

My Purim gift arrives late in the afternoon, delivered by special courier all the way from Kiryas Joel. It must have been the traffic that kept him so long. Everyone knows it's impossible to drive into Williamsburg on Purim. The streets are choked with party trucks and drunk revelers. The messenger can barely make his way up the stairs with his oversized package, wrapped and tied flamboyantly in trailing purple raffia. It's a giant cake shaped like a fiddle, with individual fondant strings and even a bow leaning on the side, with chocolates shaped like musical notes all around. "May your future be as sweet as the fiddler's tune," says the card at the top. I want to see what's in the black velvet box sitting innocently in the belly of the instrument. I slip it out carefully from under the edible strings and open it to see a heavy gold watch, its thick links shimmering in the light, the diamonds clustered around its face like a halo. Everyone crowds around me to get a glimpse. I put it on and it clanks heavily down to the bottom of my slim wrist.

"You'll have to get it resized," Bubby says. It is several links too large. I look down at the foreign piece of jewelry on my arm. I have never owned a watch that cost more than ten dollars. This one is an ostentatious display; the face is at least half an inch thick and sparkles with gems inlaid in various patterns, while the chain is formed in an intricate pattern of gold links that shift awkwardly with every movement of my wrist. In my opinion, jewelry should be dainty and feminine; it should bring attention to the wearer, not to itself. This watch is like a separate being, not an adornment.

Still, I hold my wrist out proudly to all my cousins and aunts, who *ooh* and *aah* and try to guess how much it cost. It suddenly occurs to me to check the back for an inscription, but when I do, there's nothing there. When I bought Eli his watch, I had it engraved with his name. No one else would ever be able to wear it. But it is appropriate that this watch should not have my name on it. It wasn't made for me, not in the way Eli's watch was, handpicked for his personality, the way I like it. This watch is for a girl that doesn't exist, a girl that my mother-in-law thinks she's getting. The girl that everyone wants, who is as bland as oatmeal under her heavy jewelry, who piles on the pearls and the bracelets to give herself some allure because underneath them she is as commonplace as a pebble.

I don't need this watch, or those pearls. For now, it feels nice to have them, but I know they will not be hard to let go of someday. Perhaps if they had been picked for me, it would have been different later. It would have been harder to part with something that had been carefully chosen to complement my style. But these gifts were purchased with no thought to who I was or what I might like. And when I would eventually part with them years later, I would feel relieved. My life would feel lighter as I removed each link to my past.

At the worst possible moment, a new scandal breaks. The rabbis put a temporary ban on the wig trade, because it has been discovered that most of the hair that wigmakers use to make the *sheitels* for married Hasidic women comes from India, from the temples where the women go to shave their heads and offer up their hair as sacrifices. For the women of the Hasidic community to gain in any way from the worship of idols is an unimaginable horror. It's the work of the devil, the rabbis claim, a punishment for the promiscuity of our women. Married women pranced around in gorgeous human-hair wigs and it angered God, they say, and so through the vanity of women we are all deceived and seduced by Satan. The Yiddish newspapers that arrive on our doorstep every morning contain the same angry headlines, with photos of rabbis pumping their fists righteously in synagogues throughout Brooklyn.

No more human hair, the rabbinical court announces. From now on, only synthetic wigs can be bought or sold. Until the community can determine an authentic source for human hair that's not a result of idol worship, that's all that will be available.

I curse the arrival of this new complication right before my wedding. Why couldn't it have waited until after? Now, instead of buying me luxurious, silky wigs like every other young girl gets before she marries, Zeidy will purchase only cheap synthetic ones, and I know that those look ugly, with a plastic sheen that can never be mistaken for real hair and a shelf life of no more than six months. Even when wigs do become kosher again, there's no way I will have the money to purchase them on my own. One human-hair wig can cost upward of three thousand dollars.

When Chaya takes me to the wigmaker to get my measurements, I sit sullenly in the rotating hairdresser chair, glaring resentfully at the options laid out in front of me.

"The only thing I miss," says the *sheitelmacher*, holding the wigs out on little foam heads, "is the feeling of the wind in my hair. Otherwise it's so much more convenient. I never have to wait for my hair to dry or to spend hours styling it. It's such a relief."

My hair has never been much of a difficulty, drying into smooth, lanky strands straight out of the shower. Still, I'm nervous to see how I will look in my new wigs, which can be ordered in whatever vibrant color I choose, and cut according to my preference.

I choose three wigs, one for Shabbos, a little longer so it can fit under my white *tichel*, the traditional scarf worn on Friday nights that's draped over the wig and tied at the nape of the neck. The other two are short and smart like the women in my family wear them; Zeidy doesn't allow wigs that are longer than shoulder-length.

That night there is a big bonfire in front of the Satmar shul, and all the men bring their wives' wigs and throw them in the fire, while the crowds stand around cheering emphatically. Policemen set up barriers to keep people from spilling into the roads and to prevent riots. The shouting goes on till dawn anyway, and journalists snap countless photos, much to everyone's rage.

When Zeidy brings home *The Wall Street Journal* the next morning, the bonfire is on the front cover. "Wig-burning is the new bra-burning," reads the tagline, and I don't quite understand what it means, but I know it's mocking. Zeidy shakes his head in disappointment as he reads the article.

"A fire was necessary?" he mutters to himself angrily. "So that all the goyim have to see what we're doing? It can't be done quietly? Ah, these young people, they always need something to shout about."

Chaya calls to invite me to lunch at her new house on Bedford Avenue. With Chaya, lunch is never just lunch. It's a front for an uncomfortable conversation, so the invitation makes me nervous. I dress up for the occasion, tucking one of my new silk blouses into a navy blue pencil skirt.

Her new apartment is located on the first floor of one of those recently erected buildings popping up in the formerly industrial section of Williamsburg. It has an elegant brick facade and hard marble hallways, and it feels more appropriate to Chaya's lifestyle than her old apartment on the top floor of the brownstone I grew up in. Her kitchen is lined with rows of dark mahogany cabinets, but the tiles on the floor and behind the counter are a cool slate blue. Her new home consists of large empty rooms, only minimally furnished. I sit down at the long glass table where Chaya has prepared an elegant lunch, made from scratch this morning, no doubt.

I shove the food around my plate while Chaya makes small talk. I just want her to get to the point so I can get rid of the sick feeling of anticipation in my stomach. Why does she always have to do this? Why must she drag everything out so that it becomes a dramatic situation instead of just leaving me in peace? It's as if she knows she's torturing me and enjoys it.

"So," Chaya finally says, putting down her fork and reaching for her water glass. "Your mother called."

Well, that's not what I expected. I reach for my water, sipping daintily to fill the awkward silence. I'm not going to give her the satisfaction of seeing my reaction.

"She wants to come to the wedding."

I shrug my shoulders. "Why does she all of a sudden want to show up at my wedding? That makes no sense. I haven't seen her in years."

"Well, she insists she has a right. You know, she probably thinks she can stop you from getting married, or something like that. She's a loose cannon that way."

"Well, if she shows up at the wedding, it will be a disaster. Everyone will be looking at her, talking about her. She'll embarrass me, she'll embarrass Eli's family. I mean, she looks like a goy!"

Chaya puts her glass down and purses her lips. "The thing is, she'll show up whether we like it or not. At least, if we say yes, we can set conditions. I can make sure she wears a wig and a long skirt, and I will stand next to her the entire time to make sure she behaves. If she does anything out of turn, I will see to it that she leaves."

"Well, I guess I have no choice, then." I wonder why Chaya called me here, if she's already made up her mind. It's not like she needs my opinion.

I visit the marriage teacher for the last time a week before the wedding. It's time for the lesson, that special lesson shrouded in mystery, the moment the brides whisper about but never discuss in too much detail. I am both wary and curious. I wonder what she has to tell me that my family can't bring themselves to reveal to me in person. I know it must be something big, something juicy but also embarrassing, something so secret that only she, the woman designated by the community to be the teacher of all things marriage-related, is allowed to talk about.

I perch nervously on the hard edge of my chair, looking around her dingy kitchen for a clue—to the secret but also to her personality, a hint perhaps to show me why her, why she is chosen to impart these shadowy wisdoms. Her kitchen table is littered with baffling sketches, like the designs of an engineer only less precise, eerie, somehow, with their repeated ringtoss patterns. It's the middle of August and there is no air-conditioning in her apartment; the air is heavy and thick and old, rationed frugally between us. Her tablecloth is greasy and stained, and I am careful not to brush up against it.

When she finally sits down across from me and begins lecturing about the holiness of marriage, I grow increasingly impatient; I can't wait for her to get to the good part so I can get out of here, this cramped kitchen with the smell of old sweat and sour pickles. Indeed, as I sit at her table, I begin to get a sense of who the teacher is, the life she has finished living, the way she covets my youth. I sense her loathing of my carefree existence, my bridal radiance, as clearly as I perceive her eagerness to squash it. My skin prickles beneath her stare as she begins to talk about a holy place inside each woman.

A man and a woman's bodies were created like two interlocking puzzle pieces, she says. I hear her describe a hallway with walls, leading to a little door, which opens to a womb, the *mekor,* she calls it, "the source." I can't imagine where an entire system like that could be positioned. She tries to tell me about the passageway that leads to "the source," how this passageway is entered, demonstrating with her forefinger inserted into the ring of the thumb and forefinger of her other hand, and making ridiculous thrusting motions. I'm guessing that that motion is referring to the part where they click into place. Still, I can't see where that spot, that entryway, can exist on my own body. As far as I know, the place where the pee comes out isn't that stretchy. I finally stop her.

"Um, I don't have that," I say, giggling nervously. I'm sure I don't have an opening, and if I did, it definitely wouldn't be big enough to accommodate something the size of that pudgy index finger, or whatever it might represent.

She looks at me, nonplussed. "Of course you do. Everyone does."

"No, seriously, I don't have that." At this point I'm becoming increasingly nervous. I start to question myself. Could I possibly have missed this passageway she was talking about? How could I not notice a hole in my body? I start to panic. What if they have to cancel the wedding because the bride was born without "the source"? Tears of frustration form in my eyes as I insist once again that I do not have this mysterious body part she is so industriously illustrating for me. I want her to stop making those motions, they seem so obscene and offensive.

"I don't have that thing you're talking about. I think I was born without it. How could I have something like that and not know about it? I think I would know if I had a hole down there!"

"Okay, look." The *kallah* teacher sighs. "Maybe you think you don't have it, but you do. I promise that you weren't born with some strange birth defect. You may never have noticed it before, but if you look for it, you'll find it."

I don't want to look for anything, not in that house, not with her in the next room, but she intimidates me, or rather that insinuated threat of my horrible deficiency becoming a public scandal hangs over my head like an ax and I do what I'm told. I go to the bathroom and tear off a piece of toilet paper from the roll, folding it around my right index finger. Hesitantly I explore down there, making sure to start all the way at the back and work my way slowly toward the front, searching for some indentation along the way. Nothing. I go again. Besides the natural valley my finger delicately traces, nothing gives way further. Perhaps that is as deep as it goes, I think, this puzzle piece on the man that has to click into me, that has to make a deposit at the altar of my womb.

I come out of the bathroom nodding sheepishly. Maybe I really did find it. If I did, I feel betrayed by my discovery. How could something supposedly so important have hid from me all these years? Why was I now being forced abruptly to acknowledge it? Did that mean that up until now it had not been okay to have a *mekor*, but now that I was getting married, it could make its grand entrance, suddenly "holy"? I stand in front of her, angry and confused.

I feel a little twinge when I remember that day. I want to be the woman who knows herself, her body, her power, but that moment divided my life in two. Before I visited the marriage teacher, I was just a girl, and then I was a girl with a *mekor*. I had made the sudden and shocking discovery that my body had been designed for sex. Someone had fashioned a place in my body specifically for sexual activity. Growing up in Williamsburg, I had been effectively sheltered from anything in any way associated with sex. We were spiritual beings, bodies carrying souls. The idea that I would now have to confront an area of my body I had never even thought about, let alone *wanted* to think about, on a constant basis for the rest of my life was in stark contrast to the chaste lifestyle I had been living until now. It was a lifestyle I had grown comfortably accustomed to, and my body rebelled against this change. That rebellion would soon cost me my happiness and would sow the first seeds of destruction that eventually tore my marriage apart.

Five days before the wedding, it's time for the *mikvah*. Chaya is taking me. I've caught a strange summer cold that has my throat feeling raw, and I spend the day loading up on strong, copper-colored glasses of Lipton tea that has the Flemish writing on it because Bubby thinks buying it from Belgium makes it more authentic.

Chaya tells me what to pack; the *mikvah* provides almost everything, but it's better to have your own bathrobe (theirs are skimpy, she says) and your own soap and shampoo. She hands me a Walgreens shopping bag with a loofah stick in it. "So you can reach the tough spots. Otherwise they will do it for you. I don't want you to feel uncomfortable."

I shudder in revulsion. I've heard that some pious women let the attendants wash them, but there's no way I'm going to let some strange old woman lay a finger on me.

We take a *goyische* taxi to the *mikvah*. We can't ask Tovyeh to drive us, because men are never supposed to know when women go to the *mikvah*, and we can't walk there holding our bags because it could look conspicuous. I wonder if the Puerto Rican man driving us knows the significance of the place where he is dropping us off and if he gets a lot of calls for this reason.

The building is yellow brick and built at an odd angle because it's a triangle block. We enter from a side alleyway, ringing a bell and watching a small camera whirring above us, until the buzzer sounds and a heavy metal door swings open into a well-lit hallway. There is a desk, with an aging receptionist behind it, looking bored. She brightens when I walk in.

"A *kallah*!" she says, noticing my uncovered hair. "Mazel tov! Such a special day. Let me call you our best attendant; she'll take care of you." Her face quivers with excitement, and she doesn't take her eyes off me the entire time she speaks.

She pushes a large tray toward me, filled with various nail clippers and manicure tools. "Pick," she says. "Whichever you like." As if she is offering me the choice between gold and silver, pearls and diamonds. She's still looking at me hungrily, without blinking, her sparse eyebrows lifted into gray arches above her pale blue eyes.

I don't really care. I grab a small clipper and notice the metal is chipped and scratched. I wonder how many women have used it. I put it back in the tray. "Oh, I brought my own."

I hear a door open behind me and turn. A dark-skinned woman stands in the doorway, the sleeves of her flowered housedress rolled up to reveal sinewy arms. She wears a *shpitzel* just like my mother-in-law. Only very pious women get to work here.

"*Mamaleh*," she says sweetly, ingratiatingly, and I can see instantly that her wide smile is fake, that her way of lolling her head to the side when she looks at me is condescending, and that she thinks she is better than I am, because my family doesn't wear *shpitzels*, only wigs. All this I see in that tiny empty moment before she puts her arm around my shoulder, still smiling that oily smile, and waves Chaya away with her other hand. "You can wait here, Mrs. Mendlowitz. I will take such good care of your daughter, don't worry." Chaya doesn't correct her mistake, doesn't say I'm her niece; it would be too long a story to tell her, in the anteroom, a stranger who doesn't need to know.

Mrs. Mendelson (she tells me her name right away as we walk through the set of double doors into the vast main lobby lined with velvet chaises and humongous bouquets of silk flowers) leads me down a long marble corridor, softly lit by delicate chandeliers and sconces. The corridor branches off into many small hallways, but we pass all of them because, as she says, I am going to the special room they save for brides. When we get there, I can't quite remember the route we took or how to get back, and that scares me a little, because the room is as small as a closet (I wonder what they give to the regular people) and it's frightening to think that I will be this one dot on a map, this one small person getting ready in a tiny room, surrounded by hundreds of other women in other tiny rooms, lost in the motion of things.

"You know what to do, *mamaleh*?" she asks condescendingly, standing in front of me with her hands on her hips, feet spread apart slightly as if to emphasize her authority. She's implying I might not remember everything I was taught about the *mikvah*, but I do—I studied before I came here and I've always had an excellent memory—so I smile big and fake right back at her like I know her game and I'm not going to let her belittle me.

"Of course I remember. I had a great *kallah* teacher. Thanks, though!" My voice is bright and thin, reedy with nervousness.

"Very good, *mamaleh*," she concedes. "Just press the button on the wall if you need me." The call panel flashes red next to the bathtub. One button says Help, the other says Ready. There is a small intercom as well. I nod my head.

When she leaves through the door on the other side of the room, I unpack my bag quickly and take out all the equipment I brought. I turn the taps and let the bath fill, and start at the top of my checklist. Lenses off first, and in the case. Wipe off any makeup, clean my ears, floss my teeth, and cut my nails short. In the bath I wash my hair twice and comb it, and make sure I wash the creased areas of my body very well, like the teacher said, to make sure nothing is stuck between my toes, or in my belly button, or behind my ears. The creases are very important. "Nothing can come between you and the water," she had said to me warningly. "If you find something later and there is a possibility it was on you when you were in the *mikvah*, you have to go back and do it all over again." I don't want that, so I make sure I'm clean according to the law.

When I'm done soaking and my fingers are dark and puckering like dates, I step out of the tub and wrap myself in my new blue bathrobe, made of thick plush terry, and press the Ready button on the panel. Mrs. Mendelson's voice comes crackling through the intercom immediately, as if she has been waiting to pounce the moment I pressed it. "So fast, *mamaleh?*"

I don't answer. She comes in a moment later, gliding on slippered feet. She sees me in my robe sitting daintily on the edge of the toilet and waves her hands in irritation.

"No, no, *mamaleh*, I can't check you like this, in a robe, what were you thinking? You have to be in the bathtub; this isn't the way to do it!"

My cheeks heat up and I uncross my legs. This is ridiculous. Why would she want me in the bathtub? My *kallah* teacher clearly told me that I would be checked while dressed. I try to speak but nothing comes out of my throat.

The attendant's face is stern, but there is a faint whiff of triumph about her movements, and she ushers me into the tub impatiently, saying, "I don't have time to wait, *mamaleh*. I have a lot of girls to take care of tonight. Don't be scared, sweetie, didn't your *kallah* teacher tell you what to do? You remember everything you learned, right?"

She's baiting me, trying to show me she was right, that I wouldn't remember, but I swear I do. I'm still going over it in my head, because I can't believe I would forget something like this, but it was so hot in that apartment all the time, and maybe I dozed off at some point, I don't know. It's horrible, but I feel clearly like I have no other choice but to do as she says, so

I slip quickly out of the robe and in a flash I'm in the water, knees bent and folded against my chest. My skin prickles and I can see goose bumps rise on my forearms. Mrs. Mendelson kneels by the tub, and she has such a satisfied look on her face that I can't help feeling like she won, like she wanted to win, like this is her power. It makes me angry and helpless-feeling and I can feel tears pricking at the edge of my eyes, but I want more than anything to keep my face stony, just to show her I don't care, that this doesn't affect me, that I am as strong as iron and no one can shame me into anything.

The light is so white. My skin looks almost blue beneath the harsh white light of the bathroom, the shape of my body distorted by the water, fingers fat beneath the surface and disproportionately thin above it. I keep my muscles stiff and tense, knees straining against arms, arms grasping tightly around knees, using that physical exertion to keep from showing any emotion, as she inspects my hair for dandruff and my skin for scabs.

"All right, *mamaleh,* you're ready. Put on your robe and your slippers and I will take you to the *mikvah.*" She doesn't even turn around so I can get out. I don't look at her at all now, and I keep my mouth hard and straight, nostrils flaring from the effort. My brain feels hot and swollen in my head, pressing against my eyes.

In the hallway I follow her blindly because my vision is blurry from holding back the tears. We end up in a small room with a little blue pool. This part I know, and I take off the robe and give it to her and walk down the series of steps into the water, trying not to go too fast even though I can feel her watching me, because I don't want her to see that I'm even the least bit embarrassed. No one can hurt me. No matter what they do, they can never hurt me. I am iron.

The water is relief. I can see the Hebrew blessing printed on the tile wall to my left. "Thank you, Hashem, for sanctifying me with your commandment to immerse myself in water," I mumble quietly. I dip once and come up so I can hear her say "kosher," then twice more, making sure my feet don't touch the ground for the split second of totally immersed suspension that is required. I make sure that my hair doesn't stick out, and that my body is positioned so that the water reaches everywhere. After the third time, I cross my arms over my chest like I'm supposed to and say the blessing out loud. I'm finished now.

I walk up the steps facing her and she holds out the robe like my *kallah* teacher said, but I can see her inquisitive black eyes peering above the collar, and at that moment I hate her so much and the tears I've been tamping down burst out from behind my eyes. I put the robe on and feel my eyes fill and fill and fill, and I try to be quiet and walk behind her so she won't see, but I forget about the customary kiss on the cheek, and as she turns to me to give me the blessing, she sees a tear burst out of my eye and fall down my cheek. Her eyes widen.

"*Mamaleh, shefaleh, bubeleh,* what's the matter, sweetheart, darling, little lamb? What's wrong? What can I do?" Now she's fawning over me, making it worse. I can hear a loud sob escape my throat, and I can't help myself from bawling like a child whose innocence has been snatched away.

"Oy, *shefaleh,* it's all right to be a little emotional, on the first time, it's okay, but *mamaleh,* you don't have to cry. You should be happy; this should be the happiest night of your life!"

I can't believe she thinks I'm crying out of some sort of spiritual wonderment. How crazy is this? And yet why not go along with it, let her think it was piety all along, let her think I'm some *frimmeh* freak who is overwhelmed with the holiness of this stupid swimming pool.

She waits for me as I hurriedly get dressed, then escorts me back to the waiting room where Chaya is sitting, talking to the lady next to her. She sees my reddened eyes and morose face, but Mrs. Mendelson smiles brightly again and says, "Oy, your daughter, she's such a *feineh maidel,* such a pure soul, such a saintly child. It overwhelmed her a bit, the experience, but you know how it is, your first time . . ." She nods her head like a puppet, and I watch it bobbing up and down, and for a moment that's all I can see, the quick up-and-down movement of her head. Is that a little bit of guilt I detect, or is it fear, that jitteriness that wasn't there before?

Chaya slips a tip into her hand and puts my arm through hers and leads me away. "Was it so bad?" I don't say anything. She knows what it's like, she did it too, she still does it, and I don't have to answer her.

I was right, though, about the rules. After I got married, none of the other *mikvah* attendants made me sit in the tub, only her. She was being cruel, I thought later, trying to toughen me up, perhaps, or doing what she thought was more religious, more extreme. It never occurred to me that Mrs. Mendelson might have had darker, more personal reasons for doing what she did that night. Years later the police would arrest a *mikvah* attendant who molested all the brides that were brought to her, but the story would be so shocking, no one would really believe it. After all, when a woman is telling you that you need to submit because that's how God commanded it, would you question her? It would be like questioning God.

The taxi is still waiting outside. I slide into the cool leather seat, and Chaya slams the door shut behind her. As we stop at the red light on Marcy Avenue, I am struck suddenly by the incongruity of her presence next to me. Chaya is essentially taking the place of my mother at this moment, joining me in what is considered the most important rite shared between a mother and daughter in the community. What right does she have to assume this place, when our relationship is nothing like that, when her only concern is to ensure that I behave myself and don't embarrass the family?

"What went wrong?" I ask.

"What do you mean?" Chaya says sweetly, turning to me with a bemused smile, her face streaked with light from the orange bulb of the streetlamp.

"With my mother. What went wrong?"

The car jolts forward and Chaya's face slips quickly out of the light and into the shadows.

"A nervous breakdown. She went crazy after she had you. We couldn't let her take care of you. She had to be hospitalized."

"I thought you said she just abandoned me."

"Well, it was the same thing. You know she could have pulled herself together, to be a strong mother for you. But she chose not to."

I wonder, do you tell a "crazy" person to just pull herself together? But before I can respond, the taxi drives up in front of my house, and Chaya opens my door to let me off before she continues on her way home.

Chaya goes with me to the bridal *gemach*, where I can pick a wedding dress on loan. There are only eight summer gowns in my size, all of them bedazzled with sequins and rhinestones, draped with lace and tulle, encrusted with glittering gems. It's as if someone took apart pieces of different wedding gowns and sewed them all into one dress. I pick the simplest one, which is still ornate, with a full lace skirt that ends in sharp points around my ankles and a heavy, banded midriff staggered with jewels. But the bodice is clean and white, and the high neckline dips in a V just above my collarbone. The woman at the gown rental desk marks down the date of my wedding. I can have the dress for two weeks, and I must return it, freshly cleaned, by the due date. We carry it home in a giant black plastic trash bag, making sure it doesn't scrape the sidewalk. At home, it rests upright on the weight of its own skirt, glaring at me first thing in the morning like an intruder that snuck in during the night. Its presence is so big, I fear it will overtake me, or that I will somehow disappear into it and become lost in its voluminous folds.

On the last Friday night before my wedding, I slip into the sheets just before midnight. The streets outside are silent, blessedly free of weekday traffic, and the glow from the streetlamps creates firm, steady stripes on the walls of my room. The sheets are still cool when I fall asleep, and my dream is lit by the pale fiery glow of two Shabbos candles flickering bright orange, the flames growing bigger and bigger until all I can see are flames everywhere. I am watching Bubby and my aunts Rachel and Chaya hunched over a large stockpot, stirring above my head. I realize I am in the pot, being fussed over like a fancy dish for the holidays. The stainless steel walls loom impossibly tall around me, the faces above me glowing in the distance. Their foreheads are creased in concentration and fury, the flames still crackling in angry silence around their heads. How are they not noticing they're on fire? I wonder. They stir faster and faster, and as they stir, I hear them talk about me, about all the bad things I do, about how I never make them proud. I have never heard them speak this frankly about me. Sure, I have always felt their disdain, an impalpable air that I could never quite put my finger on, but no one ever bothered to articulate the reason for it. I always assumed it was because I reminded them that the family wasn't perfect. Did my behavior really matter to them, when my background was inescapable?

This time, they say, this time she'll come out right. Sweat beads and drips from Rachel's forehead as she whisks the wooden spoon efficiently over my head. I watch the droplets splatter loudly into the liquid broth I have been distilled into. It's as if they have been given a second chance with me, a sudden miraculous solution to the long-standing problem of my ignoble status. They can make a success out of me, despite the odds, and close the book on the sad saga I represent.

They're going to bake me. I can hear them arguing about how much time I need to turn out just right. They preheat the oven to 350 degrees and pour me into an aluminum pan. The perfect sponge cake, Rachel says, only needs thirty-five minutes to attain the ideal combination of vanilla moistness and airy perfection. When I'm ready, then I can come out of the oven. I can still see them through the smudged glass pane of the oven door, tapping the watches on their wrists. I lie there, wondering why I'm not really feeling the heat. Instead I'm aware of a sense of security, ensconced in the warm, safe oven, away from their cruel, calculating stares. When the timer beeps, the oven door opens and I feel myself sliding out with the rack. I look up expecting to see smiling faces, but their mouths have fallen open in shock. There I am, a roasted suckling pig, my skin a golden, shiny crust, a small red apple in my mouth. Even I am horrified by this shameful turn of events.

I awake with a start, and my room is still swathed in darkness. I can see Rachel's angry face before me, vividly engulfed in orange flames, stirring furiously with her wooden spoon. I can feel that longing to be the perfect sponge cake and the burning humiliation of having my true face exposed.

As I turn on my side and lift my hair off my sweaty neck, I try to distance myself from the horrible, shocking image of looking down at my own self and seeing the nature of my betrayal. Surely that's not who I am. I am most certainly a good girl, and I will make everyone proud of me. If I can make this work, all my shame can be erased. No one will be able to criticize my family when I am a successful, obedient housewife.

7

Costly Ambitions

*For we pay a price for everything we get or take in this
world; and although ambitions are well worth having, they
are not to be cheaply won, but exact their dues of work
and self-denial, anxiety and discouragement.*
—From Anne of Green Gables, *by Lucy Maud Montgomery*

The morning of my wedding is so bright and clear, I can see every dewdrop
glistening on the maple leaves swinging lushly outside my window, and every
rhinestone sewn on the thick sash of my wedding gown shimmers in the day-
light. I fast all day, as is the custom, but don't feel hungry at all. I hold a book
of psalms and mouth the prayers; my duty as a bride is to use this opportunity
to hold God's ear and pray for all those who need guidance and salvation.

I am so excited to get my first professional makeover. A woman comes
to the house to do my makeup; she has a case full of glittery eye shadows
and sparkling lip glosses. The most I've ever really worn is foundation
and a little blush. She uses a metal contraption to curl my eyelashes, and
I'm afraid that my lashes will be chopped clean off. In the end, when I
look in the mirror, I can hardly recognize myself. I look so grown up and
sophisticated, my lids heavy with forest-green shadow, the mascara piled

on my lashes feeling like a weight I can't fully lift, so that my eyes appear to be not quite fully opened, in a kind of sleepy, delicate way. There must be girls out there who are excited to get married just for the experience of wearing all this makeup. Only brides are permitted to be this decorated.

My wedding dress folded neatly around me, we drive to the wedding hall, which is housed in the boys' school on Bedford Avenue. At five o'clock in the afternoon the light is still bright, and we hurry inside to avoid the stares of passersby. I'm set up on my special bridal chair of white wicker, with silk flowers entwined around its brim, and Bubby spreads the tulle skirt of my gown evenly around me, so that the lace-trimmed edge forms a perfect arc on the floor. *Flash* goes a camera. I pose quickly; there is not much time for trivialities on a day like today. A close-lipped smile, an earnest glance from behind lowered eyelids, and the camera is whisked away.

Here come the guests, my fellow classmates, home early from summer vacation especially for my wedding, dressed in their best so that they can be viewed by all the matchmakers looking for smiling young girls with rosy cheeks and dainty ankles. They line up to air-kiss me and wish me congratulations and good luck. Bubby sits next to me on the bridal platform and sniffles into a tissue with a sad smile on her face. So many people come up to me, people I've never met who say they are a friend of my mother-in-law, or the wife of my future husband's friend, and I smile benevolently to all, my eyes permanently crinkled in delight.

Every one of Eli's sisters-in-law insists on posing for photos with all their children, and I smile and tickle the smaller ones under their chins so that they giggle for the camera. I notice my mother out of the corner of my eye, standing far off looking disoriented, with Chaya holding on to her arm, a tight expression on her face. I can see my mother is wearing some sort of purple gown, her honey-colored wig slightly askew. With her standing that far away from the bride, it's likely most people won't even realize that she is my mother. Chaya promised that she wouldn't be allowed to make any sort of scene. I guess that includes making sure she avoids me.

After what seems like hours, the music strikes up, and the march begins. The women veer off to either side of me to clear a path for the parade of men entering for the *badeken* ceremony. Zeidy carries the white cloth that will soon be covering my face. After the *badeken*, I won't be able to see until the chuppah ceremony concludes, which is when Eli and I will officially be married.

As Zeidy pronounces the blessing for me to be fruitful and multiply, I bite my lip to keep from showing any expression other than the somber one I'm attempting to maintain. Gaiety would be inappropriate at this most holy of all moments. I catch a glimpse of Eli, looking strangely small beneath his brand-new mink *shtreimel,* which perches at the very tip of his head like an uneasy animal. His shoulders jut out stiffly on either side in his new black satin coat. I don't want to meet his eyes for fear I will crack a smile.

At last I'm covered, and underneath the white tarp I smile secretly to myself at this sudden pleasure of being anonymous in a crowd of people focused only on me. I fake the sound of sniffles all the way to the canopy, and someone slips me a handkerchief underneath my covering. I take it delicately, drawing it away from sight with an elegant swishing movement.

I watch the feet of the men under the canopy as I am led in circles around Eli, seven precise turns until I am left to stand beside him, still blind. Their shoes all look the same, black lace-up oxfords tapping quietly on the ground. I shift briefly under my gown, but no movement is obvious above the stiff petticoats.

After the *mesader kiddushin* pronounces the marriage blessing, Eli slips the wedding band onto my finger, which I stick out from under the heavy veil. I hear the sound of the glass breaking, and Eli lifts the veil and takes my hand, and we walk together through the crowd to our *yichud* room. The *yichud* room is a special suite set aside for the bride and groom as part of the wedding tradition, a room where we will eat our wedding dinner in private, the first place we will be alone and unsupervised. It's only symbolic, of course; we won't lock the doors. The *sheitelmacher* has to come set my wig on top of my hair and reattach my veil. We barely have time for soup.

In the *yichud* room, as is the tradition, Eli gives me a pair of diamond earrings that his mother picked. I remove the simple pearl studs I was wearing and replace them with the heavily studded squares instead. My earlobes droop slightly. He leans forward, and I think he might suddenly try to kiss me, but I stop him. "Wait," I say. "Anyone can walk in. Wait till later." The light is too bright for me to be that close to his face.

Sure enough, the *sheitelmacher* breezes in carrying my freshly set wig in a large leather case. She busies herself shoving all my beautiful, shiny hair into a white lace cap, making sure not even a strand is sticking out. Now that I'm officially married, no man aside from my husband is allowed to glimpse even a quarter inch of my natural hair. She sets the wig firmly on top of my head, pulling it down around my ears so that it is snug against my lace-encased scalp. I can't even think about what my squashed hair will look like when I finally take it off. Eli is whisked away by his brothers for some photographs, and I finish my soup alone, pecking without interest at the hunk of challah next to my plate. I know I should eat or I might faint, but I can't seem to swallow anything. I chew the same piece of bread continually, but my throat feels too dry and tight to let anything go down.

Even though I picked comfortable white shoes for dancing, I'm not prepared for the work it entails. The fabric of my dress is so stiff that my body chafes everywhere it must bend, at the shoulders, elbows, and even wrists. I make an enormous effort to keep up my smile as everyone insists on taking their turn whirling me around the dance floor. They lift me on tables and steer me through human tunnels, twirl ribbon sticks and floral bouquets above me, and I work hard to keep my eyes wide and gay.

The brass section plays lustily until one in the morning, after which most of the crowd drifts off with sentimental good-byes, leaving only extended family to stay for the *mitzvah tanz*. This is an opportunity for me to finally rest, and I drink glass after glass of water and stand in front of the air-conditioning unit in the bridal room, begging my body to cool off. I hear the pianist start up an arpeggio and I join the family outside in the main ballroom, where rows of chairs have been set up on either side to accommodate both the male and female audience. The groom, however, will sit beside me at the very front of the ballroom, to get the best view. My new nieces bring me grapes on a platter to share with him.

All the little girls whose parents have allowed them to stay this late sidle up to me and watch me out of the corners of their eyes, like I sidled up to the brides of my childhood, envious of their princesslike status. Zeidy brings me the black *gartel*, the long sash that connects me to the dancers. I hold one end and various family members take turns holding the other end. Meanwhile the wedding poet takes turns praising each family member in witty rhymes, as is the custom.

"Eli, famous for always offering to help a fellow Jew, of such generous boys there are few. He is praised for being a studious learner, let's hope he will be an equally successful earner. May he have many offspring and may they bring him much joy, soon he will be dancing at the wedding of his own boy." The rhymes are simple and ill-timed, but everyone is drunk and tired enough to find them funny.

The last dance is reserved for Eli and me, but it's not really a dance, more like a shuffle. Eli stands two arm-lengths away from me, as is the custom, only the tips of his fingers brushing mine to signify that we are married while still remaining modest. We keep our heads down because if we look at each other, I'm sure we will burst out laughing. I don't even have to move my feet, I just make the skirt of my gown shake slightly to intimate some movement. Finally the music winds down and I breathe a sigh of relief. I don't know how long I could have restrained myself from letting loose a giggle.

The wedding hall begins to empty out as my family members head back to their respective homes. Most people have to be at work in a few hours. Some come over to wish me a last "Mazel tov!" but I only smile at them distractedly. All I can think about is getting out of the dress. The creases inside my elbows are raw. When Eli's parents drop us off at our front door, I fidget uncomfortably as they exchange their good-byes, and the minute the door is shut behind me, I kick off my scuffed white pumps and start unhooking the back of my dress on my way to the bathroom. Inside I slip off the sleeves slowly because they are sticking painfully to my arms. Tenderly I finger the deep red welts along my forearms and shoulders. Who would've thought wedding gowns could hurt so much?

In the shower I wash the hair spray out of my matted hair and let it stream for the last time just past my shoulders, water dripping off the edges and burning my sore back.

I stand in front of the fogged mirror for a few minutes and the air begins to feel icy around my body. After the mirror clears, I can see my reflection peering back at me with blank eyes and I turn away from it instinctively. I come out in my bathrobe.

"You can take a shower now," I call into the dark of the apartment. Eli is in the kitchen, still dressed, uncorking a bottle of cheap kosher champagne. "Your favorite. Chaya told me," he says. I smile quickly. I don't really like any wine at all.

As he showers, I go to the bedroom with my champagne flute in hand and set it down on the nightstand. My mother-in-law has already laid out layers of cheap towels over one of the beds, and there is a bottle of K-Y jelly as well. I put on a long white nightgown.

I sit down on the bed next to the nightstand and pop open the bottle of K-Y, squeezing a pea-sized blob onto my fingers curiously. It's surprisingly cold and viscous. Carefully, I lie down on the bed so that my hips are on the towels and reach down to anoint myself gingerly with the clear, cold jelly. I don't want to get the new linen dirty. It's very dark, until Eli opens the bathroom door and light pours faintly into the apartment. He comes into the bedroom wearing a towel wrapped around his waist, and the outlines of his body are strange and new. He smiles uncomfortably before squatting on top of me like his teacher said, letting the towel roll off. I still can't see much. I ease my knees apart and he moves closer, adjusting his weight on his palms. I feel something hard nudge my inner thigh. It feels bigger than I expected it to. He looks at me anxiously in the darkness. He's nudging everywhere, waiting for some sort of direction from me, I think, but what do I know? This is as much a mystery to me as to him.

Finally he pokes, I think, in the right area, and I lift up to meet him and wait for the obligatory thrust and the deposit. Nothing happens. He pushes and pushes, grunts with the effort, but nothing seems to give way. And in fact, I can't see what should. What is expected to happen here?

After a while he gives up and rolls over to one side, his back to me. I lie there for a few moments peering up at the dark ceiling before I turn to nudge him slightly. "Are you okay?" I ask.

"Yes. I'm just very tired," he murmurs.

Soon I can hear him snoring lightly. I crawl into the other bed and lie awake for a long time, wondering if it happened, or if it didn't, and what the implications of either possibility might be.

When I open my eyes in the morning, the sun is shining weakly through the window blinds and the air conditioner is whirring sluggishly against the humid August air. I push the windowpane up a bit and lean out into the smoggy street, watching the trucks and city buses bounce up and down the series of metal plates covering the potholes and ditches on Wallabout Street. The garage doors in the warehouse across the street are open, laborers rushing back and forth across the loading docks.

Eli dresses quickly and grabs his tefillin just as his father knocks on the door, calling "*Men geit davenen.*" It's time for morning prayers. I amble luxuriantly around the quiet, squeaky-clean apartment in my organza morning robe with poppies printed on the fabric. My hair has dried all stiff and crunchy. I open the linen closets and run my hands over the brand-new towels and tablecloths smelling brightly of the lavender sachets I have tucked snugly between them. I open the sideboard and look at my new silver cutlery and china dishes, intoxicated by the idea that I own all these things.

In a minute Chaya is here with the electric razor, and we set up a stool in front of the bathroom mirror. I'm surprised by how little I feel about losing all my hair. If anything, I feel like I'm about to become an adult, about to be initiated into a new life. It's strange to watch my hair fall into the bucket, but there it goes, in fuzzy brown clumps. It's over so quickly, it's like I never had hair at all, and my scalp positively gleams under the bathroom lights. I never thought about the shape of my head before, but now that it's out there in the open, I marvel at its perfect proportions and the sudden symmetry of my countenance. I feel light and unburdened, almost as if I might rise suddenly from weightlessness, and I feel a strange yearning to hold on to something stuck to the ground, as if to avoid floating away into space. Chaya brings me a terry-cloth turban in a beautiful magenta hue, and it smells like fresh towels and feels soft and gentle on my forehead, holding me down like a paperweight.

I want to say something meaningful to Chaya, but I can't think of anything sensible, so I only smile and say, "So that's it. No big deal, huh?" feeling brave and grown-up to be speaking so calmly.

"What should be the big deal?" She shrugs, winding the cord around the razor and putting it away. "It's natural."

I reach up to feel my weightless head, stroking the knot of the turban briefly. No big deal, it's natural.

I hear footsteps in the hall. I think it's Eli, but it's my mother-in-law, lips pursed, hands folded in front of her, glancing away from the peephole.

Chaya puts the razor back into her oversized black pocketbook and ex-changes a brief air kiss with my *shviger* before scooting down the hallway.

I offer Eli's mother coffee, tea, any excuse to use my new dishes, and when she politely refuses, I insist on arranging chocolates prettily on a silver dish.

"So how'd it go?" she asks.

I smile politely but I'm confused. Not because I don't know what she might mean, but because I can't possibly believe she'd address it so di-rectly. I murmur vaguely and indistinctly, "Oh, fine," and wave away her question like an annoying fly. I think to myself, *This is between Eli and me, we can take care of our own business; he wouldn't want me to involve anyone*.

My mother-in-law's face draws tighter and she takes her hands off the tablecloth. "My husband tells me it wasn't finished."

I'm speechless. I don't ask her anything. I just sit there, mortified, feeling that weightlessness again: if I don't hold on to the table leg, I will release into the sky like a helium balloon.

The door opens before I can say anything, and Eli and his father are at the door. My mother-in-law stands up and reaches forward to air-kiss me good-bye. I don't lean in toward her, and she leaves with her hus-band, shutting the door behind her. My eyes are on Eli, but his eyes are downcast. My body feels hard on the outside but mushy in the center. *If the shell collapses, the filling will just spill out*, I think, as I look down at the untouched chocolate bonbons on the table.

"What happened?" I ask Eli. "What did you tell your father?"

He cringes at the urgency in my tone. "I didn't tell him anything; he asked me!" he protests quickly. "I was so taken by surprise, I just told him the truth. I didn't think he would tell anyone!"

"You told your father? Your mother knows! She'll tell everyone! Your whole family probably knows! My whole family probably knows by now too! What were you thinking?"

"I don't know, I *wasn't* thinking, I was taken by surprise!"

"Don't you think this is *our* problem to take care of? Don't you think this is something private that a couple should deal with on their own? Didn't you think it would be embarrassing to me, to you, to have every-one know our private business?"

I'm panicking now, thinking of the possibilities, of one person whispering to another, of the way gossip travels like lightning in my world, and all I can see now is a future of walking down Lee Avenue and having people point and whisper about me, about the girl that couldn't do it. Oh, the horror. I will never live this down.

Eli interjects, a pained look on his face. "It'll be fine. My father says we'll just have to do it tonight. We'll get it done, and once it's done, no one will be able to say anything. We'll try to leave the minute the *sheva berachos* is over, so we won't be too tired. Maybe that was the problem last night, maybe we were too tired!"

"Maybe," I say, but I know that's not it. That wouldn't explain my womb's failure to open its doors at that very loud and persistent knock. My strange, rebellious womb, that doesn't want guests.

In the afternoon, Eli suggests we take a nap so we can be rested for later, but I stay awake watching his blank sleeping face, his hand tucked restfully beneath the pillow. The doorbell rings and I pad out into the living room to press the intercom button. It's Chaya, and I press the buzzer to let her in.

"I heard what happened," she says, after she is seated at my new dining room table, stocking feet crossed neatly under her chair. I wait for her to come to my defense, to say something soothing.

Her face is hard when she continues. "If there's one thing that makes a marriage work," she says, "it's that a man must be king in the bedroom. If he is king in the bedroom, then he feels like a king everywhere else, no matter what happens."

She pauses, looking intently at me, her hands clutching the handles of her black bucket purse. "You understand me?" she asks, waiting for confirmation.

I nod, too flabbergasted to say anything.

"Good," she says, firmly, standing up and smoothing her skirt. "Then everything will be taken care of. I'm not even going to tell Bubby and Zeidy about this; why give them more bad news in their old age and fragile condition?" I hear the implications of that statement and feel immediately guilty.

Still, as the door shuts behind her, I wait for it to hit me. *How exactly will everything be taken care of?* I wonder. Does she have a plan? Because I don't.

The best part of the seven days of blessings after the wedding is getting to wear the clothes. The bride is always the best-dressed person attending the seven nights of festivity and good wishes, a custom designed to bestow luck on the new couple. I wear a different outfit every night, each of which was carefully shopped for and altered by a seamstress so that it fits my figure like a glove. My wigs are all freshly set and sprayed.

Throughout the parties, my new sister-in-law Shprintza, herself newly married as of two months ago because she didn't want to wait for us, as is the custom, glowers darkly in the corner, quivering with some sort of sad bitterness I can't quite understand. But I ignore her, because I am, sadly, so focused on the task we haven't managed to complete all week.

The days after my wedding, which should be the happiest of my life, become consumed by the effort to consummate my marriage. But as each effort results in failure, Eli becomes more and more anxious, and as a result, his family exerts more and more pressure on us to be finished with it. By the third try, Eli can no longer muster any eagerness from his own body, and I cannot submit to something that isn't there. He explains to me the process of his arousal, and we stay up until five a.m. trying to calm his nerves and relax him enough so that he can try, but by the end of the week we are both driven near mad with desperation.

In yeshiva, Eli says, the boys would jerk each other off. Because there were only men around and no girls, the sight of a boy could get him aroused. After many years, he explains with a sigh, to switch suddenly is weird. "I don't even know if I should be attracted to you. I didn't even have an idea of what a girl looked like before I saw you."

I'm suddenly horribly self-conscious. I took for granted that he would be excited at the mere glimpse of me. But now I see my body through his eyes—foreign, mysterious, and confusing.

At the end of the week the rabbis say to call it quits because I am bleeding from all the irritation, and technically speaking there's no way to tell if that blood is coming from the splitting of the hymen, therefore rendering me impure. They rule that I am now *niddah* and must proceed like any other married woman to count seven clean days, or fourteen cloths, before immersing myself in the *mikvah*.

The process of cleaning up so I can try again takes two weeks, but a week before I have to go to the *mikvah*, I wake up with a terrible itch on my left arm. I think it's a bite from a mosquito, and I scratch furiously all night in between brief dozing periods, but when I wake up in the morning, I can see a litany of angry red pustules all along my arm and shoulder. I have never seen anything like this bizarre rash, and I make an emergency appointment with the local health clinic on Heyward Street. Normally I don't use the doctors at ODA medical center, since the clinic, which is run by the Hasidic community but funded by the government, is open to all patients and is always crowded and dirty. However, I can't get an immediate appointment anywhere else.

Dr. Katz looks me up and down and squints carefully at the rash but can't seem to come to a clear diagnosis for quite some time. Eventually he says he's eighty percent sure it's some form of chicken pox but can't be absolutely sure, and he prescribes an antiviral medication just in case it is.

"This only works if you take it within forty-eight hours of an outbreak," he says, "but I'm pretty sure this is still early on. It won't get rid of the virus but it will reduce its severity and length."

I really can't quite believe I have chicken pox. I was vaccinated as a child, and I've been exposed to it since then, so why now? I feel ridiculous even telling Eli. But now I can't go to the *mikvah*, which I was dreading anyway, and I can take a little vacation from all the stress I was under. No one can argue with chicken pox.

The spots spread and show up on my left leg, the left side of my abdomen, and, finally, the left side of my face. It's as if someone drew a line in red marker down the middle of my body and told the spots to stay on one side. They itch terribly; I bathe in oatmeal and slather multiple anti-itch creams over everything. I'm embarrassed to be seen on the street with my face in such a state, so I am stuck at home until it clears up.

"It's a good thing you are *niddah* now," Eli says. "I can't touch you anyway."

Three weeks later the spots are still there, although they are starting to scab over. I wake up in the middle of the night with severe abdominal pain and vomit for hours before Eli calls his friend, an EMT, and asks him what to do.

Michoel is part of the local Hatzolah organization, which has its own ambulances and paramedics. He says that anytime a woman has abdominal pain, the policy is always to take her to the hospital in case it has anything to do with her uterus. We are dropped off at the NYU emergency room, which is largely populated by locals looking for painkillers. No one attends to me for a while except to give me something for my fever, but when a doctor finally sees me, he pages the specialist in infectious diseases to come down and examine me. The doctor, a diminutive Asian man with a creased forehead and oily skin, tells me I have orbital shingles, which he claims, looking at Eli's religious garb, I probably caught in the ritual bath.

Thinking back to the pool of warm water I probably shared with hundreds of women, I shudder. It never entered my mind that I could contract a disease by fulfilling one of God's commandments. I was always taught that one could never be hurt by way of a mitzvah, a commandment; its merit would protect us.

I feel like I've been cursed. Since Eli and I got married, everything that could possibly go wrong has. I inherited Bubby's tendency to be superstitious, so is this a sign? If so, it's a bit late in coming. I could have used the warning a little earlier. It's not like I can do anything about my circumstances now.

There are eight floors in my apartment building, and about twenty apartments on each floor, most of them housing newlywed couples just like Eli and me. Still, what are the chances that Golda should end up living right down the hall from us?

My old friend, the one who got caught in the *gan yehudah* with me all those years ago, has grown up into the beautiful woman I always thought she would be. Her eyes are even shinier than they used to be, her body rounded out into pleasant curves but her waist as small as ever. Her manner has changed: she is shy, soft-spoken, nothing like I remember her. She invites me over for coffee after her husband leaves for shul in the morning. Like all newly married women, we fuss over her dishes and linens and pore through her wedding album. She takes me into the bedroom to show me her gorgeous mahogany bedroom set, with its brooding armoire and stodgy dresser. The small room is dwarfed by all that furniture.

She sits down on one of the beds, smoothing the coverlet with a slim, graceful hand. She looks up at me, her face pained.

"You should have seen it the night of the wedding," she whispers. "There was so—so much blood." Her voice cracks on the second sentence.

I don't know if I understand what she's trying to tell me. If she's talking about losing her virginity, I'm not sure I want to hear it. I can't bear to hear yet another successful wedding night story, not when I still haven't managed to shed a drop of blood.

"There was blood everywhere—on the bed, on the walls. I had to go to the hospital." Her face creases suddenly and I think she is going to cry, but she takes a deep breath and smiles bravely. "He went into the wrong place. It ruptured my colon. Oh, Devoireh, you can't imagine the pain. It was so bad!"

I'm flabbergasted. My mouth is probably hanging wide open. How exactly do you rupture a colon?

"You know," she hurries to explain, "they tell them in marriage classes to go really fast, before they lose their nerve, before we get too scared. So he just pushed, you know? But in the wrong spot. How was he to know? Even I wasn't really sure where the right spot was."

"How are you feeling now?" I ask, deeply moved by her story.

"Oh, I'm fine now!" She smiles widely, but her eyes don't crinkle the way they used to, and her dimple barely flashes. "My husband's going to be back any minute, so you should probably go." Suddenly she's in a rush to ferry me out the door, as if she is afraid to be caught in conversation with a neighbor.

Back in my apartment, I go into the bathroom and close the door. I sob into a towel for twenty minutes straight. Where is Golda's family, I want to know, in all of this? Why hasn't somebody, after all these years, after all these mistakes, decided to take a stand?

A kosher Chinese restaurant opens down the street. The rabbis rage against this appropriation of gentile culture, but the young couples who live in our neighborhood love the opportunity to try something new, and although we don't have the guts to be seen eating there, we order takeout and Eli goes by to pick up the order after evening prayers.

I plate the spareribs in a bright-red, jellylike sauce on our brand-new, silver-rimmed china plates. Eli and I sit across from each other at the kitchen table; I watch him tear at the ribs while I pick at my food. I haven't been able to keep anything down lately, so I've stopped eating. I think I may be very sick with some strange disease, even now that the shingles have mostly passed, and that maybe it might have something to do with my locked-up vagina.

Chaya talks to the rabbis, and they send us to their specially approved sex therapist. It's a married couple, actually. The lady doctor speaks to me, and the man speaks to Eli. Afterward they put us all in one room and show us plastic body parts that Velcro together. The doctor painstakingly explains every small part of my reproductive system to us. I don't see how this helps. It makes it all the more clinical.

As she explains my down-there area to Eli, I feel a bit better that I'm not the only one they seem to be blaming at the moment.

Then the male doctor announces he is going to examine me to make sure everything is as it should be. At first I protest. Having never had a gynecological exam before, I panic and refuse to get on the table. Finally the doctor says he will use anesthetic; he applies some lidocaine before exploring with a gloved finger. After a moment of uncomfortable poking around, he pronounces his diagnosis. "You have two hymens. You're going to need surgery."

I have two virginities, it means. Eli tells his mother what the doctor said, but she scoffs at him. When it comes to surgery, she says, you don't take one doctor's word for it. You ask a second opinion. She gives Eli the number of her gynecologist in Manhattan, a high-risk specialist who delivered all her children.

Dr. Patrick has an office on Fifth Avenue that overlooks the snowy expanse of Central Park, and peering out from her window, I can see the taxicabs slicing through the slushy roads, some coming to a stop in front of the Pierre at the signal of the valet. I feel very small here in this office, in this uppity section of Manhattan, knowing beyond a doubt that the nurses and doctors look down at me for being married at seventeen, to a man who wears black velvet hats and long silk coats, whose *payos* swing energetically with his movements.

Dr. Patrick's face is stern and furrowed in concentration as she shoves the steel speculum into me and steers this way and that. "You may have a septum," she says. "There seems to be some scarring, and that can happen with scarring sometimes. It's like another wall in the vagina. We'll send you for an MRI to confirm." She looks up at me as she says this, but she doesn't appear to expect a reaction. It's like she already assumes I don't have any real feelings on the matter. She bustles importantly out of the room, and as I'm getting dressed, the nurse comes in to give me the prescriptions, her face unsmiling. I don't know why here in this office I feel so unbearably ashamed just to exist, when I never feel like that in Williamsburg.

When I get my first MRI, I discover I'm claustrophobic, and I cry so hard in the tube that my body shakes and they can't get a clear image, and they yell at me from their little intercom, "Keep still!" The MRI is inconclusive, says Dr. Patrick. Sometimes longitudinal septums don't show up on MRIs. There's nothing to be done, she says, except visit another therapist, and she gives us a referral.

Eli has stopped approaching me the way he used to in the beginning, when every night held the possibility that our long string of failures might be broken and that he might still somehow be able to pick up the pieces of his shattered masculinity and make something of our marriage. While we are going from doctor to doctor, he feels there is no point, not until we know what's wrong. I think that he may be hoping something is seriously wrong, anything to propel the blame away from us, from him. Although I never really believed it when they told me it was my fault, I think he did. He takes what his family says very seriously.

Now he comes home from work later every day, and he runs off to evening prayers as soon as he gets home. In the beginning he would skip prayers all the time just to be with me. I don't mind, I let him go, but when he comes back, I reprimand him for abandoning me. I want to be left alone, but I don't want to feel unloved. Which is it?

While he is gone, I take long baths. My new bathroom has become a great consolation to me, after all the trials of the last few months. It has a big tub and shiny expensive tiles, and with some scented candles placed strategically around the room, it becomes my personal oasis of peace.

Eli sometimes comes home to find me still in the tub. "You'll turn into a prune," he says. I check my fingertips, but they don't look especially wrinkled. After I finally come out of the bathroom, I always feel dizzy and weak. It must be the heat of the water.

One night I get in the tub as usual and run the hot water, relishing the warmth on my constantly cold feet. But after a few minutes, it feels as if my entire body is burning up. My face, which is not even near the water, feels like it's on fire. I get out and try to cool off, but I can't seem to chase away the sensation. It rises in waves toward my chest and head, and because I do not understand what is happening, I begin to feel panicked, my pulse racing quickly. Within minutes, my dinner is propelled up my esophagus, forceful fountains of vomit splashing into the toilet bowl. It's the first time in my life that I've vomited without feeling any sort of stomach upset. I have no idea why it happened, and for a while I convince myself there was something wrong with the food, even though Eli suffered no such effects. He always says he has an iron stomach.

After a while, Eli renews his efforts. The rabbis have told him to keep trying, regardless of what the doctors say. Our lives become clearly marked by the clean days and the unclean days: two weeks in which we gingerly approach each other, knowing the attempts are futile, and two weeks in which we carefully avoid each other, making sure not to violate the laws of *niddah*. The pattern has me feeling perpetually unsettled. At the end of each two-week period of forced intimacy, I find myself finally adjusted to the new tone of our relationship, only to be thrust back into the *niddah* state, feeling discarded and unwanted.

It feels like a form of psychological torment for Eli to alternate between wanting to be next to me and wanting me as far away as possible. I cannot understand what his true feelings for me must be if it is so easy for him to snap back and forth, shut off and turn on. Why can't I exhibit the same self-discipline? Eli lives by the letter of the law; it seems that God's commandments are his one true love. He only wants me when I fit into the parameters of his pious devotion to halacha.

My feelings are such fragile, scared creatures; they must be coaxed out slowly, and by the time they get comfortable, they are sent into hiding again. Soon I cannot bring myself to reach out to my husband at all, because I dread the day when he will once again reject me. I find that I've become very cold; each day that passes, people recede further and further away from me until they feel like specks in the distance. My own body becomes detached from me as well, and I can make it do things without feeling as if I am present.

The impulse vomiting has been happening a lot lately, and I find that the only way to avoid it is to stop consuming food. I can't throw up if there's nothing to get rid of. Giving up food is easy because I have completely lost my appetite. The sight of a chocolate bar, once such a temptation, makes my intestines curl. Because I cannot eat, I lose weight. I only notice this when others point it out to me, remarking about how big the clothes I purchased only a few months ago have become, skirts slipping from my waist to my hips, sleeves skimming my knuckles instead of wrists. Everyone has always made fun of my plump cheeks; now they have become drawn and pale.

If I become surrounded by too many people, I start to feel my heart beat fast, and my limbs are overtaken by a quivering sensation of weakness. I fear that I may have a terrible illness. If I do try to force myself to eat something, within moments I am vomiting profusely, unable to stop dry heaving for hours. My body feels as tired and wretched as an old woman's.

My doctor performs many tests, sends me for X-rays and CAT scans. One day in his office he gently offers me a handful of white pills, a kind look in his eye. "They're Xanax. Take them every time you start feeling sick. They will make you feel better."

"What are they for?" I ask hesitantly.

"Anxiety," he answers.

"But I'm not worried!" I protest. "Why would I need those?"

"Maybe you don't feel anxious," the doctor explains, "but your body does, and your symptoms won't go away until you address the problem."

I can't bring myself to take the pills from his hand, so I get up and put on my coat, ready to leave his office.

"Well, if you won't take pills, at least let me give you a referral." He hands me a white business card. "She's a good friend of mine; she might be able to help you."

"Biofeedback," the card reads. "By Jessica Marigny."

The office is in a doorman building on the Upper East Side, just off Park Avenue in the most genteel of neighborhoods. In the waiting room I am assaulted by glitzy magazine covers, their pages thumbed by women with long, manicured nails and gleaming, bare legs.

When Jessica invites me into the examination room at the back, I'm surprised to find it lacking in the usual equipment. There is no table to lie down on, only a comfortable chair. To the right I can see some machinery, but not what one would usually find in a doctor's office.

Jessica attaches wires to my palms with little pieces of gray tape and presses some buttons on the machine they are attached to. Instantly a number pops onto its small screen, ninety-eight, but the number changes rapidly—ninety-nine, one hundred two, one hundred five.

"Stressed out, are we?" Jessica says with a smile, tucking a curtain of blond hair behind her left ear.

I smile back, unsure of her meaning.

"Those numbers reflect your stress levels," she says kindly. "Biofeedback is about learning to read your body's signals and understanding how to respond to them. I'm going to teach you how to recognize when you are having anxiety and how to regulate it so that it doesn't make you sick."

For an hour each week I sit in her chair, learning how to breathe so that I put pressure on my adrenal glands, learning how to clear my mind and relax my muscles, until I can watch the numbers on the screen go down of their own accord.

"Just remember, you are always in control. Your anxiety can never get the best of you unless you let it," she tells me.

As I leave after my last session, Jessica gives me her usual parting words.

"Mind over matter," she says, tapping her forehead. "Mind over matter."

Eli watches as I spend my evenings lying on the couch, concentrating on the breathing exercises. His presence instigates waves of anxiety that

I am forced to battle nonstop, fighting each upsurge with a powerful breath. I feel as if I am putting up a poor fight, the fight of someone under siege who knows that she will run out of energy before her enemy ever will and that defeat is inevitable. Still, I keep doing the exercises. The anxiety never goes away, but I can hold it at a distance, always keeping my eye on it should it decide to creep up on me and catch me unawares.

Sometimes at night I am half awakened by a violent hallucination in which my blankets and sheets are trying to devour me. I race from the bed and cower in the kitchen until the feeling of being attacked fades somewhat, although it still feels as if the air itself is trying to smother me. The room seems to bend and twist in its efforts to crush me; even the chair underneath me feels precarious. I feel as if I have no physical refuge. What a curse it is not to feel safe in one's own body, when everything else is going wrong. My body should be the one thing I can rely on; instead it has become my worst enemy, undermining my every effort.

Eli has been watching me go through my panic attacks but he doesn't understand them. Perhaps he thinks that I am going crazy and that I will never recover. One day in June he doesn't come home from work, and when I try calling his phone, he doesn't pick up. I wait till late in the evening, but he still hasn't been in touch, so finally I call his mother to see if she knows where he is, but before I even ask her, she says coldly, "Eli isn't coming home tonight."

"What do you mean?"

"I mean he doesn't want to come home to you anymore. And he doesn't want to talk to you."

I hang up the phone in shock. I call my aunt Chaya, who already knows what's going on. She says my mother-in-law thinks Eli should divorce me because I can't have intercourse. I can't understand how Eli could decide to do that so impulsively, that he could choose his mother over me, without even telling me in advance.

Suddenly I feel a well of anger surge up in me where previously there was fear. I don't know who or what I'm angry at, but I am enraged by the unfairness that seems to have characterized my entire life up to this point, and I am fed up with being blamed for everything.

"Fine," I say, hardness in my voice. "I'm not going to fight it. If he really wants a divorce, he can have it. I don't care." I hang up the phone before she can say anything.

I do care, deep inside, because I'm afraid of being on my own. If my husband divorces me, I will have no home, no friends. I will probably never be able to remarry. But I don't think about those things, because his betrayal is bigger than all of that, and I stay awake until dawn, frozen with numbness.

Is it fair, I think, that because I have the vagina, the receptacle, I have to do all the work? What if I had the penis; would anyone blame me for not being able to put it somewhere? What about all those nights that I stayed up with Eli comforting him because he couldn't maintain his own erection? Am I responsible for that too?

I drive myself crazy with these thoughts, but I don't know who to be angry at first: Chaya, for always telling me what to do without ever earning that right; Zeidy, for being clueless enough to think I could ever be happy married off to a boy from a dumb, fanatical family where I was the only married woman who didn't wear a *shpitzel* or hat; Eli, for being a spineless husband from the start, for blurting out the truth to his father without even giving us a chance at privacy; my mother-in-law, for constantly butting into our business and gossiping to her daughters about me behind my back, for marrying Eli to me and then telling him he could have done better; my father-in-law, who seemed to take distinct pleasure in our failure to consummate our marriage and who uses every opportunity to lecture Eli about halachic sexual practices. The list goes on and on, until in the dark before dawn, I fear I may be entirely consumed by rage. I muffle my wails so as not to wake the neighbors.

At seven a.m. Eli comes home. He prostrates himself in front of me with apologies, but I can't hear any of it. All I see are his lips moving, and all I can think of is his lack of character and strength. In my heart I have already cut him out, and I know that if I stay married to this man, every day will be a performance of a good, loving wife, but I will never care for him as a human being again. Mutely, I nod at whatever he says, and he hugs me gratefully when I agree to take him back.

His mother has told him not to let me read any more library books, as if my illicit glimpses into their pages were the cause of all our problems. If I ever want to read again, I must revert to the wiles of my childhood, and the thought of such deception now tires me. I am too old to fight for these small freedoms. It was never supposed to be like this.

I have to get rid of all my books. I used to be so excited by the way they lay nakedly on the table near the sofa, by the way I lived in my own home and no longer had to hide the evidence of my preferred pastime. Now I can't afford for anyone to see them and report back to my mother-in-law. I put them all into a big plastic garbage bag that Eli will take to the Dumpster outside his office.

I thumb my well-worn copy of *Anne of Green Gables* before placing it in the bag along with *Watership Down* and *Jane Eyre*. Anne was plagued like all the beloved female characters of my youth, but she was my favorite, because for all her spunk and mischief, she earned the undying love of those around her the way I always wished to. I thought it would be Eli, finally, who would love me despite my inability to be ordinary, the way he promised to when we first met and I warned him I would be a handful. But perhaps what he meant by being able to handle me was not love but the power to make me bend to his wishes and conform to his world.

Eli tells me it was his sister Shprintza who was behind his sudden disappearance. Now that he thinks he's back in my good graces, he is anxious to blame all the unpleasantness on someone else. He says he found out that Shprintza had been bad-mouthing me to everyone in the family all along, making up lies about me. So they convinced him to leave me, because they believed her. I remember her bitter, angry expression at my *sheva berachos*, and it suddenly makes sense to me.

"Do you think she was just jealous that we stole her thunder?" I ask Eli. After all, a newly married woman is fawned over by her family and friends for a full year before she must surrender the attention to the next bride. Instead, she was forgotten as soon as I got married. Still, it had been her choice; she could have waited and stolen my thunder instead. I don't think I would have minded it.

"I don't know," he answers. "It could be that, but it could also be that she's jealous that you are closer to me than she is. We were always so intimate with each other when we lived at home. Maybe she feels like you are a threat to our relationship."

"But she has her own husband! And he was your best friend! Shouldn't you feel threatened that she's getting in between you two?"

"No, with me, it's different. It's like she married my best friend so she could always be in my group. You know she had her eye on him all along. She told the matchmaker to suggest it."

I can't believe Eli's sister would be so manipulative. It sounds like she was always obsessed with Eli. The idea of it makes me distinctly uncomfortable, but I don't know why. Still, I'm not willing to pin all the blame on her. The fact that Eli couldn't see through his family's manipulations worries me. How could he have turned out to be the weak-willed man I was so sure he was not? And why, after discovering that Shprintza was the culprit, was he not taking her and his family to task over their actions? At the very least, he could do *his* husbandly duty and stick up for me.

Because I promised Eli I would figure out a way to take care of our problem, I make an appointment to see the sex therapist Dr. Patrick recommended. The therapist says she can tell from the way I squirm on the table that it's in my head. My head, she says, has more power over my body than I give it credit for. My vagina closes up if my mind wants it to, and no matter how much I convince myself I want it to open, my subconscious knows best, and it is in control.

It's called vaginismus. She gives me a book about it. I read that the condition is most common in women who grow up in repressive religious environments. I begin to understand that years of hiding from my body has taught it to hide from me.

There is something called muscle memory, the book explains, that the body uses to retain skills like walking and swimming. There is a reason why you can't forget how to ride a bike. Even though you can't remember it, your muscles do. They kick into action the moment you put your feet on the pedals.

If your leg muscles learned to walk, they can't unlearn it. You can't ever erase the memory without undergoing a great trauma. In the same way, the author explains, if your vaginal muscles were told to clam up, that sort of muscle memory is going to be hard to overcome. So it's more than just the mind that has to be convinced: it's the actual muscle.

The first thing I must do, the book says, is obtain a plastic dilator kit, a series of long tubes of varying widths to be inserted as practice. The process can take months, continuing until the very widest tube can be inserted comfortably. The idea is to train the muscles of the vagina to loosen naturally. The act is accompanied by special breathing procedures and muscular exercises.

I'm supposed to go to the therapist and do the dilators in her office, but it's too humiliating, so I find a kit for sale online and have it shipped to the apartment. It arrives a week later in a nondescript white box, the tubes nested inside each other in a velvet drawstring bag. They are beige-colored, with only slightly narrowed tips. The instructions say to use lots of lubricant.

Every night while Eli is at evening prayers, I lie on my bed and practice. The first two weeks it is a long struggle just to get the narrowest tube in, the one that's barely the width of my finger, and I have to lie there with it inside me for a while, and then practice sliding it in and out while keeping my breathing as relaxed as possible. It is grueling and boring work.

Eli comes home and asks about my progress every night. It takes three months for me to get to the largest dilator, but no matter how long I practice with that one, it never gets less painful. It seems I'm doing all the right things physically, but mentally and emotionally nothing is changing, and I begin to understand that that is the core issue here.

For our first anniversary, Eli and I go see a hypnotist show in Las Vegas. We don't tell anyone where we are going because people would disapprove; Eli tells his mother we are going to California so I can rest. After the show the hypnotist offers to cure people who smoke, or hypnotize people to lose weight. When we get back to our hotel, it hits me that perhaps this could work: I could hypnotize my vagina open!

When we return to New York, I make an appointment with a licensed hypnotherapist in midtown Manhattan. It costs two hundred and fifty dollars, she says, but she's confident she can cure me. I lie down in her chair as she plays soft music and instructs me to breathe deeply. The session lasts one hour. I don't feel hypnotized, but you never know with these things, right?

I tell Eli we are going to try again for real. When I go to the *mikvah*, the woman who inspects me has seen me before, and she glances curiously at my flat stomach. *"Shefaleh,"* she says, "don't worry, honey. Some-times it takes time." I pretend to smile gratefully.

At home I change into a lacy nightgown because I want Eli to be re-laxed and not too nervous, as after all this time he is not very confident ei-ther. I pretend his penis is the tube, and it works, even though it hurts a lot, stings and burns up and down in a rhythm, but it's nice that it's over fast, that he can make it quick. He's so happy, he laughs and cries at the same time for what seems like forever, and his body shakes violently above mine.

Afterward, he rolls over on his back and puts his arms behind his head, a satisfied smile on his face. He is still a little out of breath.

"What does it feel like?" I ask softly. I'm genuinely curious.

"What? You mean the actual experience?"

"Yes."

He turns and looks at me, trying to find the words.

"It's like the best feeling in the world." His eyes are wet.

"Hmmm." I don't say anything else, but I wonder, if it's the best feel-ing in the world for him, why isn't it for me? Why does it get to be so great for the man and so much work for the woman? Will I ever like it?

Well, anyway, I'm glad it's done. I call Chaya the next day and tell her, and she calls everyone to relate the good news. I'm past caring about privacy anymore. I'm past caring about anything.

On Friday night Eli wants to do it again. He's so excited at this new thing in our lives. He comes into bed after the Shabbos meal, and his breath smells strangely of Coca-Cola.

"Did you drink soda?" I ask him. "You smell like cola soda."

"No! What are you talking about? There's no soda in the house. How could I drink cola?"

"But you smell like Coke! It's so strong! Go brush your teeth at least."

When Eli comes back, he still smells pungent, like warm soda with the gas gone out. I can't bear to be near the smell of it. He thinks I'm making it up, but it's more real to me than the sheets I'm sleeping on.

When Eli comes home from the synagogue the next morning, he says to me, "Maybe you're pregnant. My friend in shul says sometimes pregnant women smell weird things that aren't there."

I can't be pregnant, not this fast. Does it really work like that? Is it that easy? It hardly seems possible. But then again, pregnancy is not a result of an accumulation of intercourse; all it takes is one time. Why not the first time? I guess it is possible.

We buy a test after Shabbos is over, and the two pink lines show up within five minutes. I guess we are pregnant. I feel instantly that it's a boy. I go straight to the bookstore the next day to buy pregnancy books and spend the whole week on the couch reading. I resolve to do no drinking at all, even though my sister-in-law thinks a little bit is fine. I'm going to have the healthiest pregnancy, the healthiest baby. This, at last, is in my control.

I ignore the fact that I don't feel any emotion at all, even while Eli is practically weeping with happiness and tearing his hair out about who he should tell and whether he should wait the required three months before letting anyone know. I busy myself with thinking about practicalities, like how we are going to get all the supplies we need and where we will shop for them and how I will soon no longer fit into any of my clothes.

I can hear Eli on the phone with his mother in the other room. I smile secretly to myself. I guess he really couldn't hold it in. Soon he comes into the dining room and sits next to me on the sofa, putting his hand on my belly. "She cried," he whispers. "She's so happy, you should've heard her. She thought this day would never come."

Right. Because I'm eighteen and have few fertile years left ahead of me. She thought we wouldn't "fix" our little problem until I was forty. Well, Chaya got pregnant for the sixth time at forty-two. I shake my head dismissively. What a pair those two are, Chaya and my mother-in-law: both drama queens.

"You know," Eli says slowly, "now that you're pregnant, you're clean. Like for the next nine months. You won't have to go to the mikvah. I will be able to touch you all the time."

I snort with laughter. "That's what you're so happy about? Since when do you worry about the mikvah? I'm the one that has to go, not you."

"I know," he says, "but you always tell me how you hate it. I'm happy for you."

He's happy for himself. He just discovered what sex feels like and now he gets nine unrestricted months. There is no rest for the weary.

8

Justice Prevails

The Talmud asserts that God himself prays. "What is God's prayer? 'O, that My mercy shall prevail over My justice!'"
—From A Treasury of Jewish Folklore,
ed. Nathan Ausubel

I decide I can't possibly raise a child in our apartment in Williamsburg. It's too small; there is no room for a crib or any toys. I want a backyard and trees; I was spoiled even growing up in the city by being able to live in a private brownstone with its own garden as opposed to the housing projects that most of my friends lived in.

I am so tired of living in Williamsburg. I can't believe I still have to put up with all the staring and judging, the endless gossiping of the neighbors, the impossibility of keeping anything private. We can't even sneak out to go bowling without fear of being followed by some curious busybody. This isn't what I signed up for. I wanted more freedom from marriage, but in Williamsburg, even a grown-up married woman is still under as much scrutiny as she was when she was a child. Even Eli isn't used to the cramped conditions of Brooklyn; where he grew up, people were more spread out. It wasn't like you could put your ear to the wall and hear the couple next door fighting about groceries.

I'm constantly trying to figure out a scheme to change our living situation. Eli has difficulty adjusting to change; he is by nature averse to any sort of risk taking. For weeks I lay the groundwork, reminding him how tedious his two-hour commute to work is and how deeply that will cut into his time with the baby. All his brothers and sisters live upstate, I point out. There's nothing keeping him here.

Eli calls his brother to see what he thinks. Of course Aaron is instantly enthusiastic, rattling off a long list of reasons for Eli to move. He even knows of an apartment that's available, and he can make sure we get it at an excellent price. When Eli and I take a trip to see the apartment, I'm not thrilled with its condition, but I figure once we move up here, I can find a better place later on. For now, I'm just delighted at the prospect of leaving everything I hated about Williamsburg behind.

When I tell Aunt Chaya about it, the boxes are already halfway packed. Still, for some reason I feel I have to formally notify her. Surprisingly, she seems approving of the idea. She gives me an appraising look when I deliver the news, and says only "Monsey? I think it could be a great idea for you to move there." There's emphasis on the uncertainty in that statement, but at least she's keeping an open mind. Maybe she is tired of having me around as a burden. In Airmont, a small town just outside Monsey, I will be far away from everyone's mind, and for the first time, I will be truly independent.

Our new apartment is on the bottom floor of a ranch-style house on a little dead-end street just off the New York State Thruway. My city soul is soothed by the sounds of passing traffic at night, combined with the incessant chirping of crickets.

I love the country. I can't imagine ever living in the city again, with its prying eyes and confining quarters. I walk along Route 59 to the commercial area to do my shopping, but after a while I worry that I won't be able to walk everywhere when I get bigger, and some women in Monsey drive, I know. Even my sister-in-law has her license for emergencies, although her son's school won't let her drive, officially speaking. But I am not as religious as she is, and I have no kids in school yet, and I decide I want to take driving lessons. I convince Eli that it would be good for us; on long road trips I could help with the driving.

Steve is my driving teacher. He's Jewish, he says, but not religious, a middle-aged bachelor who lives in the basement of an old woman's ranch house, drinking beer from a can and watching football. I don't tell him that I'm pregnant because he makes derogatory remarks about Hasidic women as baby machines, and I don't want him to see me that way. I wake up early so I can get the vomiting out of the way, and by the time he honks his horn outside, my stomach is usually settled enough for me to hide the queasiness.

I wait for him to crack jokes about female drivers, but instead he teaches me to be strong and aggressive and not to let other drivers intimidate me. After a scrape in a parking lot I contemplate quitting. All my life I have heard mocking tales of clumsy women drivers, and somehow I still feel as if I don't have the right to be on the road. Steve comes by and insists we get back in the car immediately, and even though I'm terrified, I obey him, and he takes me out on the highway. I can't believe he feels safe enough with me to brave the 65 mph speed limit.

When we get back, Eli is sitting on one of the lounge chairs on the front lawn waiting for me, and Steve looks out at him and says, "That's your husband?"

I nod yes.

"Huh. He looks like a hip dude."

When I get inside, I tell Eli what Steve said and we laugh hysterically at the idea of my husband, with his long, swinging *payos*, being called a "hip dude" by anyone.

My driving test is administered by a grumpy old man who makes little muttering sounds at every turn and glowers at me the entire time, but I pass. Even Steve is a little surprised, I can tell.

Now I'm so excited, I want to drive everywhere, and even when my belly bulges into the steering wheel, I still drive, following maps up to Orange County and down into New Jersey, just for the sake of exploring. On Sundays we drive up Route 9W and take pictures of the Hudson River snaking below us. Eli loves taking pictures, but I hate posing in them. I don't want to remember what I looked like when I was pregnant.

We go to visit my mother-in-law in Kiryas Joel, and she scowls when she sees how big I am. She keeps pulling my hem down over my knees whenever she passes the sofa, as if to say I'm immodest for being so obviously pregnant in her home. I am rather large; people keep asking me if I'm having twins. Dr. Patrick says it's because I was underweight when I got pregnant, which I was, but only by five or ten pounds. The anxiety of the first year made me lose a lot of weight.

Now I'm so big I can't find any clothes that fit, and my *shviger* wants me to wear tent dresses, but I think, *Just because I'm pregnant doesn't mean I want to look ugly.* I get migraines now and can't bear to wear a wig for too long. I started growing my hair in too, because I don't have to go to the *mikvah* anymore and no one is checking up on me. It's still short, maybe two inches.

After a monthly checkup at the doctor's office in New York City, I stop into a salon. I take off my wig and ask the hairdresser if she can do something with it, maybe some highlights and a cute short haircut.

"Oh my God, you have virgin hair!" she squeals. Her hair is streaked red and slicked back like a boy's.

"What does that mean?" I laughingly ask.

"It means your hair has never been dyed or cut in any specific style, so it's like a clean slate." She doesn't mention my wig, but later, while she's cutting my hair, she says the salon gets a lot of cancer patients growing their new hair in and that she has a lot of experience dealing with hair this short and I shouldn't worry.

At the end of the day I have a reddish pixie cut with thin honey-colored streaks at the tips. I look different, what Zeidy would call promiscuous, but I like it.

Eli doesn't seem to notice anything different about me, but later he asks me if I think I'm going to shave my head again, because, he says, the hair peeks out of the edges of my turban and people can tell, and he doesn't want anyone saying bad things about me, about us.

"Who would say bad things?" I ask. And although he brushes away my question, I know he's talking about his sister. We hear stories from other people all the time about how she goes around spreading slanderous rumors about us, but we haven't said anything to her partly because we feel pity for her. I know she's just doing it out of jealousy, except I'm not sure what it is we have that anyone could be so jealous of. Shprintza became pregnant right after she got married and already has a fat baby boy named Mendel after Eli's grandfather.

"What are we going to name the baby?" I ask Eli. "You know the first one is the wife's pick, but we can only name it after a dead family member, so there's not that much to choose from. Let's at least pick something that's cute and not too serious. Nothing kids will make fun of."

After poring over my family tree, I settle on my great-uncle, Zeidy's brother. His name was Yitzhak Binyamin, and everyone is always talking about how smart and amicable he was. The literal definition of the Hebrew moniker is "he who brings laughter, the son, the right hand." The possibilities for endearing nicknames are endless: Yitzy, Binny, Yumi, all of them great for baby talk.

When the ultrasound tech told us it was a boy, Eli cried. He held my hand and said to me that he had always wanted a son so that he could give him what he never got from his own father. Eli's father is the coldest and most distant person I have ever met, and I'm glad Eli wants to be different, but I wonder if he even understands how much like his family he is, how he subconsciously models his father's behavior. He promises me he will be the best father I can imagine, and in that moment, I believe him, because the tears are real.

I marvel at the picture the nurse prints out for us, at the tiny babylike form with his hand curved toward his mouth, thumb hovering near his lips. It's so hard to believe that something that lifelike could be growing inside my innocent belly.

I start to develop tiny red marks all over my abdomen. They look like little veins. They're stretch marks, but not the usual ones that run up and down the sides. Instead it looks like hundreds of little rubber bands snapped in my skin.

When the baby starts kicking weakly, I lie on the couch and lift my sweater so I can poke back at that ever-growing mound, pushing at the little lumps that appear in random areas of my abdomen. At times I wonder, *Is this an elbow, a heel, or perhaps his tiny little head pressing up against my stomach?*

Sometimes I get in a mood, and I climb into bed and cry, and when Eli asks me why, I say it's because the neighbor's piano playing is too loud and I can't sleep, or because we have no bathtub and I miss being able to take a bath. Eli says his brother tells him pregnant women cry a lot and that I shouldn't worry, because apparently I'm nowhere near as bad as his sister Shprintza, who cried every day for nine months. I don't know if he's just saying that to make me feel better, though.

Hasidic men aren't allowed to masturbate, Eli repeatedly tells me. As a result of this rule, he explains to me, I am obligated to satisfy him so that his sexual frustration doesn't build up. If I refuse, I would be forcing him to sin, thereby carrying the burden of his wrongdoing.

Whenever Eli feels libidinous, which is quite often lately, he approaches me much in the same way I imagine a dog pounces on a leg of furniture, rubbing himself insistently against my body as if I were a lump of wood to be used for the pleasurable sensation of friction. I can't explain to him why I tense like a taut guitar string at his fumbling attempts at release, because he can't understand why I would want to deny him pleasure. But I dread his humping sessions more than actual attempts at penetration; in the moments that I cringe motionless beneath the scraping movements of his body, I feel my dignity and sense of self-worth slip away.

The more obviously pregnant I get, the more excuses I have to avoid sex. Even Eli is frightened of hurting the baby. He has this bizarre idea that the baby might be able to see him from the inside, and even though I know how ridiculous that is, I don't tell him what I read in the pregnancy books; instead I let him continue thinking that, and the respite is welcome.

Still, if I want something, I know the best way to get it is to receive Eli's advances. Sex softens him for a little bit, makes him inclined to let me have things my way, and it feels nice to have him smile at me the way he does after we do it, rather than have him glowering at me resentfully for everything I do wrong. He gets grumpy when denied.

As soon as it's over, Eli gets dressed and leaves. Always. The minute his desire escapes him, it's like he forgot why he ever got into bed in the first place, and he rushes out of the house like he's late for an important meeting. The contrast between his eager attentions and his sudden disappearance is disconcerting. To me, it feels like all he ever wants from me is to feel physically satisfied, and the minute he does, he leaves me alone. I hate him for making me feel so small, but when I tell him how I feel, he laughs me off. You're being ridiculous, he says. What am I supposed to do, hang around? If we're finished, I might as well go meet my friends in shul. Is there anything else you think I should be doing? he asks me. Please tell me. But if there isn't, then don't make me feel guilty for every move I make in this house.

The truth is, I don't want him to hang around. I don't want him in my bed in the first place. But I wish it weren't so obvious to me what my role is in this household. I wish I could be ignorant and believe that my husband cherishes me for more than just the simple pleasures my body provides.

When I am six months pregnant, Reb Chaim from Yerushalayim comes to town. He's a famous kabbalist from Israel who visits the United States a few times a year, and when he does, everyone bends over backward to get an audience with him. This year Eli got one for me, through a friend of his, because of my pregnancy. I have no special desire to see a kabbalist, because I'm skeptical about mysticism in general and have been questioning my belief in God for a while. And secretly I have always been afraid of people who profess to be all-seeing; I don't know if I want to be seen.

My stomach has formed itself into a neat little ball under my sweatshirt, and with my hands in my pockets I cradle it protectively as I wait for the rebbe to see me. It is two a.m. by the time I am ushered in, and the rebbe's wife sits in the corner so that we won't be breaking the laws of gender separation by being alone in a room together.

Reb Chaim asks me to write down my birthday and spends a few minutes making calculations on a piece of paper.

"Where are your parents?" he asks. "Why aren't they with you? You're not an orphan, I can see, but they are missing nevertheless."

I explain to him briefly about my parents.

"There is a secret surrounding your birth," he pronounces. "The blood ties are not blood. With the birth of your child, everything shall unravel. The truth will surface. You shall come to know yourself through your son."

He asks me what I plan on naming the baby and pronounces his approval of my choice. "Remember," he says, looking directly at me with a penetrating stare, "this child will change your life, in ways you can't begin to understand. Even when you think things are meaningless, your path has already been mapped for you. You are a very old soul; everything in your life is laden with meaning. Do not ignore the signs. Remember the number nine. It is a very important number for you."

I nod my head earnestly, but inside I'm thinking this is ridiculous, that there is no way this man, who has never met me before, knows what I am really like.

Before I leave the room, he looks up and asks me to wait.

"Your *shadchan*," he says, "your matchmaker, she's not happy. She feels she didn't get paid enough money for her work. She has been saying bad things about your family and your husband's family, and her bitterness hangs like a cloud over your marriage. You and Eli cannot be happy, cannot be blessed, until she is appeased."

I don't even know who our *shadchan* was. I will have to ask Eli if that even makes sense. At home Eli is waiting up anxiously, curious about my meeting with Reb Chaim. He is taken aback when I tell him about the bitter matchmaker.

"I will have to ask my mother," he says, pensive. "I never even thought about it."

The next day Eli calls his mother to let her know what Reb Chaim said. She is immediately defensive, saying she paid the matchmaker a thousand dollars, which is considered average. But Eli was a hard boy to match up, older than most.

Later my mother-in-law calls Eli back, saying she asked around and heard that the rumors were true, that our matchmaker is complaining to people that she was underpaid. An unhappy matchmaker makes for bad luck; everyone knows that. Eli says it's up to us to appease her, but we don't have the money to pay her.

I wonder if perhaps she is the reason I've been so cursed from the start of this marriage, if her bitterness is directly related to our discontent. Would God allow such a simple justice system to operate within his greater system of reward and punishment? Surely one malcontent could not have the power to wreak such destruction. If Eli and I were being punished for something, it was not for a dissatisfied matchmaker. I could think of a long list of reasons that would rank higher.

Toward the end of my second trimester I gain twelve pounds in one week. My stomach balloons out in front of me and weighs so much I have to place both hands under it to support myself when I walk. The weight of my belly drags down on my back and shoulders, causing me excruciating pain. As I enter my third trimester, I become increasingly inactive, unable to perform simple tasks without difficulty. Stuck on the couch, I feel bored and frustrated. The highlight of my day is the gossip Eli brings with him when he comes home from work. I have been reduced to the yenta housewife I always hated, yearning to know everyone's business.

When Eli comes home one evening after prayers with a furrowed brow, I am alight with desperate curiosity. Hoping for an interesting piece of news to brighten my day, I make him some tea and ask him what the men are saying in shul.

"You know that Bronfeld guy, from down the road? His son got kicked out of yeshiva."

"What for?" I ask, surprised.

"For getting molested." Eli's voice is heavy.

"What are you talking about? Tell me everything," I insist.

"You know the weird guy with the limp from the shul up the road?"

"The old guy, right? Yeah, I know him. So?" I nod impatiently.

"Well, Bronfeld's boy was acting weird in yeshiva, so the principal called him into his office to ask him what's going on, and he said that this old guy, who's been giving him bar mitzvah lessons, was molesting him for months."

"No way!" I gasp, shocked but also hungry to know more. "But why would he kick him out for that? It's not his fault."

"Well, the principal told the boy's father that he can't have him in yeshiva because he could corrupt the other kids. And now they say no yeshiva wants to touch him."

Eli is quiet for a moment, stirring his tea. "I mean, sometimes I think, you're never safe, you know? It could be anyone. Your next-door neighbor. An old family friend. How do you protect your children from this?"

"I still can't believe the old man is a child molester. How do they know for sure?"

"You know, actually, the men in shul were all saying it makes sense. I mean, we all thought he was gay for a while, because of the way he was always sitting too close to you . . . Besides, he used to talk about buying this boy expensive gifts and stuff. I mean, it was odd, you know? It was definitely odd."

"Are they going to report it?" I ask.

"I think the boy's father doesn't want it publicized. It will make it so much worse for the kid, having everyone know. But someone will take care of it, you'll see."

Indeed, several days later, the old man mysteriously disappears, and rumor has it his family pressured him to go into hiding. While he is gone, a few people in the community sneak into his house and go through his things. Eli tells me they found shoe boxes stuffed with pictures of children in various stages of undress. It appears, he says, from the evidence, that he's been molesting kids all his life. They could number in the hundreds.

The accused pedophile comes back home a few weeks later, when his family thinks the buzz has died down, and every day I see him take his daily walk, his frail, bent body moving slowly. I am both repulsed and astounded that a man of his age could still perpetuate such an awful obsession. Each time I drive by him, I am overcome by the urge to roll down my window and spit, but the worst I ever do is sidle up to the curb, slowing down as I approach him and glaring straight into his eyes. He always looks as though he doesn't notice, and his self-satisfied smile burns into my memory.

"He's too old to go to jail," Eli says, and I am incensed.

"He's not too old to molest, but he's too old for jail?"

Hasidic people always say they are renowned for having compassion for their fellow Jews. What a liberal form of compassion it is, to me, if it can be so indiscriminately extended to people who are guilty of terrible crimes. And yet, that's exactly the kind of love Hasids profess to have for each other, a love that doesn't discriminate, a love that doesn't have to be justified. Justice is a celestial concern in this community's view; our job is only to live as harmoniously with each other as we can. Do unto your neighbor as you would have him do unto you, and when he doesn't fulfill his part of the deal, let God take care of the rest.

Eli invites different people each week to come to our house for Shabbos. We prepare a big spread and I make a large pot of greasy *cholent*, complete with marrow bones and cheek meat just the way all the men like it. I don't mind working hard if it means we will have guests over. It's always more interesting to listen to what they have to say than to sit at the table making stilted conversation with my husband. The people who live in our neighborhood are nothing like the stuffy people I grew up with. Many of them are the rebels of their families, and they've moved here for the same reason I chose to, to get away from the watchful eyes. And also, living in Airmont means they're not a thorn in their parents' sides, constantly reminding the elders of their children's lack of desire to live up to the expectations others have of them. When they visit their parents, they pretend to be as devout as they need to, but here in this small town, no one sees what they're up to, and certainly no one reports it.

Of course this week all everyone is talking about is the old pervert. No one can believe the guy is a child molester. Some people talk about how there were hints; others say they know his children and it's not possible. My neighbor Yosef says the man survived the Holocaust as a young boy because he lived under the protection of a Nazi guard in the concentration camp, ostensibly cleaning his house but really being repeatedly molested by his protector. With his blond hair and blue eyes, it was easy for the Germans to overlook it. Yosef says that's why the guy became a molester himself, that we should have pity on him. I listen carefully to all the details. I can't get my head around the shoe box full of photographs. Who could be so twisted as to take those pictures? Who could be stupid enough to keep them around as evidence? What makes a man do such things? But most of all I wonder about halacha. There's a Jewish law for everything. The Torah offers a punishment for every crime, no matter how insignificant. But what about child abuse? What about pedophilia? Is there a halacha for that? Is there a rabbinical procedure?

But the Torah doesn't talk about what to do with a man who wants to have sex with children, it seems. It talks about men who have sex with other men, and men who have sex with animals. Those are the unforgivable sins. But there is nothing said about the sexual abuse of children.

When I voice my indignation at the dinner table, Eli tries to explain it to me. He says in the olden days people got married very young. There wasn't really a clear distinction between a child and an adult the way there is today. Women were being married off at age nine, so was it really feasible to set up laws against cohabitation with children? There was no social taboo in place.

Today there is all this sensitivity, he says derisively. Now you're considered a baby up until the minute you turn eighteen, and then suddenly you're an adult? Semantics, he claims, waving his hand in a gesture of contempt. The others chime in, agreeing with him. I watch the men slurp up the chicken soup I made so lovingly this morning, dumping chickpeas and sliced radish into their plates and mashing it together with the noodles and squash. They're eating my food at my table, but I might as well be invisible. Women have no real place in a conversation. They should be busy serving food and cleaning up.

I look down at my own plate, feeling my cheeks redden self-consciously. Eli always reprimands me for getting too heated at the Shabbos table. Why do you have to be so angry about everything? he always whines. Other women don't behave like you. Can't you just relax?

But I worry. I worry that if no one around me takes anything seriously, who will? The Talmud says, "If not me, then who? If not now, then when?" If I should follow the advice of our rabbis in everything I do, shouldn't I follow this particular verse as well?

It seems that all my pregnancy is good for is compounding my anxiety about everything. The more I hear about the horrors of the world I live in, the more unsure I feel about bringing a child into it. Only a few years ago I was free of all this knowledge; I have only recently discovered how dangerous it is out here, but I have not yet figured out how to navigate those dangers securely. How can I possibly protect a child?

A few weeks later it is Eli's own brother who becomes the focus of local gossip. It's all anyone can talk about at the Shabbos table. Everyone knows he's been sneaking around with a Sephardic girl from Williamsburg for three years now, but her father found out and now he won't let his daughter out of the house.

My brother-in-law Yossi is the rebel of his family, the bad boy who smokes Marlboros and talks back to his father, who shaves his beard close and keeps his *payos* hidden behind his ears. His out-of-control behavior has everybody horrified.

This Shabbos we are guests at my in-laws', and I watch as Yossi overdoses on cognac before the morning meal has commenced. By the time my father-in-law is ready to pronounce the blessing on the wine, Yossi has collapsed on the floor. "Is he breathing?" my father-in-law asks coolly, and Eli's brother Cheskel leans casually over to check.

His face is white when he looks up. "We have to get him to the hospital."

The Hatzolah ambulance comes to take him away, and we are all stuck waiting at home until Shabbos is over to find out what happened to him because of the no-phones rule. Cheskel calls the minute Shabbos is done and says Yossi got his stomach pumped at Cornwall Hospital but he is doing okay. Eli and I drive to the hospital to pick him up, and Yossi emerges from the double doors with his stomach hunched inward, as if it is painful for him to stand straight. His face is pale and sullen. He refuses to talk.

We all know why he drank too much. He's been drinking a lot lately, depressed about this girl he knows, because it's time for him to marry but he only wants to be with her. She's a beauty with black hair and pale green eyes framed by long lashes, whose father wants her to marry a good Sephardic boy with dark brown skin and an earnest manner.

For Yossi to marry Kayla would be a big scandal, because in the Satmar community Sephardic is considered lower-class, and Ashkenazi Jews don't marry out of their class.

Yossi lies in bed for a week and refuses to get up, so their mother calls Eli and asks him to come talk to his brother and try to convince him to get over this. Eli comes home later that night shaking his head in bewilderment. "He won't get over this girl. He says he won't come out of bed unless he can marry her."

"So tell your mother to just let him marry her, for God's sake! She's being so stubborn! Really, what's the big deal?"

"Everyone will talk about it. If Yossi marries a Sephardic girl, the whole family will be affected. Everyone will think there's something wrong with him."

"So your mother will let Yossi kill himself just to prevent a little gossip?"

Eli reluctantly agrees to talk to his mother. Eventually she consents, saying that if the other side agrees to the match, she won't do anything to prevent it. Eli has a meeting with his brothers around our dining room table one night, and they agree to get someone to talk to Kayla's father. I think the battle is over, but after Shabbos I hear Yossi is back in bed and won't talk to anyone.

Eli and I go visit him together, and I marvel at how identical they look, except for the fact that Yossi wears his *payos* curled around his ears and trims his blond beard very short. Eventually we manage to pull it out of him. Apparently Kayla's father took her to a Kabbalist who told her that terrible things would happen to her in the future if she married Yossi, like warts and diseases, and then Yossi's friend found out that Kayla's father paid the Kabbalist to say that, but Kayla won't even talk to Yossi because she's scared.

I sit down on the chair next to Yossi's bed, pulling my shirt down over my pregnant stomach, and look earnestly into his eyes.

"Look at me," I say emphatically. "You know Kayla for how long? Three years? You think one moment of fear is going to just erase that? That's not how it works. If she's that crazy about you, she will get over this kabbalist thing. Just give it a couple of days and she'll be calling you, I promise."

Yossi sits up on one elbow, looking at me pleadingly, his strawberry-blond hair mussed under his black velvet yarmulke. "You really think so?"

"Of course! If this is the real thing, no kabbalist is going to get in the way of it, I promise."

Sure enough, three days later she calls, and she promises him she will fight her father. Eli's brothers get people to put pressure on Kayla's father and he gives in, agreeing to allow the match.

The engagement is fast and hush-hush, and a wedding date is set for six weeks later, to avoid too much scandal. There are rumors that Kayla is pregnant. Surely that's just idle gossip.

We stay at Shprintza's house in Kiryas Joel the weekend they get married. I hate staying there, because she is all sweetness to me as long as Eli is around, but the minute he leaves for shul, it's like she switches personalities. It disgusts me that she can be that two-faced and unashamed of it.

I have to drag myself and my pregnant belly in my ugly maternity dress up the hilly inclines to the synagogue where my mother-in-law is hosting the *sheva berachos*. I haven't been doing very well lately—I've been feeling ill and tired most of the time—and pasting a smile on my face after that difficult walk is hard. Friday night when I get back to our room, I have a hard time sleeping because my stomach is cramping and I feel sick. Finally at three a.m. I roll out of bed and get to the bathroom just in time to vomit. The force of it is so violent that stomach debris shoots out my nose and I can feel the little veins around my eyes strain and pop.

Eli hears me and comes out to hold my head, which is something he is used to doing for me. The pain in my stomach doesn't go away. I'm six months pregnant. I tell Eli we have to call the doctor, even though it's Shabbos. For a life-or-death matter, phoning is allowed. We call on my cell phone and leave our information with the answering service and wait for the return call.

The doctor on duty listens to my symptoms and tells us to come in, that stomach cramps and vomiting in pregnancy are usually a sign of labor and it's too early for me to be in labor. Eli says to ask if we can wait until Shabbos is over in twelve hours. The doctor says it's up to us and how we feel. I can tell she doesn't understand why we called if we want to wait to come in. Kiryas Joel is at least an hour away from the hospital.

When I put down the phone, Eli begs me to wait until Shabbos is over.

"If we leave now, everyone will know, and my mother will go crazy from worry, and it will ruin everyone's *simchah* from the wedding."

I want to throttle him. Does he not hear himself? How do I contend with his view of reality? It's obvious to me that he doesn't think he is asking for much. Is it that he is naive and ignorant, failing to realize the urgency of the situation? Or is it that he has, once again, put his family before me?

Because I don't want to wake up Shprintza and her husband, I agree to wait as long as I can. I don't want to fight with Eli and give his sister more ammunition to bash me. After Shabbos is over, we pack up as if everything is normal and drive to the hospital. First the nurse shepherds me into a room full of pregnant women who think they're in labor but probably aren't; she hooks me up to a machine and tells me she'll be right back. Within moments I hear an alarm bell clanging at the nurses' station and she is back at my side, looking at the monitor. She shows me a strip of paper with lines wiggling wildly across it. "Are you feeling this?" she asks, mouth agape.

I nod my head.

They wheel me into a private room that has a little plastic incubator near the bed, with holes in the top like the ones they have for premature babies. At the time, I don't really register the implications of its presence.

The doctor gives me little injections in my thigh to stop the contractions, and the medication leaves me feeling really woozy. I start hallucinating or dreaming, I can't tell which.

Eli drags two big plastic-upholstered hospital armchairs together to create a bed and promptly falls asleep. I toss over the wires attached to me all night, repeatedly woken by the nurse who comes to check my blood pressure. The baby's heartbeat goes *boom-boom* on the monitor, and footsteps patter up and down the corridor outside. I watch a pregnant woman waddle slowly past my door, one hand on her lower back. She looks sad and lonely.

When the doctor discharges us two days later with a prescription for terbutaline and bed rest, we don't tell anyone about the incident and go back to our routine, except that Eli is a little nicer to me now and doesn't complain if the dishes aren't washed or dinner isn't on the table when he gets home.

I spend the next few weeks on bed rest. Eli comes home early on Fridays to prepare for Shabbos, tidying up the house and warming up the challah he purchased because I'm not strong enough to bake and cook anymore. One rainy Friday I'm lying in bed, reading *What to Expect When You're Expecting* for the umpteenth time, when I hear Eli muttering agitatedly in the kitchen. He's on his phone, speaking in hushed but anxious tones. I wonder what it could be about.

After he puts down the phone, I amble into the kitchen and lower myself gently onto a kitchen chair.

"Who was on the phone earlier?" I ask innocently.

"My brother Cheskel. You know he's an EMT, a Hatzolah member. He just had a call before Shabbos, and by the time he got there, the boy was dead."

"A boy? What do you mean? What happened?"

"He told me they told him not to tell anyone, but he called me, he said, because he was traumatized. He doesn't know how he can sleep tonight."

"Why? What happened?" I straighten my back in expectation.

"When he got there, the father pointed him to the basement, and the boy was lying there in a pool of his own blood. His penis was cut off with a jigsaw, and his throat was slit too. And the father wasn't even upset. He said that he caught his son masturbating."

It takes me a moment to process the implications of what Eli is describing to me.

"So he killed his son for masturbating? And then he called Hatzolah? I don't understand!"

"No! Don't jump to conclusions. Cheskel told me he doesn't know for sure what happened. He said the neighbors told him they heard loud arguing coming from the house. When he called the dispatch, they told him to go home and keep quiet about it, that they would take care of it. He said they buried him in thirty minutes and they didn't even issue a death certificate."

"So they're not going to report it? They're going to let a possible murderer roam free to protect their reputation?" I can feel a twinge in my lower back and remember suddenly that I'm supposed to be resting for the baby. "Oy," I say. "What is this world, that we only punish for trivialities like wearing a short skirt, but when someone breaks one of the Ten Commandments, we keep quiet?"

"Ah, you can't know for sure. The Torah says there have to be two witnesses for a man to be tried for murder. What are you gonna do? You can't bring back this dead boy anyhow. And you better not tell anyone about it, because Cheskel could get in big trouble for talking to me. Please don't get him into trouble; you don't know what these people are capable of."

"I do now. I know exactly what they're capable of."

I'm dying to say something to someone. I restrain myself at the Shabbos table, because I know Eli would never forgive me if I brought it up, but just this week no one has anything interesting to share, and I can't help but wonder if someone else is holding their tongue too.

I will hold that secret to my chest for a long time, but I have many nightmares about it, only in my dreams the boy is my own son, and Eli is standing over his prostrate, bloodless body with a look of vicious satisfaction on his face. In the dream I am always paralyzed, my limbs suddenly frozen, my tongue limp and apathetic. I wake up in the middle of the night and immediately put my hands over my belly to feel the baby's kicks. I'm worried that with all this stress I will end up like Aunt Chavie, who was in her ninth month when the baby just died all of a sudden in her belly. I'm constantly checking for signs of life in my abdomen. What a hostile environment this baby must think my body to be. I imagine he will always resent me for it.

I communicate wordlessly with the burblings in my womb. *I don't want to bring you into a world where silence is a cover for the worst crimes*, I tell him. *Not if I can't protect you from it. I won't keep quiet forever, baby, I promise. One day I will open my mouth and I will never shut it again.*

I get so big, none of my maternity clothes fit anymore except one blouse with pink flowers on it. I need to buy more maternity clothes, but I have to buy modest ones at the Jewish shops, which are expensive, and we don't have the money.

I get mad when Eli says that, because if we can't afford maternity clothes, how can we afford baby clothes? And all the other expenses that come with having a child?

I'm still a teenager. The work I do teaching rudimentary English to high-school-aged girls barely pays for groceries. Eli works as a laborer in a warehouse, but we don't always manage to cover our bills. How, I ask him, does he see things getting better for us as a family?

"None of my brothers are entrepreneurs or businessmen," says Eli. "The Feldmans are workers and wage earners; we aren't cut out for anything else. I'm trying my best."

I find myself unable to comprehend that way of looking at oneself, as unable to supersede the accomplishments of one's family. I always set high standards for myself; why can't he? If he won't plan for our future, for my baby's future, then I must take it upon myself to change things.

I know as a woman I will never get paid even half as much as a man if I work in the Hasidic community, but the only way for me to get a job elsewhere would be to get a degree. Then maybe I could be a nurse or a real teacher. Those jobs would still be okay for me to have. After my baby is born, I promise myself, I will look into getting a degree, so I can give my child a better life.

I don't know how I will convince Eli to let me do it, but I'm determined to figure it out one way or another. However, before I can even start doing my research, Dr. Patrick tells me it's time to go to the hospital. At one of our routine appointments, she taps my knee with a little metal hammer and it jumps wildly.

"Hmm . . . extreme reflexive action." She takes my blood pressure. "One thirty-five over eighty-five." She removes the band from my arm, ripping it off in one swift motion. "I think it's time to get this baby out."

Stunned, I take the elevator down to the street, where Eli is double-parked.

"We have to go to the hospital," I tell him.

"What do you mean? What happened? What's wrong?"

"Nothing's wrong, I think," I say slowly, "just I have some sort of problem with my blood pressure, I don't really know, but it can't be a big deal because otherwise they would make us go in an ambulance, right?"

Eli nods his head. I direct him across town to St. Luke's–Roosevelt Hospital, where we take the elevator up to the labor and delivery ward on the seventh floor. We pass the birthing center, where women balance themselves on giant plastic balls, breathing through contractions. I manage to laugh at the sight.

I get checked into a pretty room with flowered wallpaper and a pink quilt, with a view of Midtown. The doctor comes in as soon as I've changed into my gown. She has very short blond hair and a pair of rimless glasses perched on the edge of her nose.

"So your doctor asked me to speak to you," she says, "and tell you the reason we admitted you is that you have preeclampsia, which is dangerous for the baby. Think of it as your body having an allergic reaction to the little person inside you. It's seeing it as a threat, and we can't have that, because your baby needs a friendly environment."

"Oh," I say quietly. "So what happens now?"

"Well," she says cheerfully, "we are going to gently induce labor, which is fine, because you are far enough along. We will start by administering medication directly through your cervix, which should help dilate your cervix a little bit while you sleep. In the morning we will give you Pitocin intravenously, which will induce contractions. When they get painful, you can have an epidural inserted, so don't worry."

"Okay," I say. "So I'm going to have the baby tomorrow?"

"Yes, ma'am!" she sings, as she smears blue gel on my straining belly, and I can detect a trace of a southern accent. I can't believe that by this time tomorrow I will have a real live baby instead of just a pregnant stomach.

The doctor leaves. Fran, who introduces herself as my nurse, starts typing my information into the computer. She flips her dark hair over her shoulder as she turns to me.

"How old are you, sweetie?" she asks. "You look so young!"

"I'm nineteen."

"Wow! I thought you were in your twenties, but you're even younger."

She skips a beat. "Well, good for you, getting a head start." I smile weakly because I know she doesn't mean it; she's judging me.

Twenty-four hours later, Dr. Patrick shakes me awake with a big smile on her face.

"It's time!" she sings loudly.

A black male nurse holds one of my legs because Eli can't touch me anymore, and his hands look shockingly dark against my pale skin, in a way that feels horrifyingly taboo. I wonder how this is better, having a black man looking at my most private area instead of my own husband. But I'm impure now, and it's not about me, it's about keeping Eli pure.

Suddenly I feel the most incredible pull in my belly, as if my very guts are being sucked out of me. The huge weight in my abdomen slides out of me in a split-second motion and my entire stomach collapses so quickly that I feel as if I just fell from a great height. The force of it knocks out my breath.

Dr. Patrick asks me if I want to see the baby now or wait for it to be cleaned up.

"No, just clean him first. I don't want to see him yet." A glimpse of squirming, slimy pinkness makes me want to vomit. Eli is already over by the crib, peering between the shoulders of two doctors. I want to remember that feeling, of having my guts sucked out of me, but the force of it is fading fast. I've never felt anything like it in my entire life. I will wonder for years if that moment was the only one in my five-year marriage when I was ever fully alive. It made my every other waking moment feel false and numb, like a hallucination. I think it was that moment that served as my wake-up call, that made me start fighting again.

Dr. Patrick reaches in and pulls the placenta out and sets it on the table next to her. She asks Eli if he wants it, because some Jews bury the placenta to honor it. I shake my head no when he looks at me. The Talmud calls it the "tree of life" because of the treelike pattern on its surface and because of its ability to give life to a child. It looks disgusting sitting there, quivering on the tray. We are not taking that home with us.

In a minute they bring the baby to me wrapped in clean blue blankets, and I can see the top of his head, with minuscule blond curls stained dark by moisture. His face is scrunched up, but he has the most golden skin I have ever seen on a newborn baby. Eli is tearing up next to me, but I'm calm.

"Hello," I say to the little bundle. "How are you feeling?"

That's all I do for the first hour. I talk to him, jabbering on about everything and anything while the baby looks up at me with dark liquid eyes never wavering from my face. As I talk, I try to make the connection between this tiny person in my arms and the body it just came out of, but I can't shake the notion that this baby has just been arbitrarily dumped in my care and that whatever was in my abdomen until now was actually mere stuffing.

Shouldn't I feel maternal? Why do I feel like this baby is a stranger, when I spent months poking my tummy, giggling as limbs bumped up against the walls of my uterus? I talk, thinking that with words I can convince myself, convince him, convince everyone that I'm in love.

After a while the nurse comes in to check on me, frowning when she sees my stomach. I'm not contracting properly, she says, and massages my belly to get the process started. The flesh on my abdomen reminds me of a waterbed, the skin flapping sloppily around as she kneads it like challah dough.

Postpartum pain is worse than I imagined. The stitches Dr. Patrick sewed after everything was out sting really badly, and the nurse won't give me anything stronger than ibuprofen. I try to hook the baby onto my breast to feed, but then a wave of pain comes over me and I almost drop him. My vision blurs and I fall back onto the pillow.

After my two days of recovery are up, Eli drives me to the new-mothers' home in New Square. I will stay there for two weeks, and Eli will pick up the baby when it's time for his circumcision and bring him back right after.

I'm not allowed to go to the bris, because they don't want the mother to suffer emotional distress—or worse, get hysterical—from watching her son get cut. Eli won't even tell me how it went, if he cried, but when the baby comes back, he sleeps for eight hours. I stand over the newly named

Yitzy like a hawk the entire time, terrified he will never wake up. There was a baby in the other room that turned blue because the rabbi wrapped the bandages too tight. I check and recheck the gauze wrapping over and over again, making sure it's loose enough not to cut off Yitzy's circulation. The attendant tells me not to worry, that the drops of wine they use as an anesthetic can cause this kind of sleep. "Go to sleep," she urges me. "I will watch him. Don't worry so much."

All the other women at the home sit around the common room eating, claiming the extra calories are necessary for nursing. I have no appetite, and no milk either. They have to bring in a lactation consultant to help me, but Yitzy won't latch on, because even if he tries, nothing comes out. I sit for hours at a time with him, trying to get him to eat, but nothing works. In the end they have to give him formula, and I'm ashamed, because none of the other mothers have a problem. I'm the only first-timer here this week; the rest of them are experienced. I'm the only one with a book, too, and they stare at me when I retreat to a sofa to read instead of joining them in conversation over snacks.

By the time I leave the convalescent center, all the swelling from the birth has gone down, and the bleeding has subsided somewhat. I put on the shiny black trench coat that I used to wear before I was pregnant, and it fits comfortably. I've gotten so used to the constant distortions of my body that I no longer recognize this newly flat form. It feels nice to walk outside though, suddenly weightless, the balls of my feet bouncing gently on the asphalt driveway.

Eli has cleaned the apartment thoroughly, and when we get home, everything has been set up for the baby. We've received gifts from some of his friends—a baby swing, a bassinet, and lots of small stuffed animals. I put Yitzy in the swing, and his head lolls immediately to the side. We try to support it with blankets. With his eyes closed, he has the most perfect little face, relaxed in slumber, full golden cheeks and smooth forehead. When he opens his eyes, he looks weird, scrunching his forehead until it wrinkles deeply, his mouth forming a squished O shape. Eli jokes that he looks like an old person, with that worried face. I like watching my baby when he looks peaceful. It makes me feel peaceful too.

• • •

Because Eli and I are both descended from Israelite lineage, Yitzy has to have a *pidyon haben* ceremony when he is four weeks old. This is an ancient custom dating back to when Israelites had to redeem their firstborn sons from the Temple priests, who had the right to retain every Israelite firstborn to work in the Temple.

Today the process is symbolic but nonetheless considered very important. My mother-in-law has rented an elegant hall and has hired a catering company to present an elaborate meal to all the guests after the ceremony is concluded. She sends over a special outfit to dress the baby in, an expensive, all-white affair that was designed specifically for the occasion. When everyone has arrived and the perfunctory *Kohain*, a man of priestly lineage, has been procured, Yitzy is placed on a gold tray and all the women take off their jewels and drape them on him, as is the custom. He is then carried to the men's side, dripping in pearl necklaces and gold brooches, where the ceremony will be performed. I can see his tiny, squashed little face turn toward me, his wide, alert eyes following me as he is carted away.

Six men grasp the tray with my newborn son on it and hold it aloft. Yitzy lies still and quiet, and the women marvel at his calm demeanor. The ceremony is quick, and after the *Kohain* pronounces his special blessing over the baby, Eli and his brothers bring him back to me. Once in my arms, he looks up at me and starts to fuss, and my mother-in-law remarks on his good sense of timing.

Six weeks after the birth, Eli is already pestering me about the *mikvah*. I haven't even thought of starting to count the seven clean days. As far as I know, I'm not really bleeding anymore, but I haven't actually been able to muster the fortitude to inspect the situation down there. I suspect it is greatly changed, and not for the better.

The process of counting out fourteen pristine white cloths is an odious one, especially when my life now revolves around the baby's erratic schedule. I dread what will surely be an endless stop-and-start process, with trips to the rabbi every time a suspicious stain shows up on my underwear. Shouldn't I feel psychologically ready to look at my vagina before I decide to open it for business again? And then there is the matter of birth control. It's not allowed, of course, but my aunts have all told me that if I "nurse clean"—that is, breast-feed consistently and don't get my period—I'm very unlikely to get pregnant. I don't know if I'm willing to test those odds.

I tell Eli that I want to get Dr. Patrick's approval before I decide what to do. I leave the baby with him in the waiting room so that I can have some privacy with the doctor. The sign on the back of the door to the exam room lists at least twenty forms of birth control. Dr. Patrick sees me looking at them as she fills out my chart. She shoves some free samples toward me. "Just in case," she says. I pocket them gratefully.

After the exam, she takes off her gloves and smiles at me. "You're all set," she says. "I give you the green light." There's more warmth in her voice than there ever was, and I wonder if it's because I've been initiated into the club of mothers or if it's because she feels bad for me. She thinks I will be in and out of her office for the next twenty years, popping out babies and generating excellent income for her practice. Well, we'll see about that.

I go to the *mikvah* a week later. I'm self-conscious about undressing my new body in front of the attendant. My stomach is still pouchy, and there are tiny red stretch marks on my thighs. It feels like the basic structure of my body shifted, as if my hips had realigned themselves and my spine found a new curve. Nothing about the way my body moves is familiar anymore. My prepregnancy body was that of a starved teenager. This new one feels like the body of an old woman.

I shouldn't have worried. The attendant has obviously seen way worse, for she seems as placid as ever. I like the attendants here in the Monsey *mikvah* so much better than the ones in Williamsburg. They are less nosy and more efficient. I am never at the *mikvah* for more than an hour.

If Eli notices any change in my body, he doesn't show it. I can tell how excited he is when I get home to find the lights dimmed and rose petals sprinkled on the bedsheets. I have to giggle silently, because I can't wait to find out which particular sibling gave him that advice. With something like this, I always know he got it from somewhere. It's funny because the laws say that what's between a man and wife has to be kept private, but everything always turns out to be a family matter.

There's a bottle of kosher champagne on the nightstand, accompanied by the plastic flute glasses we picked up at the local Walmart. It's my first sip of alcohol in a year and I feel instantly light-headed. Eli is already moving his hands up my legs. I can feel his beard tickle my neck. As I lie back and try to relax, I comfort myself with the knowledge that Eli will be extra nice to me for the next few days. He always is after sex.

I have a problem. I woke up feeling itchy down there. The itch builds over the next few days, until it feels as if someone has lit a small fire in my underwear. Soon I am swollen and irritated, and Eli has to take me in to see Dr. Patrick again only a week and a half after my last appointment. She looks surprised to see us but performs the examination with Eli still in the room. When she lifts her head from under the sheet, there's no smile. "You have an infection," she says. She wheels her little stool over to the counter and writes a prescription. She hands it to Eli. "You have to take this pill," she says to him. "It should clear up anything you have."

She turns to me and pats my leg. "Give the medication a week to work and you shouldn't be having this problem again."

"Wait," I say, "why is he taking a pill?"

"Well, whatever it is you have, you're getting it from him. If I only treat you for this, he will just keep giving it to you." She doesn't offer any additional explanation.

I'm confused. The idea of an infection down there is new to me. Until now my problems were strictly psychosomatic. More important, they stemmed from my own body, not someone else's contagions. I can't wrap my mind around this new concept, the passing of bacteria from Eli to me. It doesn't even cross my mind then that the infection could have originated outside our relationship.

I feel resentful at yet another complication in our sex life. Why am I always the one suffering? Eli doesn't have any symptoms at all, and he's the one who's giving it to me! It doesn't seem fair.

It occurs to me suddenly that I may not be the only secretive one in this marriage. I've become so concerned with myself, I've never stopped to think that Eli might not be inclined to share all his thoughts and feelings with me either. But even as I acknowledge the possibility that Eli could be deceiving me, I also realize I don't really care. If something is distracting him, then that can only work in my favor. Freedom from Eli's watchful eyes could afford me a brighter future.

9

Up in Arms

And now I see with eye serene
The very pulse of the machine;
A being breathing thoughtful breath,
A traveller between life and death; . . .
—From *"She was a Phantom of Delight,"* by William Wordsworth

After all the fuss about the new baby has died down, I begin to realize that I've become a mother. It never really hit me until now, because I was too busy to even think about it. Secretly, I'm consumed with anxiety, because I don't *feel* like a mother, and how could I be such a horrible person as to look at my own son and not *feel* anything at all?

The more I try to bond with the baby, the more detached I feel. I don't understand how love can develop between me and a tiny, scrawny-limbed thing that alternately cries and sleeps in my arms. What if I have no love to give? Could I be so damaged by my childhood experiences that I was drained of the ability to love anything? It was one thing if I couldn't manage to love a man I was arbitrarily arranged to marry. It was a whole other thing to feel detached from my own child.

I always thought that when I became a mother, I would finally feel what it was like to love something wholly and intensely. Yet now, although I perform the part of the doting mother, I am painfully aware of my own emptiness.

A part of me is afraid to get too attached. Lately I've been thinking about leaving Eli, leaving this life I've always lived. What if I want to stop being Hasidic one day? I will have to leave the baby behind too. I couldn't bear to love him and then leave him. I go through the motions of parenting, but even while I feed and change him, even while I soothe him endlessly in the night, I protect the part of myself that wants to give in to motherhood yet remain untouched on the inside.

What a performance new motherhood is, I think, after yet another stranger on the street stops to coo at my baby. I paste a proud smile on my face and play the part they expect me to, but I feel hollow inside. Can anyone see that I don't really feel it? Can they see that I'm cold, that I'm unreachable?

I return to Williamsburg in the summer to visit Bubby and show off the baby, and I wear my long wig with the curls in it and a pretty dress that I bought from Ann Taylor and had lengthened so it would cover my knees. Still, it's pencil slim, and I like the way my hips curve out gently beneath its thin cotton fabric.

Walking down Penn Street pushing the baby carriage we got as a gift, I hear a little boy, no more than six years old, whisper to his playmate, *"Farvus vuktzi du, di shiksa?"*—"Why does this gentile woman walk here?" I realize he is referring to me, dressed too well to fit into his idea of a Hasidic woman.

His older friend whispers back hurriedly, "She's not a goy, she's Jewish. She only looks like a goy," and the incredulous but sincere response, "How can it be? Jews don't look like that," makes me start. He's right, I realize. In our world, Jews don't look like gentiles. They look different.

I remember being a small child, playing in the street in the summertime. Sticky with sweat underneath my layers of clothes, I squatted idly on brownstone stoops with the rest of the neighborhood children, slurping slushy freeze pops and ogling the people who walked by. Each time an immodestly dressed woman passed, we would sing a familiar ditty:

"Shame, shame, baby . . . Naked, naked lady . . ."

This mocking chant was such an ingrained ritual with us kids, I never stopped to think about what that song meant until now, but I remember that our common scorn for outsiders brought us together and made us feel special in our difference. We were all one big, holy, modesty-patrol gang. And we had muscle too: sometimes we'd throw things, not stones but pebbles, maybe, or trash. Our favorite activity was pouring buckets of water out the second-story windows onto unsuspecting passersby. By the time they had looked up in shock and anger, we had already ducked back inside, giggling like mad.

Years later the tables are turned. Now I walk down the streets of Williamsburg and hear young children mock me, not loud enough for me to turn around and address their disrespect, but loud enough for my cheeks to redden. When had I been cast out? Suddenly I no longer belong; I am an outsider.

Even the smallest steps toward independence have consequences. I can hardly imagine what the people in my hometown would say if they knew what I was planning on doing with my future.

I stopped going to the *mikvah*. I used to get stomachaches in the week leading up to it because I was so nervous. I hated the questions most, the women who always had to know where you were in your cycle, if you had miscarried, if you were trying to get pregnant again, always wanting to know your business. And the stares too, if you were wearing makeup or nail polish, like they were better than you somehow because they didn't interest themselves in such foolishness.

So now I leave for a few hours on *mikvah* night, bringing a magazine with me to keep myself entertained. Sometimes I just park the car in front of the Starbucks on Route 59 and watch the modern Orthodox girls study for exams.

The law says Eli can't have intercourse with me if I don't go to the *mikvah*, but he's never hesitated, so I don't know if it's because the strength of his desire exceeds his religious fear or if he doesn't suspect I would deceive him in such a terrible and unforgivable way. The Torah says awful things about women like me; it calls me a Jezebel, a truly evil seductress, dragging my husband into sin with me. If I were to get pregnant, the child would be impure his whole life.

But I'm not going to get pregnant. Because I'm on birth control, and I don't ever want to go off it again.

Eli likes foreplay more than I do. Before sex, he wants to kiss and touch, and feel loved. But since we're always fighting or giving each other the silent treatment, the time before sex is not exactly romantic.

"If you know it's fake," I say, "why do you still want it? Do you really think this sort of affection can come from a genuine place if we were arguing at dinner?"

He takes to cleaning up the kitchen while I am ostensibly at the *mikvah*, so that I will come home and be pleased that my housework is done. How simple he must think me, that I can be so easily made pliant and happy by the prospect of fewer chores.

So we kiss, before. Not for long. I take to biting, for some reason I can't understand, and he tries to teach me to kiss slowly, but I don't like sloppy, wet kissing, with the scruff on his face burning my chin and the skin above my lip. After a few moments of biting, he gives up and moves on.

He wants to make the experience last as long as possible. I just want it to be over as fast as possible, and he knows it and doesn't care.

I'm beginning to wonder if I'm becoming an atheist. I used to believe in God, then I believed in him but hated him, and now I wonder if it's all just random and doesn't matter. The fact is, there are all these people out there who aren't Hasidic going about their lives, and no one is punishing *them*.

I check out a documentary from the library about gay Orthodox Jews struggling to reconcile their faith with their sexuality. The people interviewed talk about wanting to be Jewish and gay at the same time and their struggle with the conflict inherent in that identity, and I wonder at their desire to be a part of a religious community that's so intolerant and oppressive. At the end of the movie as I watch the credits roll, I recognize my mother's name in the list of contributing voices. Rachel Levy. And sure enough, as I rewind the film, there she is, seen for a brief moment stepping off a curb, saying, "I left Williamsburg because I was gay."

Is that what Chaya meant by crazy? I am flabbergasted. The worst part is that I'm sure everyone knew but me. Is it that I buried my head in the sand? It just never even occurred to me.

Before the Shavuos holiday I look up her address and order a large bouquet to be sent to her for the holiday, with a special card attached. I'm not ready to talk to her, but I want to do something nice, something I would want my daughter to do for me.

She calls me a few days later, but I don't pick up the phone, so she leaves a message on my answering machine, thanking me for the flowers. Her voice holds the wonder of a surprised child, laced with the harder inflections of a thick-skinned adult.

This woman is my mother, I marvel, listening to the scratchy message play back on my machine. This woman, who is as different from me as night from day, gave birth to me. I feel nothing at all. I wonder if that's just me, unable to feel connected to anyone, even my flesh and blood.

In the fall, after I have lost enough baby weight and Yitzy has started sleeping through the night, I start researching colleges. I'm determined for us to have a better life. Hannah, the modern Orthodox woman who lives next door, advises me to look into adult programs—easier for a mom like me to work with than a traditional undergraduate environment. She went back to get her degree at Ramapo College in New Jersey, and they were very accommodating.

I research colleges nearby and I come up with Pace, Sarah Lawrence, Bard, and Vassar, all with adult education programs. I download applications, but the Sarah Lawrence website has a number to call to schedule an interview, so I jump on that first. The woman on the other end of the line sounds calm and indifferent and tells me to come by the first Monday in March, because it is too late to apply for the fall session.

I prepare the essays in advance, handwriting them first before typing them up. The first two are autobiographical. I think to myself, *This is my shtick. I gotta use whatever I got.*

I don't tell Eli that I am applying to college; instead I say I want to take a business class but that I probably won't get in. He doesn't object. I'm sure he's thinking, *Who would take a chasidisher into a gentile college?*

The day I drive down to the Sarah Lawrence campus is cloudy and wet from yesterday's rains. Newly sprung leaves hang heavy off the oak trees, dripping onto concrete pathways. Students wearing galoshes walk in groups across the lush green lawns, lugging artfully creased leather knapsacks and nonchalant attitudes. I park in the main parking lot and walk with my head down across Wrexham Road to the address I was given on the telephone.

In my short black wig and long skirt, I look more different than even I expected; everyone is wearing jeans. If I could wear jeans, I think, I would never wear anything else. I wish I could throw away all my skirts and just wear pants for the rest of my life.

Jane is matter-of-fact in the interview. "We'd love to have you," she says, "but it all depends on your level of writing skills. This is a writing school; there are no exams, no grades, just essays and evaluations. For us to accept you knowing you don't have the capability to perform at this key level would be cruel to you."

I nod my head understandingly. "Absolutely. I totally get it." I hand in my three carefully crafted essays and ask her when she thinks I will know whether or not I got in.

"You'll be getting a letter in the mail within a matter of weeks."

Sure enough, two and a half weeks later the envelope arrives, on ivory stationery stamped with the Sarah Lawrence logo. "We are pleased to announce that you have been accepted into the Continuing Education program at Sarah Lawrence College." I hold the letter in my hands all day, imagining myself as a Sarah Lawrence student, maybe even in jeans and a J. Crew jacket to match.

I finally call my mother to tell her that I got in, because I think this is something she will want to hear. I know that she doesn't approve of my life among the Hasidic people, and I think that this will be my small way of telling her that I do want something more. I hear the pride in her voice when she congratulates me, and also the underlying question about whether my choice of Sarah Lawrence reflects my sexuality, something she doesn't articulate. All she says is, "I hear that's a very gay-friendly environment." It's not like it's genetic, I want to tell her.

Business classes, I tell Eli. I will learn bookkeeping and marketing and things like that. So I can get a good job somewhere or maybe open my own business one day. He just wants to know how much of my time it will consume and if I will be home to pick up Yitzy from day care and cook dinner as usual.

In April the college hosts an open house to introduce us to the professors who will be teaching classes to the adult students this summer semester. I already know just from looking at the syllabus that I'm going to choose the poetry class, because I've always wanted to be able to read, understand, and talk about poetry and famous poets, and I've never met anyone who knows anything about it at all.

James, the poetry professor, has neat salt-and-pepper hair that spikes upward over his tall forehead, a barely perceptible gap between his two front teeth, and a long, lean body encased in a preppy knit sweater and the kind of jeans people wear when they go riding in New England, or so I think. He looks exactly like the kind of person who reads poetry, and when he talks, his voice is slow and thick like honey pouring off a spoon, the perfect voice for a poem.

After the event is over, I ask him if it matters that I never studied poetry before, or if there's anything I can do to prepare, but he says many of the people who take his classes know nothing at all about poetry. "Ignorance is more common in this area of study than you might think," he says, smiling slightly. I feel privileged just to be speaking to him.

I order *The Norton Anthology of Poetry* from the local library. On the first Monday in June I put on my sheerest pair of beige stockings and my blue Prada espadrilles that I found on sale, drop Yitzy off at day care, and drive over the Tappan Zee Bridge and the Hudson River flattened below it to Westchester County. The sun glares brilliantly off the white water and the rooftops lining the shoreline, and the concrete roadway shimmers in my rearview mirror. In my car the air conditioner hums beneath the roar of the speakers playing Europop. I roll my window down and let my arm dangle out in the summer air, nodding my head and tapping my fingers on the steering wheel to keep rhythm. I suck in the pouch of stomach left over from my pregnancy, trying to see my former waistline behind the shadows of my long-sleeved T-shirt.

My classroom has little dormer windows that throw squares of sunshine onto a large round table, but there are only three of us seated around it when the professor starts the class. I never imagined the class would be so small.

James introduces himself and then asks us to say a few words each. My only other classmate is a middle-aged man named Bryan, with a swarthy face and dark skin, a ring in one ear, and skinny arms that dangle out of a wildly emblazoned T-shirt. He says something about traveling with someone named Mick Jagger, and a show called MTV, but I don't really understand what he's talking about, except that he loves music and smoking. He excuses himself every so often to take a drag outside the building, and it makes me wonder what it is about him that makes him unable to go for an hour without a cigarette.

I don't say much about myself, except to mention that I'm Hasidic, and James turns to look at me with surprise and interest on his face.

"That's so funny," he says. "My father-in-law is Hasidic. He wasn't born that way, but he decided to become Hasidic later in life."

"What kind of Hasidic?" I ask. There are different versions, like Hungarians with *shtreimels* and Russians with pointy felt hats and exposed fringes.

"I think he is Lubavitcher." That's the Russian kind.

"Oh," I say. "I'm Satmar. They're completely different, but it would be hard to explain."

I can't understand why anyone would give up a life on the outside for a life full of limits and deprivations. I wonder what James really thinks of his father-in-law.

We start the class by reading a poem by William Wordsworth called "Anecdote for Fathers." James reads it aloud, and I can hear the reverence he has for the words in the way he speaks them, and it makes me hear them differently too, so that each word becomes a universe of meaning. Wordsworth's language is flowery, but the rhymes are tight and even, each stanza packed like a small pincushion. The story of a father strolling with his son seems simple and clear enough, and I begin to think that poetry, after all, is not so very difficult to read. James asks us to uncover the mystery of the poem, as Wordsworth tells of a young boy who chooses the green seashore over the woodsy hills of a farm for the simple reason that the shore lacks a weather vane. At this the father in Wordsworth's poem rejoices, "Could I but teach the hundredth part / Of what from thee I learn."

"What is it about the boy's choice and its explanation that has so moved his father?" James asks. "Is the weather vane really such a satisfactory explanation for his preference?"

I can't figure it out at first, but James says everything in a poem is deliberate. Nothing is casually thrown in, like you might find in a novel. Therefore if anything catches your attention, it is always for a reason. That is the first and foremost lesson in poetry.

The poem, says James, is about the nature of children and what they can teach adults, and about the very lack of reasoning required in life: all one needs is an instinct, a feeling. Not everything has to be explained.

It's a lesson I never expected from this poem, the idea that one should value instinct over logic, emotion over intellect. But it makes sense now, looking back at my own childhood and the way I've always trusted my gut even in situations where logic clearly called for restraint. Every brave leap I've taken in life I can trace to a feeling, as opposed to a rational thought. In fact, the very reason I am here at Sarah Lawrence is an impulse I had months ago. True, I don't know how long I will be able to stay, or what this education will afford me, but I'm trusting in the lessons of my own childhood and choosing not to rationalize my decision.

This poem was a reflection of Wordsworth's desire to move away from logic and intellect and move toward the emotion and romanticism that was beginning to qualify the poetry of his time. Wordsworth, says James, was the first great Romantic.

I raise my hand to ask a question. "How is it," I ask, "that a man living during that time period would be comfortable expressing himself in such flowery terms and still keep his masculinity intact? Isn't romanticism a feminine trait?"

James laughs at my use of the word *flowery*. "I don't think anyone would call Wordsworth 'flowery,'" he says with a grin, "but I see where you are coming from. All I can say is that at that time, poetry was a man's world. So no matter how 'flowery' Wordsworth would get, he was still doing a man's work. No one could see that as feminine. We can talk more about it when I meet with you for conference, something we'll do once a week after class to talk about your individual work and research."

What a wonderful thing, I think, to take one's masculinity so for granted that there is no need to fear being stripped of it. Are the lines that divide the men and women in my community in place because that fear has come to exist for some reason? Maybe, in a world where women outside the community have more freedom, masculinity is suddenly a thing that can be stripped.

In our conference after class, James asks me if I've ever read any Yiddish poetry.

"I wasn't aware there was any," I say, surprised.

"Oh, there are lots of Yiddish poets, and most of them have been translated into English. It might be interesting for you to read both versions and see how well the language translates."

On my way home I think how remarkable it is that my first professor at Sarah Lawrence knows so much about my little world. I had been expecting complete ignorance.

Yitzy stretches his plump arms toward me when he sees me at the door to his day care center, his face lighting up in joyful recognition. His happiness makes me feel inordinately special; I can hardly understand why he adores me so much, but it's the first time in my life that I've felt truly loved. The sound of his giggle is constant, and he always waits expectantly for me to laugh along with him; I can't help but smile. Often I look at him and wonder at how he ended up so perfect; surely it is not to my credit. I sometimes think that he was given to me as a sign that I am not trapped after all.

But although Yitzy is wonderful, I remain hurt and distracted by what is going on between me and Eli. Our marriage is fraught with strife; one of us is always sullen. Our arguments seem to erupt out of nowhere and fizzle out just as unpredictably.

Friday night is the night Eli and I must have sex. It's the night everyone has sex. In the Talmud it says a traveling merchant must have intercourse with his wife once every six months, a laborer three times a week, but a Torah scholar has intercourse on Friday nights. Because

Hasids consider themselves primarily scholars, we follow that school. I don't particularly like it, because I always feel full after the Shabbos dinner, and tired. Eli wants to have sex regardless, even if we've been cold to each other only moments before. I cannot comprehend his ability to separate physical intimacy from the general tone of our relationship.

Lately Eli has been criticizing the way I prepare the food. He thinks I don't pay enough attention to the laws of kashruth, the Jewish dietary laws. Sometimes I put the meat knife down on the dairy counter by mistake, but I know that's not really breaking the law, it's just frowned upon. Breaking the law would be putting a meat knife in a hot dairy dish, like a cream soup. Then I would have to throw away the soup and the knife.

I tell Eli that any rabbi would tell him to put the laws of *shalom bayis*, peace in the household, over the laws of kashruth. His criticism sparks arguments, and then it ruins the entire Shabbos meal I worked so hard to prepare, because instead of telling me how much he likes my cooking, like a good Jewish husband is supposed to, all he sees are the mistakes I make. Then after the Friday night dinner is over, I can sometimes refuse sex, because there is a law that a man cannot have sex with his wife if they are fighting; he has to apologize first, and Eli doesn't always want to apologize.

When Eli is not angry, he is very calm. Everyone thinks he's such a nice husband, because when we are in public, he brings me glasses of water "in case I'm thirsty." At home I have to get the water myself.

Little things make him angry, like if the kitchen cabinet won't close because I put the cereal box in the wrong way when I was in a rush to get to school, and then he'll slam doors or throw books on the floor, but afterward he won't even remember that he got mad.

Just before his second birthday I decide to toilet train Yitzy. My friends say he's too young, but I've read that it's the best age to try, that the older children get, the more recalcitrant they become. My neighbors have three- and four-year-old sons that are still in diapers.

I stay home with Yitzy for two weeks. The first day I keep Yitzy in the bathroom all day for as long as I can, reading books to him about going to the bathroom, and when he finally gets distracted for a minute and lets a small stream of urine out, he looks up at me, his mouth crinkled downward in shock, and I clap enthusiastically.

Although he's already accomplished it once, getting him to do it a second time proves to be even more difficult. When I ask Eli to take over for an hour after he comes home from work, Yitzy squirms and tries to get off the seat, but I tell Eli to make sure he doesn't get off until he does his business.

After a few minutes I hear crying coming from the bathroom and I open the door to see what is going on: Eli gripping Yitzy's shoulders and shaking him back and forth in anger.

"Stop that right now!" I say, seeing the fear on my son's face. "What's wrong with you? He's two years old! You think he's going to go to the bathroom if you threaten him? You could ruin everything!"

I don't let Eli participate in the toilet training after that. I don't let him bathe or dress our son either, because if Yitzy gets squirmy and tries to slip out of his father's grasp, Eli will lose his temper. When that happens he does strange things, like pushing Yitzy away with force even though he is only a toddler. It makes me very angry and I always threaten to call the police, but I never do.

The one time I called the Ramapo police, it was because one of our next-door neighbors drove by and yelled at me through his rolled-down window, "What's wrong with you Jews? Why can't you be like everyone else?" and Yitzy started to cry. But the cop didn't believe me because, he said, he had known that man for years now, and he would never say such things.

The cops don't like that the Hasidic Jews live in Airmont. When elections roll around, we swarm the voting booths, checking the slots the rabbis tell us to, electing politicians who will allow us to bend zoning regulations and manipulate funds and resources for our own agendas. I don't blame the goyim for hating us. I just wish there was a way for me to tell them how much I want to be different and how trapped I feel in this costume, this role.

Since I moved to Airmont three years ago, the community has grown. It used to be a small group of Hasidic families that had migrated from places like Williamsburg and Kiryas Joel, where the lifestyle was too rigid and extreme for them to be happy. A few young couples, like us—wives who wore long human-hair wigs and jean skirts, husbands who drank beer and smoked marijuana on poker nights. Someone called a "bum" in Williamsburg was now just another lapsed Hasid in the sprawling, diverse Jewish community of Rockland County. The difference between living in Airmont and living in Williamsburg is that as long as you don't talk about it, you can break the rules. You can have the privacy to live the life you choose as long as you don't draw attention to yourself. I drive, I paint my toes with red nail polish, I sneak out to see a movie sometimes, but no one really notices when you live on your private little piece of land and mind your own business. Still, it's not enough. Eli thinks I will always find a reason to complain, no matter how much freedom I have. He thinks I'm incapable of being happy.

The problem is, with each restriction lifted, I find another one lying just behind it. And I can't help but be reminded all the time that there are some things I will never be able to experience. I can't bear the thought of living an entire lifetime on this planet and not getting to do all the things I dream of doing, simply because they aren't allowed. I don't think it will ever be enough, this version of freedom, until it is all-inclusive. I don't think I can be happy unless I'm truly independent.

On Shabbos I put Yitz in the stroller and walk to the synagogue to pick up Eli after prayers, and when the men spill out the front door, they stare unabashedly at me, at my tight black dress and black high heels. If you dress up, you get attention. Here the Hasids don't look at the ground when a woman passes. But they aren't any better, because instead they make lewd remarks and dirty jokes. That is the extent of their enlightenment.

My neighbor Chavi, who lives just a ten-minute walk down the road, styles my wigs for me. I just purchased my first extralong wig from her, made from virgin human hair that has never been chemically treated, so it falls soft and wavy down my shoulders. Still, no matter how carefully she cuts it and how expertly she arranges it around my face, I can still see the obvious, harsh hairline, and I can't imagine how anyone could think it's my real hair.

Sometimes when I go to the mall with Yitzy in his stroller, I feel as if his blond hair and blue eyes and his innocent, all-American face not yet marked by side curls bridge a little bit of the distance between me and the other people in the mall. Yitzy makes everyone stop and coo at him with his perfect baby face and pudgy limbs, while I stand by in my wig and long skirt, pretending to be normal.

I've started taking my wig off in college, even though my hair underneath is always a little matted. The wig makes me self-conscious, as do the skirts, but I don't own any normal clothing, and thus far I've been scared to be seen buying any. I go to the T.J. Maxx in White Plains and peruse the jeans rack nervously, not understanding the differences among all the shades of denim and all the styles and pocket designs. I choose a pair with big brown loops embroidered on the pockets and white fade marks at the hips and try them on. They're a bit long, but with heels they would be perfect. I marvel at how different my body looks in the jeans, so curvy, so powerful.

When I get to class on Wednesday, I take off my long black skirt in the car. I'm wearing my jeans underneath. In the classroom, my friend Polly squeals excitedly, "Oh my God, you're wearing jeans! Are they Sevens?"

"What?"

"The brand—they're Sevens, right?"

"I don't know. I got them in T.J. Maxx for fifteen dollars. I liked the color."

"That's a great deal for a pair of Sevens. You look so cool!"

When the class starts, I can't hear anything the professor is saying because I keep looking down at my legs and smoothing the denim with my fingers. When I walk out of the building, the gardeners working outside whistle as I walk past, and I look down at the ground automatically, scolding myself for attracting attention. Surely this doesn't happen to every girl when she wears jeans, I think.

At home I crumple them up and stuff them under my mattress so Eli doesn't find them. I'm not sure I can lie my way out of this one.

Polly is my new best friend at Sarah Lawrence. She has brilliant blond hair and a dimpled smile, and she wears beautiful clothes and talks animatedly about everything. She is a character straight out of the books I read wistfully when I was younger, and I ache to have hair as yellow as hers, eyes as blue, teeth as white as milk. When I first introduced myself to her, I told her I was Hasidic, and she looked at me and laughed, as if I were joking. But then she realized I wasn't kidding, and she slapped her hand over her mouth and wouldn't stop apologizing, but I didn't mind. I was flattered that she couldn't really tell I was different. She thought my wig was my real hair.

If I had a nose like Polly's, my life would be different, I know it. It always comes down to the nose. Bubby says that's how Hitler identified the Jews from the gentiles. He sure would have had an easy time identifying me. I associate my lot in life with my nose. Polly's life suits her nose, so it makes sense. You have a pointy nose, good things happen to you.

In January, Polly takes me to her neighborhood in Manhattan and we go to a restaurant. She loves food; she used to be a chef before she and her husband opened a chocolate factory. I think to myself, *I will eat everything but the fish and the meat, and it won't be so bad even if it isn't kosher.* When we arrive, I can see that the ceiling is so tall because the people inside are long-legged, with noses lifted high in the air, and I feel fascinated and slightly intimidated by my surroundings. Even the waiter is devastatingly handsome, his walk a smooth rock from hip to hip. "Gay," Polly mouths silently behind his back, and I nod in understanding, wondering what it is about him that makes her identify him so easily.

The host comes over to our table to ask if everything is in order, and Polly flirts shamelessly with him, teasing him about his strangely styled hair. I watch bashfully, my eyes averted. When he leaves, Polly leans in excitedly. "He was totally checking you out! Didn't you see that?"

"See what?" I ask, bewildered.

"Oh, you'll learn in time."

Checking me out? For what? I sneak a glance at the tall, dark man standing at the front of the restaurant. To me he looks generic, like every other gentile. With their clean-shaven faces and trim haircuts, they all look like the same alien species. Surely a man like that could never be interested in someone like me, not with my Jewish nose. Men like that are interested in women like Polly.

When the food arrives, it is plated beautifully and looks terribly exotic. I can't help breaking my own rules, and I end up trying a cold cut that looks like turkey pastrami, but afterward Polly tells me it's prosciutto, which is pig. I excuse myself to go to the bathroom to wait for the vomiting to set in, because that's what my teachers used to say happens to people who eat *chazer* meat.

My stomach feels fine. In the bathroom mirror I can see my wig and long-sleeved blouse and I am almost surprised by my reflection, as if I expected to see someone as glamorous on the outside as everyone else in the restaurant. Tamping down the feeling of smallness that has started to rise within me at the sight of my reflection, I abandon the traitorous mirror and walk back out into the restaurant with a painfully straight back.

I return to the table and start sampling the other dishes. I eat as if having returned from war, victoriously. Lamb spring rolls, beef carpaccio, salmon ceviche, what strange food gentiles eat! I don't understand the concept of raw meat and fish, but I try it anyway. It's funny, I say to Polly; most Hasids who go off the path just go to McDonald's for a burger, but I'm eating gourmet *treif* cuisine.

"That's how you do it, though," she says. "Even when you break the rules, you do it with pizzazz." I like the sound of that. A glamorous rebel, that's me. On the way back we stop into a sunglasses shop and I buy a pair of tortoiseshell frames by some designer Polly says is awesome, and when I put them on, I look like a supermodel in the mirror.

I look sideways at Polly and wonder if I can ever be as self-assured as she is.

"I don't want to be a Hasid anymore," I announce suddenly, after we leave the shop.

"Well, then," she says, "you don't have to be."

I don't see how I can be anything else, though. It's the only life I'm allowed to live. Even if I were willing to give it all up, how would I go about finding a life to replace it?

The older Yitzy gets, the more I worry about his future. When he turns three, he will get his own set of *payos* and start going to cheder, a school where boys go to learn Torah from nine to four o'clock every day. I don't think I could bear seeing his childlike perfection marred by the side curls and prayer shawl he will have to wear, or the fact that his life will suddenly be full of male influences while I am relegated to the background.

How can I condemn my son to a life of smallness and limitation? How can I allow him to be imprisoned in a cheder or yeshiva for the rest of his childhood while I am allowing myself the opportunity to broaden my own limited horizons? It doesn't feel right. I can no longer imagine abandoning him to this narrow, stifling life when I want so much to have a free one.

Still, we are both trapped. I have nowhere else to go, and no means or resources to change my circumstances. Instead, I live my other life in secret, keeping my thoughts and opinions locked up in the part of my brain I have reserved for my new, rebellious identity.

On the outside, I keep kosher and dress modestly and pretend to care deeply about being a devout Hasidic woman. On the inside, I yearn to break free of every mold, to tear down every barrier ever erected to stop me from seeing, from knowing, from experiencing.

My life is an exercise in secrets, the biggest secret being my true self, and it has become of utmost importance to me to hide this self from Eli. When I was younger I would write down my thoughts in journals, but after I got married I stopped because I was worried my writings would be found and read and that Eli would be able to see inside me through them. Now it has become more about hiding my new discoveries from him; I don't want to leave incriminating evidence around, revealing the changes brewing inside me.

There are so many thoughts roiling around in my mind that writing becomes a matter of necessity. I decide to start an anonymous blog so I can post entries online and use the web as my private journal. I make sure the entries can't be traced to me. I title the blog "Hasidic Feminist" and it is mostly inspired by the work I do at Sarah Lawrence, bits of writing spurred on by my feminist readings in philosophy class, and portions of essays written in my theater and writing classes.

The first thing I choose to write about is my struggle to consummate my marriage. I never actually admitted my prolonged virginity to anyone, and normally I wouldn't consider publicizing it, but a phone call I received a week ago changed my mind. An unidentified woman from Williamsburg called me, saying she had gotten my number from my aunt Chaya, and confided in me that her recently married daughter was having issues consummating her marriage for eight months already, and did I have any advice to offer?

I was taken aback by her request because I had always seen myself as uniquely problematic in the larger scheme of vaginal health, an anomaly not just in my community but in the world. Yet here was a mother, worried about her daughter's inability to perform sexually and the apparent lack of a concrete reason for it, floundering for some kind of explanation, some assistance. I gave her whatever advice I could, even though I myself haven't begun to fully understand why I went through what I did.

It feels strangely freeing to post the story of my giant defect out there for everyone to see, anonymously, of course. After I post my story online, a swarm of comments appear, most of them written by other people like me, rebellious Hasids, some ex-Hasids, some modern Orthodox Jews, and even some gentiles. I don't know how all these readers discovered my tiny little blog, my little speck in cyberspace, but they all seem to have a lot to say.

Some are disbelieving. They don't understand how a girl could go her whole adolescent life without noticing her vagina. Others are empathetic. Still others report similar experiences. The readers debate with each other, using my blog as a forum, and for me, perusing their conversations is a thrilling experience. I feel somehow at the center of something great, and yet safe behind the screen of my computer, unable to be seen or held accountable.

"How will you keep your child?" my readers ask. No community will let you leave with your child if you're not religious, they say. "I'm a lawyer," one comment reads, "and I know for a fact it's never been done."

They warn me that no rabbinical court will let me leave with my son. Even if I were to keep all the laws, I still wouldn't be considered devout enough to be a parent to my child. They cite examples for me, names of other women who've tried, but their comments don't scare me. I know that I am different from these other women, that I have something they didn't have. I don't know how, and I don't know when, but one day I will be free, and so will Yitzy. He will be able to go to a real school and read books without fear of being found out. Subconsciously I have started to say good-bye to the people and objects in my life as if preparing to die, even though I have no real plan. I just feel strongly, in my gut, that I'm not meant to stay here.

I visit Bubby and Zeidy for the last time in March of 2009, for the holiday of Purim. I still don't know if I will ever really get to leave, but I think that just in case I do decide to make my exit, it will be easier if I cut ties sooner rather than later.

The house I grew up in is falling apart. I don't know if it's because Bubby and Zeidy don't have the money anymore, or if they simply lack the energy to keep up with the maintenance this sort of building requires. It saddens me that such a beautiful brownstone building with so much history should be left to rot. How appropriate that just as the very foundations of my faith are nearing total collapse, the foundations of my childhood home disintegrate as well. I take it as another sign that I am on the path I was set on long ago by a force greater than my own. God wants me to leave. He knows I was never meant for this.

The paint in the hallways is peeling, and the linoleum on the stairs has been completely worn through in many places. Bubby wants to sell the house to a developer who has already offered a seven-figure sum, but Zeidy is too proud to relinquish control on the best investment he ever made. He's trying to figure out how he can turn the situation to his advantage.

Already I can see there are things I don't have to say good-bye to because they no longer exist. The Bubby and Zeidy I remember from my childhood have aged dramatically. Bubby no longer has that vibrant energy that she once had; her step is slow and plodding, her eyes glazed over in disorientation. Zeidy is more absentminded than ever, his speech lacking the alacrity and precision of his younger years. Everything I loved about my childhood home has gone to tatters.

My father walks in during the festive Purim meal, eyes bloodshot, obviously drunk. He sees me and makes his way over, and I swallow in anticipation of his loud greeting. Instead he falls heavily over me in a sort of hug and slaps his arm around my neck. It's heavy, and his grip tightens. It's almost as if he is choking me, and the smell of liquor is so thick I can't breathe. His dirtiness makes me feel dirty too, the kind of dirt you can never scrub off. I will be happy to be rid of my duties to him;

I never understood why I had to perform the part of a daughter to a man who never tried to be my father.

Eli watches the whole scene without saying anything, and for once I wish he would step in and be a man, maybe distract my father at least, instead of leaving me to fend for myself. Afterward he looks at me with his mouth open in surprise, but I keep my face blank.

It's strange to look around the dining room table, groaning with the weight of platters of smoked meat and wine decanters, at the people I call my family—aunts, uncles, cousins, and distant cousins—and think that maybe in a year's time they will have become a faint memory. It's clear that they take my existence for granted, that by now I am no different from all of them, married off, with a toddler to take care of, the weight of a wig on my head. For all intents and purposes I am tied down. But truthfully, all those assurances are in the mind, and if my mind cannot be tied down, if my dreams cannot be diminished, then no amount of restraints can really guarantee my quiet submission.

I wonder what they will say about me when I'm gone. Will they feign shock, or will they nod conspiratorially and say they knew all along that I wasn't quite right in the head? A child like me, damaged from the start—what else could I have become?

The women in the adult program at Sarah Lawrence go out for lunch after classes. They are mostly white, wealthy women in their thirties or forties, able to spend the money on exorbitant tuition fees and Prada bags. I am the anomaly, a twenty-one-year-old woman with a baby, who each time slaps on the same pair of jeans in the car, with hair still getting used to the sunshine.

Materialism, I discover, is no different in the secular world. I remember the girls I went to school with as a child, dressed in Ferragamo shoes and Ralph Lauren separates that had been altered to adhere to the modesty guidelines. I long for the same status symbols now as I did then, if only because I understand that those symbols command the kind of respect the world never seems to show me.

I sometimes join my Sarah Lawrence classmates for lunch if I have time, listening quietly to the descriptions of their lives, their talk of lavish vacations, their worries about their children's private schools, their complaints about the cost of a gym membership, and I wonder if one day I will be privileged enough to have problems like these, a husband who works too much, a house that's too big to maintain, a flight to Europe that even in first class is exhausting.

Surely an ordinary person like me has no real future. If I do leave, and shed the visible parts of my Hasidic identity, what life will I have as a gentile? A single mother, struggling to raise a son in the most expensive city in the world, without a family to help, without a husband to take out the trash, without a dollar in a savings account or food stamps in my pocket. Because I promise myself now that if and when I leave, I won't just become another family on welfare, as in the world I left behind, where mothers who give birth to more mouths than they can feed trade WIC coupons for cash at the Jewish Financial Exchange.

Polly, her blond hair now cascading down suntanned shoulders, confides in me that she too grew up on welfare, in poor, run-down Utah, with a mother who joined the Jehovah's Witnesses and a father who clutched eightballs of cocaine in his shivery fist.

"You?" I say, disbelievingly. "But you seem to have it all."

"I only got this way about seven years ago," she says. "After we opened the chocolate factory, it was as if the heavens finally rained down the happiness. But I always knew my day would come, you know? I waited for so long to get *my* share, *my* reward, after what seemed like a lifetime of watching other people of privilege indulge in luxurious lifestyles. It came in the end, but the time before it still seems like forever."

I'm only in my twenties now. Who knows what could happen in ten years? Even if I have to be poor and miserable for a decade, at least there is still the possibility for that kind of miracle, the kind that happens to people like Polly, who *deserve* happiness. Can I really close the door on that chance?

"You have to manifest it for yourself," the blond diva says wisely. "I spent years believing against all odds that it would happen for me. I still wake up every morning knowing even better things will happen. If you believe it against all odds, it comes true. It's the power of the universe."

Even though Polly, too, left religion behind, she still has her own system of faith that she carried with her. Can anyone survive without faith, however it is labeled? No matter how you live your life, it seems, you need faith to get by, to get ahead.

But what is it I want to get ahead to? Do I really want to give up my life so I can have the life that these women have? Are they really that different from me, these housewives? Besides the obvious things, like bigger homes and nicer clothes, in many ways these women feel as trapped as I do. We have all come to Sarah Lawrence for the same reason, to find a way out to something more satisfying.

I can never be completely fulfilled by a pair of jeans or designer sunglasses. Sure, those things are nice, but what I want is to achieve something, to leave my mark on this world. A crater-sized hole, I said in my college application. Maybe I will always struggle, but luxury has never been my goal. It is luxury that leads to sin, Zeidy used to say, because it makes us comfortable and lazy, turns our bones soft and our minds numb.

There were rebels before me. When I was growing up, there were a few here and there who broke the rules openly, and everyone talked about them. But where are they now, these rebels? No one knows. They leave so that they can go out to clubs and drink and do drugs and behave in uninhibited ways, but there is no *menuchas hanefesh*, no serenity, in such a life. Zeidy used to tell me that serenity was the most important thing one could achieve in life, that it was the secret to happiness. I don't think he ever felt he had achieved it, but perhaps he came close. For everyone, he said, it's a different journey. Where do I travel to find peace in myself?

Zeidy spent his life in pursuit of *harchavas hadaas*, a broadened mind. How to broaden my mind in a world that is so narrow, both inside and out?

When Eli travels for a week in the early spring of 2009, I am alone in the house for the first time. If I can't manage one week on my own, there's no way I can contemplate a lifetime of independence, so I steel myself to make it work. I have always been somewhat ashamed by my night terrors; when darkness descends, every stir or creak sets my teeth on edge, and I lie awake clutching the blankets until first light.

There is a big part of me that thinks I can't make it alone because of my anxieties. I am convinced that because I'm a woman, I'm fragile, and I will always need someone to take care of me, especially because I have a child. I think, *How will I take care of him on my own when I am sick? Who will help me if I don't have a husband? Could I seriously give up the security I have now simply for the sake of freedom?*

But on Shabbos afternoon, as I sit on the lawn surrounded by my neighbors and listen to their idle gossip, I am reminded of the yawning gap that is my life, of the burning hunger inside that gnaws at me when it isn't satisfied. I think I'd rather be scared and alone than bored. I think the universe knows that too. I think I was meant for something different from this.

Lately I have been spending hours sitting between the library stacks and thinking about my future. Looking at the books lining the shelves, I remember how I coveted the privilege to read as a child, how much I risked for knowledge, and how the joy of reading always outweighed the fear. I used to marvel at the innate right those authors felt they had to speak their mind in whatever way they saw fit, to put down on paper their innermost thoughts, when I couldn't contemplate a day that I would not feel compelled to keep secrets.

I am so tired of being ashamed of my true self. I am exhausted by the years I have spent pretending to be pious and chastising myself for my faithlessness. I want to be free—physically, yes, but free in every way, free to acknowledge myself for who I am, free to present my true face to the world. I want to be on this library shelf, alongside these other authors, for whom truth is a birthright.

Polly has been sending my blog around to everyone she knows in publishing, and I'm determined to pursue any connection. I've gotten an e-mail from a literary agent already, and I am overwhelmed with the enormity of this opportunity and the terrifying possibility of its disappearance. How can I prove myself worthy of publication?

I drive into the city to meet Patricia, whose office is on the chichi streets of the Upper East Side. In the car, I slip off my long black jersey skirt to reveal new trousers I bought at The Limited, and under my long-sleeved sweater is a cap-sleeved silk shirt with tiny flowers on it. As I get out of my car and take the ticket from the man in the parking garage, I can feel the cool, smooth fabric of the trouser legs slide down my calves, covering my high-heeled black pumps. My heels click loudly and confidently on the pavement, and my stride feels wide and loose in pants. In the reflection of the windows on Madison Avenue, I look impossibly tall and powerful, like I've never looked in a dowdy skirt.

At the corner of the designated street, I can already see Polly talking to a slim brunette woman at one of the outdoor tables at the café. I approach the table and say hello, and while Polly greets me enthusiastically as always, Patricia at first seems not to know who I am. After a moment she realizes that I am indeed the Hasidic woman seeking literary representation, and her mouth falls open.

"You are nothing like I expected," she says, her eyes wide. "You're so glamorous."

"Well, that's only because of Polly. She corrupted me." I smile, secretly overjoyed to hear her confirmation, to know that I blend in here, that I look just like everyone else. To think, on the Upper East Side, I finally know what it feels like to not stand out in the way I always have. Polly reaches her hand out in the direction of my hair, hovering over it slightly.

"Are you wearing the wig?" she asks in a low tone. "I can't tell."

"No, it's my real hair." I laugh. "My wig is in the car." I find it funny that she can never tell the difference, when my wig is bushy and curly and my real hair is fine and straight.

"You two are just like Betty and Veronica," says Patricia, smiling at the both of us.

"Who are they?" I ask innocently.

"Oh my God, you don't even know who Betty and Veronica are? The *Archie* comics?" Polly asks. Even after all this time, she still can't believe it when I blank out at cultural references.

Patricia gives me some titles of books to read, books about writing, about publishing. The next step, she says, is to write a proposal. It's like a sales pitch for my book. We use the proposal to sell the idea, and then once I sell it, I can write it. I go home resolved to use every free hour to work on the proposal. Patricia said a good proposal can take up to a year

to write, at minimum three months, but I'm determined to write the fast-
est proposal ever written. If this book is my ticket out, I want to cash in
on that ticket as soon as I can. Already I have grown too big to fit back
into my old world.

On September 8, 2009, I stay late at Sarah Lawrence to hang out with
some friends. I'm feeling energized by the prospect of abandoning my
life. I have set everything in motion and now it's up to me to take that
first step. I know it will be very soon; I may just be waiting for Eli to tip
me over the edge, or for some kind of sign, perhaps, but from who? Then
again, it's preposterous to think of myself now as that girl from Williamsburg, to whom everything was a spiritual message.

Feeling jittery, I impulsively decide to bum my first cigarette. I try
very hard to hold back the cough because I know coughing is how ama-
teurs react and I want to seem smooth and natural, so I suck in a tiny
puff and keep it in my mouth for a second before letting it out in a thin
stream, so it's like it never entered my lungs at all.

As I stand outside the college library, cigarette dangling nonchalantly between two fingers, I watch the people passing me in all direc-
tions. Their gait is so purposeful that I am struck with envy. I want to
walk with such purpose toward each moment; I want to face my future
with as much certainty and entitlement as these men and women, whose
eyes gaze in my direction but never quite settle on my own.

I'm wearing jeans and a V-neck, and my hair is long and straight and
snakes around my shoulder to dangle like a thick, dark ribbon down my
side. I must look just like everyone else here. Finally, the blessed feeling
of anonymity, of belonging; are they not the same? Can anyone see past
my nonchalant poise to the nervous joy underneath?

I'm so happy to be a part of this place! I want to shout to the tower-
ing oak trees lining the entrance to campus. I want to twirl around and
around with my hands in the air and skip around the lawn. I'm never
going to be that awkward girl again, the girl with the wig and the skirt
and painfully self-conscious manner. I'm going to be normal, so normal
no one will ever know. I'm going to forget I was ever different.

It takes me an hour to get back to Airmont, so I leave before I get too tired. The highways are dark and empty, and I put in the mix CD that a friend from school made for me. The Pierces play softly as I tap my fingers on the steering wheel, keeping time with the beat. Just as I come off the Tappan Zee Bridge and veer onto the New York State Thruway, I hear a loud popping sound, and before I can look around, my car starts spinning wildly out of control. I can hear the squeals of protest coming from the road, and the car spins so fast that the night colors blur across my windshield. I brace myself with arms stretched out taut against the steering wheel, and I watch my windshield shatter prettily on impact, as the car hits the barrier and flips over clumsily, each impact sending a fresh jolt of pain through my tense body. In the last few seconds, it's clear to me that I'm going to die, and I think it is a just way to end my life, that I should die as I stand on the cusp of freedom. *There really is a God, and he's punishing me.* That is my last thought before everything goes black.

I wake up and it takes me a few seconds to realize I'm upside down and my head is touching concrete. The car is flattened, so I can't open the doors, but there is shattered glass everywhere from the passenger seat window. I slowly release my seat belt and start feeling around for my purse. As my eyes adjust to the dark I can see its contents have spilled everywhere, and my BlackBerry is missing the trackball. I try to figure out how to maneuver the phone without it, but I'm in too much shock to complete a call. I suddenly realize that if I stay in the car longer, it could explode, and I think, *I must get out.* At midnight the road is silent, except for the hushed whizzing of the occasional speeding car. No one has pulled over. I grab my wallet, phone, and keys and start easing my way out of the car, doing a slow crawl on my belly in the dark, feeling the glass cut into my knees and palms. After I finally pull the whole of me out onto the pavement littered with the debris of my crushed car, I pat myself all over as if to confirm that I'm in one piece. "I'm okay," I tell myself, over and over, trying to reassure myself. "I'm okay." And then questioningly, "I'm okay?" I can't stop saying it. After a few minutes someone sees me leaning against the barrier and pulls over.

The cops keep asking me if I'm drunk, and I laugh hysterically because I've never been able to stand alcohol, but they think I'm laughing because I'm that drunk, and they treat me roughly. Everything hurts so much, but mostly I'm so distracted from their questions because I can't figure out why I'm alive. Why would this accident happen to me if I wasn't meant to die?

I watch from the road as they tow away the crumpled mess left of my car. Watching it go is like saying good-bye to my own battered body. I look down at myself and my skin feels brand-new, like it was ripped off and grew back on its own. My new bionic limbs are miraculously intact after an accident that should have left me broken in half.

That's all I can think about in the hospital. I'm filled with searing confusion. I don't understand what this means. That something like this should happen to me, only a few days before I'm supposed to leave my past behind for good, only makes sense if it were meant to stop me from doing so. Is it meant to scare me into obedience? I look down at my body and marvel at its ability to survive something so frightening, and I gaze lingeringly at my limbs as if there were magic blood coursing in my veins. How extraordinary it is, to be alive when one should be dead.

The accident happened as the clock struck midnight, when the date changed to 09/09/09. Nine, that's what the Kabbalist told me; nine, the number of death and rebirth, endings and beginnings, is the sign I was supposed to look out for. I may always look back on this day as the one that divided my life in two.

Eli comes to see me in the hospital and I'm furious with him. He had been telling me that the tires on the car were too thin, but he had refused to have them changed. He claimed he couldn't afford it.

"But you could afford to lose me?" I ask bitterly. "Yitzy could have been in that car."

But Eli shows no signs of remorse. He refuses to accept any responsibility for the accident. I don't want to see his face anymore. I tell him to go home, I will call a friend to come stay with me. I never want to see his face again.

Could this be the sign from God, then? That clean break with my past that I was looking for, the emphatic separation between one life and the other? Maybe the fact that I'm not dead is the big miracle I always thought would come my way. Only now can I truly feel invincible, after I've been through the worst. I am no longer nervous, no longer uncertain. I have no past to cling to; the last twenty-three years belong to someone else, someone I no longer know.

The next day I sign a contract to write a memoir about a person who no longer exists, someone I will be sure to honor with a last remembrance. My two identities have finally split apart, and I've killed the other one, I've murdered her brutally but justly. This book will be her last words.

Before I leave Airmont for good, Eli and I go to a religious marriage counselor together, to see what we can do about our marriage, or rather, what remains of it. Eli thinks that by seeing a counselor he is finally showing a desire to make things better for us, but it comes too late. I already know in my heart that I'm never coming back.

Still, I go through the motions. I tell the counselor about the first year of our marriage, and how Eli left me because I couldn't have intercourse, and how he never stuck up for me when his family put me down. I say I can never forgive him for that.

The marriage counselor, himself only a rabbi and not a therapist, tells Eli we need to see a professional. "Your issues," he says, "are not the normal, superficial conflicts that occur in a marriage. You're not arguing about who is taking out the trash or who isn't being loving enough. I don't know how to help you get past something like this. It's pretty serious."

Afterward Eli turns to me and says, "We should just get a divorce, no? It's not like this is ever going to work."

I shrug my shoulders. "We could get a divorce, if that's what you want."

I rent a tiny white Kia and stuff it with as much as it can hold. I put Yitzy in his little booster seat and I notice how he looks around at the boxes and garbage bags I have squeezed into every inch of space. He doesn't say anything, only pops his thumb in his mouth and promptly falls asleep as soon as we're on the highway. As we stall in traffic on the Tappan Zee, I grip the steering wheel tightly, instantly reliving the sounds and sensations of the crash just a few days ago.

I bring my diamond ring and some of my old wedding gifts to a jeweler in Westchester, who gives me a pile of cash in exchange. I watch him bag up the last five years of my life like I might somehow be coming back to pick it all up again, and I ask him what he's going to do with it. We'll probably just melt it down, he says. I exhale in relief. It feels good to know that those items won't show up on someone else's wrists or neck, that they will disappear forever. I never should have had them in the first place.

In the beginning I feel saddened by some of the things I had to leave behind. The jewelry was easy to part with, but the dishes and linens I shopped for so lovingly five years ago, the friends I worked so hard to make, the entire extended family network I was once a part of—those are harder to disengage from. It feels new and strange to suddenly have to make do with so little, and there is a quiet panic in me at the thought of having so few possessions to tie me down. The feeling of rootlessness is etched into my muscles like the soreness that sets in after intense exercise. I yearn to feel weighed down again by life, instead of feeling this free-floating aimlessness that ignites flames of pure terror in my soul.

After I left, I changed my phone number and didn't tell anyone my new address. I couldn't risk being tracked down. I needed some time for myself, time to settle in, time to find some sort of security. However, the first thing I notice is the closeness that develops suddenly between me and Yitzy in this new space. We have to get to know each other, out here in the strange world where we know no one else. I feel as if I wasn't allowed to be his mother until now, when there is no one getting in the way of an honest relationship between us.

The first thing I do is teach Yitzy English. We read books together and watch *Sesame Street*. He learns quickly, and I'm grateful that I can do this for him when he is still young enough to adapt smoothly. I am horrified to think about the possibilities had I been forced to stay any longer.

Within weeks Yitzy is like a whole new person, speaking a charming, childlike English. We sleep in the queen bed I purchased after I left, and before we fall asleep, we have lovely conversations. He worries about me, and I can tell, by the way he gives me impulsive compliments. "Your hair is pretty," he says, noticing its newly uncovered state. I know his effort to make me feel good means that he understands that I'm going through something difficult, and the evidence of that knowledge breaks my heart. I think he is too young to be so observant and concerned with our situation in the world.

Yitzy hasn't asked about his dad yet. Only once did he look up at me after swooping gleefully down the playground slide, fixing inquisitive eyes on me and asking seriously, "Daddy and you aren't fighting anymore, right?"

"No, no more fighting," I said with a smile. "Mommy's happy now. Are you happy?"

He nodded his head quickly and ran off to join the other children at the monkey bars. His new short haircut, free of side curls, made him look just like every other American kid, and I felt a profound satisfaction at seeing him blend in, knowing he felt the kind of easy social comfort I never had.

It was shame that kept me as far away from Williamsburg as I could get, that first year. Every time I glimpsed the familiar Hasidic costume from across a busy city street, I would cringe inside, as if I were the one being spotted by an outsider. I couldn't bear to be reminded of my past. I discovered quickly the true opinions of outsiders who interacted with Hasids; people described them to my face as pushy, offensive, and unhygienic, never guessing that I might be taking the criticism personally. I was too horrified to tell anyone where I came from, but eventually the truth would always surface, and panic would always accompany that moment.

It takes a long time for shame to fade away, but surprisingly, underneath it there is pride. When I finally did return to Williamsburg as my new self, I was wrapped in a scarf and sunglasses to avoid being recognized, but I strolled through the outskirts of my old neighborhood awed by the sense of distance I now felt toward what had once been my only home. I finally saw my life with estranged eyes, and suddenly my past struck me as wildly colorful and exotic. What had once seemed to me the most intolerable version of mundane life was now transformed into a rich and mysterious history. I had spent my childhood longing for the suburban backdrop of a stereotypical American upbringing because nothing could have seemed more foreign at the time, and later I discovered that those American girls searched vigorously throughout their formative years for unique experiences that would define them as different, a struggle they found endlessly frustrating. They view me with a somewhat jealous eye, because despite its difficulties, my life has marked me indelibly with the tattoo of distinctiveness.

It was while walking along the recently renovated Kent Avenue that I reflected on how neatly the tables had turned. The landscape of my childhood had drastically changed. The run-down warehouses had been replaced by shimmering glass condominiums, and hipster men in tight jeans hunched over their bicycles as they whisked past me. I realized that everything I had dreamed of as a child had come true. I had stood here once, at the river's edge, longing to be transported to the other side of it. I had longed to find purchase in that world of toppling height and breathtaking brightness and renounce any connection to Brooklyn. I still don't like visiting Brooklyn, no matter which part of it, for that reason. Too much time spent there and I begin to feel trapped. But I visit occasionally, simply for the pure thrill of delicious memory and the satisfaction of knowing that part of what makes my fairy-tale ending so glorious is its very improbability. Even Roald Dahl could not have dreamed up such a journey as this. I have freed myself from my past, but I have not let go of it. I cherish the moments and experiences that formed me. I have lived the story.

What twenty-four-year-old gets to say that to herself, that all her dreams have come true? What more could I truly ask of life? There are days when I am full to bursting with gratitude for having come so far, farther than I ever even dared to anticipate. And although the excitement of trying new things fades with repetition, the excitement of freedom never fails to gratify me. Each time I exercise it, I feel a separate joy that curls through my limbs like syrup. I never want to give up even a fraction of that wonder.

Epilogue

When *Unorthodox* was first published in February 2012, it unleashed a furious backlash from ultra-Orthodox Jews. On message boards and websites established to discredit and attack me, Hasids posted rants in which they accused me of lying, and the religious proclaimed that I had embarrassed the global Jewish community by airing our dirty laundry. One Hasidic editorial compared me to Joseph Goebbels and warned that I could be a catalyst for another Holocaust. I have been called the next great anti-Semite, and numerous suggestions have been made that I date Mel Gibson.

Few of my critics had actually read the book, but the content of *Unorthodox* didn't matter to them as much as the fact that I was a woman who had dared to speak out. Why all the anger? Have I really inspired so much fear just by telling my story? The truth is, I'm among the first to lift the lid on a very insular Jewish sect; its members are highly motivated to keep the nature of their lifestyle secret, and the existence of this community is a troublesome issue that many Jews would like to ignore. Admittedly, I make no apologies for going public. After controversy, discussion inevitably follows, and I have always had high hopes that such dialogue would bring reform and change to fundamentalist Jewish culture. I care so deeply about the rights of women and children, and I am keenly aware of how those rights can be violated in the community I grew up in. It is my belief that bringing transformation to these radical groups is in the best interest of the greater society that supports them.

Why did I decide to speak up? Someone had to do it, and it turned out to be me. Although my first instinct was to keep my past a secret, I am glad I published *Unorthodox*. I no longer have to struggle with the shame and anxiety that come with being an ex-Hasid. Instead, telling my story has empowered me. It feels good to come clean, and to know that I am inspiring other people to do the same. It was wonderful to watch as fellow rebels came forward after the book's publication, some writing insightful articles in support of education reform, others consenting to be interviewed about abuse. I'm encouraged by their efforts, and I know that this is just the beginning.

Back when I was Hasidic, I'd always heard stories of women who left the religious community and lost their children in ugly custody battles. When I decided to leave, I knew I wouldn't let that happen. The dean of Columbia Law School told me my chances were slim to nonexistent, and although the president of the Woman's Bar Association agreed to represent me, she wasn't feeling confident either. However, through a combination of careful planning, risky legal strategy, and fiercely leveraged publicity, I managed to obtain both a religious and civil divorce and custody of my son. In fact, my divorce judgment was on the eve of Passover 2012. I went to a Seder and celebrated my liberation, along with the liberation of the Jewish people. At twenty-five years old, three years after I left, two years after I finished writing my memoir, I was finally free.

How did I create a new life from scratch? I had nothing. My adviser at Sarah Lawrence warned me that divorce was the quickest road to poverty; she questioned if I was willing to take that giant leap into the frightening unknown world of single motherhood without any support to fall back on. She was right to ask; the family and community I had known all my life would be lost to me forever the moment I left. Although there were others who had abandoned the Hasidic community, they were mostly men, unsaddled by children, and they chafed at my desire to get somewhere fast, instead of living the party life.

I had no work experience, at least none that counted. I had no college degree. I had to balance getting an education, raising my son, and supporting us financially with learning how to navigate a foreign world. I was looking for a new place to fit in, but I didn't want to trade a repressive past for a future just like it. I traveled across America in an effort to learn more about the country I had been born into, and the landscape that I had never known. I searched for a community of people that would understand and accept me. In the end, I returned to New York and discovered that it was the city I could best call home.

Leaving a religion, a community, and a family comes at a high price. I had to learn to find peace even in the face of hate and abuse coming from my former community. I ended up turning to the same resources I had relied on as a child: I read books, and the stories served as fuel to help me barrel through those hard times. I found friends and family to replace the ones I lost. I now feel loved and cherished in a way I never thought possible. I still identify as Jewish, because it's my cultural heritage, but I don't derive any spiritual nourishment from Judaism. I'm trying to give my son a clean slate in that sense; I don't want my experiences coloring his perceptions. When I watch him explore the world without fear or confusion, I'm thrilled that he is enjoying the childhood I always dreamed of. If he grows up and decides to become a rabbi or a Talmudic scholar, I'll know that he came to his Judaism through personal choice, and that makes all the difference. For now, we're both enjoying our flexibility and independence.

Although my first few years in the outside world were rocky, and I still cringe at some awkward memories, it has become clear that I do have what it takes to navigate secular society. I have claimed my place in the world, and against all odds, the skyline I once gazed at so longingly has become my true home. People want to know if I've found happiness, but what I've found is better: authenticity. I'm finally free to be myself, and that feels good. If anyone ever tries to tell you to be something you're not, I hope you too can find the courage to speak up in protest.

April 2012
New York City

Afterword

Ten years ago this evening, I sat on the sofa in my two-room garret apartment in New York, my three-year-old son asleep on the double bed squeezed into our tiny bedroom, and opened my banged-up laptop to the beginnings of the manuscript that in only a few short months was to become *Unorthodox*.

I was writing in fits and starts then, mostly in the evenings, when my college classmates went out to bars and restaurants while I, for lack of childcare, stayed in. I remember the future felt oddly compressed, like an accordion with all the air let out of it. I felt capable only of imagining the coming week; at most, the coming month. I was lonely and scared. During the day, having a small child to take care of kept me distracted from the worst of it, but in the long and empty evenings I had nothing but my manuscript, which felt like both a gift and a curse.

In November 2009, I had written something like 20,000 words; the largest part of my task was still in front of me. I was twenty-three years old, and I had never written anything serious before, not even a newspaper article or a short story. I felt I had set myself up for an impossible goal.

Writing a book was part of a much bigger plan, a necessity if I was to truly be free to start a new life with my son outside of our community. The publicity it would bring me would serve as a tool, my lawyer had explained, would provide me with leverage against people who would normally render me voiceless and therefore powerless. It was all about convincing them to let me go, that I wasn't worth the battle.

Naturally I knew I was a very lucky young woman to have been offered a book deal at my age, especially given my inexperience. However, I remember thinking that had I had the luxury of choosing, I would have liked to become a writer only once adequately prepared for it. I've since learned that there is no adequate preparation for writing except the act itself. Yet at the time, the practical reasons for writing the book weighed so heavily on me that they made writing feel less like a creative act of expression and more like the knotting of a rope ladder that would lead me to safety. This wasn't real writing, I thought. Real writing wasn't something one did to secure · one's survival—and surely my readers would be able to tell.

And yet on that windy fall evening ten years ago, for want of anything better to do, I opened my laptop and began to type, telling myself to do my part and let fate do the rest. I didn't write what I had originally planned to that night, didn't hew to my outline's calls for strict chronology. I simply sank into a childhood memory and wrote as if I were back in that moment once again. Then I sank further into another memory and yet another one, and the process began to feel intuitive, like I could shut off the part of myself concentrated on outlines and chapters and characters and all the other things I had learned in college writing workshops and just trust some long-lost inner voice. And somehow, four hours later, I looked up and it was midnight, and half of my manuscript was finished.

All these years later, working on my first novel in German, I still find myself waiting weeks, if not months, for that ghost to haunt me again, periods of time when sitting down to write means feeling stuck in my logical brain, stuck constructing stories like rope ladders, until finally she returns, and my fingers move feverishly over the keyboard while the rest of me is paralyzed, in some kind of trance. Time seems to stand still, and I feel as if I float outside of myself. That ghost has returned over the years—not as frequently as I would have liked, but with time I have come to understand that she has always been ready and willing, and that it is I who have not always been tolerant of her presence. Because she is from the past, and the rest of me is very much trying to be in the present, so as not to be burdened by anything that came before. We are two women, one lost and one found, still trying to find a way to work together to tell a story.

Toward the end of *Unorthodox*, I write about feeling as if I had murdered my old self in order to make room for my new one; my memoir would be her very last words. Yet ten years ago, I was neither in my past nor in my present. I was in a state of limbo, and *Unorthodox* is the book it is because of this, because it was written in a frightening yet magically weightless in-between place. Had I taken the time to prepare, had I waited to write it when I was older—say, now—it would certainly have gotten done, but it would not be the book it should have been, and it would not have that raw, wrenching impact readers tell me it's had on them. The reason *Unorthodox* feels so raw is because it was, because I was in a raw place while writing it, and that's not something that can easily be re-created in retrospect.

After shedding my old self, I didn't suddenly discover a more authentic version underneath. When you carve yourself out of your entire life, you are not left with much. It takes a decade to build both a new self and a life to go with it, and had somebody told me how hard it would be, I might not have undertaken the challenge at all.

Yet I never expected it to be easy either. I had no fairy-tale ending in my head and I think that helped. Happiness has a way of playing hide-and-seek when you actively pursue it, but it often surprises you when you least expect it. I found my version of happiness in Berlin. If someone had predicted that ten years ago, I would have found the thought hilarious bordering on insane.

I've been living in Berlin for five years now. I'm not the only one of my kind to find a home here. Berlin is full of all kinds of refugees and runaways, including a community of formerly Hasidic and Orthodox Jews. Part of that is just Berlin being itself: a city the locals like to joke was built on sand and swamps, without roots, perfect for those who've uprooted themselves, as well as those who've been uprooted against their will. But the other part is simply that your past becomes far more bearable to you when you've physically left it behind. New York City is still the stuff of dreams for many young people, but for me it was a backyard full of skeletons, a maze of familiar faces and triggers for bad memories. What others seek in New York I've found in Berlin.

This past summer production wrapped on a four-episode miniseries inspired by the book I wrote ten years ago. The series was filmed in my native language, Yiddish, on Berlin sets, by an incredible team of German-Jewish, American-Jewish, and German women. (Some men were involved as well.) Bringing the story of *Unorthodox* to the screen is a dream that took root in Berlin, and that was, I am certain, only possible here. Finding the women capable of bringing so much wisdom and passion to the project—and so much willingness to explore new territory—is something I could not have imagined before coming to this city, to a place where creative expression knows hardly any conventional boundaries.

One of the biggest surprises of creating *Unorthodox*, the Netflix series, was how it magically attracted so many men and women with backgrounds similar to my own. They came to work as actors and extras, as consultants and translators, so that at some point being on set felt like attending an especially emotional reunion. In the end, the story told in the series, while inspired by the events in my own life, is also much bigger than that. It is the story of so many people rolled into one, a story that could be mine or anyone else's—even yours. Where small details have been changed, themes of pain, conflict, loneliness, and humiliation remain the same. As a result, watching *Unorthodox*-the-book become *Unorthodox*-the-series was like watching my own life story become part of a larger cultural narrative, a phenomenon I've found deeply gratifying. When I was younger, I read books about rebellious Muslims and Christians, and later watched movies about them too, but it was always a stretch to see myself in those stories. The greatest triumph of *Unorthodox*-the-series is its ability to serve as a template for a journey that many have traveled and yet for which there is still no detailed map.

In the past decade, leaving the ultra-Orthodox community has gone from being an anomaly to a movement. I used to be able to count the names of people who'd left on my fingers. Now they number in the thousands, disappearing into the anonymity of cities all across the world, reinventing themselves as best they can, some of them showing up in Berlin to work as extras on a set where their native tongue is spoken, where they can count on instant recognition, and where the story they're helping to tell feels a lot like their own. For the former rabbi and the teenage runaway, the Fulbright scholar and the midlife turnaround, there is a truth in those scenes we were shooting that spoke to each of us in a primal way.

When I first watched all the episodes after picture lock a few weeks ago, and finally grasped the full extent of what we had created together, I realized that *Unorthodox* was no longer mine. I had set it free, and in the process, it had set me free.

November 2019
Berlin

Acknowledgments

This book is a result of many people's efforts, least of which is my own. I would not be the writer I am today were it not for my agent and mentor, Patricia van der Leun, whose advice has always steered me in the right direction. I am grateful to my editor, Sarah Knight, who turned my manuscript into a book worth reading. I am in awe of the whole team at Simon & Schuster who took the time to help me make this book the best it could be. I thank Molly Lindley, to whom I am forever indebted for her dedication and efficiency; you untangled all the knots for me, a first-time author still feeling her way in the dark. Thank you to Brian, Kate, and Jessica, for your enthusiasm and patience. Thank you to Nancy Singer, Monica Gurevich/Julie Metz Ltd., Sybil Pincus, and Peg Haller, who are responsible for making this book actually look like one. I have felt spoiled by all of you.

Thank you to Carolyn Ferrell, for allowing me to use your writing workshop as a personal sounding board for the early beginnings of this memoir. Your guidance, as well as the thoughtful feedback of my classmates at Sarah Lawrence, was invaluable. Special thanks are owed to Katherine Quinby Stone, Adam Singer, and Julia Sternberg, whose sincere relationship with my work meant the world to me. You were my first readers.

My gratitude to Sarah Lawrence, the institution that gave me my first opportunity to make something of myself, is indescribable. Thank you, Joann Smith, for giving me the chance at a quality education. Thank you to the wonderful professors who pushed me to discover myself, to Carol Zoref, Ernest Abuba, Neil Arditi, and Brian Morton. Thank you,

Paulette, for being at the same place at the same time, so that I could be inspired by your courage and faith. Without you, I would not be where I am today. The same applies to all the wonderful men and women who were my first friends and allies in a strange world; I will forever be grateful for your support and understanding.

Thank you, Diane Reverand, for convincing my agent to give me a shot. Thank you, Amanda Murray, for being the first person in publishing to believe in my book wholeheartedly. The same goes for David Rosenthal, who took the time to meet with me, a gesture that touched my heart.

Thank you to Sandra and Rudy Woerndle and Kathryn and Jon Stuard, who extended a helping hand to me when I was still struggling to find my footing. I am grateful for the support of the wonderful group of women I met in Midland, Texas.

I would like to thank Patricia Grant for taking me on pro bono even when the odds were stacked against me. You inspire me to be a stronger, better woman.

Thank you, Juliet Grames, BJ Kramer, Joel Engelman, Malka Margolies, Claudia Cortese, Amy Donders, and Melissa D'Elia for being great friends and mentors at the same time. Also, many thanks to my fellow rebels, whose stories of both hardship and triumph helped lessen the pain of isolation from my family and community. It's been an incredible journey, one that would not have been possible without even the smallest contributions from my fellow travelers.

I am so fortunate to have my son; from the day he was born he became the inspiration for this journey, and if it hadn't been for his coming into my life, I would not have found the strength and determination to accomplish what I did. I can't wait to watch you grow up into an incredible young man, and I hope I can be the mother that you deserve to have.

Lastly, I thank my mother, who has supported me throughout all my writing efforts, even though I know it can't have been easy for her. I consider myself lucky to have the freedom to write this book, and I hope it makes a difference in the lives of others. Thank you for reading.

SIMON & SCHUSTER
READING GROUP GUIDE

Unorthodox
Deborah Feldman

Introduction

Raised in the cloistered world of Brooklyn's Satmar sect of Hasidic Judaism, Deborah Feldman struggled as a naturally curious child to make sense of and obey the rigid strictures that governed her daily life. From what she could read to whom she could speak with, virtually every aspect of her identity was tightly controlled. Married at age seventeen to a man she had met for only thirty minutes and denied a traditional education—sexual or otherwise—she was unable to consummate the relationship for an entire year. Her resultant debilitating anxiety went undiagnosed and was exacerbated by the public shame of having failed to serve her husband. In exceptional prose, Feldman recalls how stolen moments reading about the empowered literary characters of Jane Austen and Louisa May Alcott helped her to see an alternative way of life—one she knew she had to seize when, at the age of nineteen, she gave birth to a son and realized that more than just her own future was at stake.

Questions and Topics for Discussion

1. The heroines in the books Deborah read as a girl were her first inspirations, the first to make her consider her own potential outside of her community. Which literary characters have inspired you?

2. As a girl, with two absentee parents and an outspoken nature, Deborah was systematically made to feel different or "bad." How did the structure of Satmar Hasidic culture make her feel such shame, and how did this shame serve to subjugate her?

3. When Deborah learns that King David—a revered historical figure who supposedly did no wrong—is a murderer and a hypocrite, she writes, "I am not aware at this moment that I have lost my innocence. I will realize it many years later." What is the line between innocence and willful ignorance? How did Deborah's ability and willingness to question authority and think for herself change the course of her life?

4. The cloistered Satmar community is located on the outskirts of New York City, one of the most racially, spiritually, and culturally diverse places in America. How do aspects of the outside world enter Deborah's consciousness, and how do you think these glimpses of life outside her insular community affected her development?

5. Deborah writes of the various ways she was restricted and constrained by her religion, but her grandparents found solace in the strict Hasidic community after the Holocaust. Were there any positive aspects of her tightly knit sect?

6. How was Deborah's life affected by gossip and the fear of scrutiny from her friends and neighbors? How have other people's judgments and criticisms affected your own life?

7. How much were Deborah's Bubby and her aunts responsible for the unhappiness in her life? How much free will did they have, given their cultural restrictions?

8. When it is time for Deborah to find a husband, her ordinarily stingy Zeidy starts spending money. How does this rampant materialism conflict with the community's values of modesty and simplicity? How does this kind of materialism differ from and how is it similar to materialism in secular life?

9. Discuss your reaction to the fact that Deborah's mother fled the community. How different do you think Deborah's life would have been if her mother had not left?

10. Even though her marriage is arranged and she has very little say in the matter, Deborah originally views her impending nuptials as an opportunity for freedom. Was she naive? Did her marriage to Eli constrain her even more than she already was?

11. Deborah's description of going to the mikvah is one of the most harrowing in the book. How did her experience at the ritual baths expose the most glaring hypocrisies of her religion?

12. How did Deborah's responsibilities shift when her son was born? What do you think ultimately led her to summon the courage to leave her community?

13. Deborah writes about the abuses that are allowed to run rampant in the Satmar community—from her own father's untreated mental illness to pedophilia. From Deborah's account of life in the Satmar Hasidic religion, do you think the community will ever be able to change or be reformed?

Enhance Your Book Club

1. Food was a major aspect of Deborah's family and religious life. Try out some recipes for Eastern European delicacies, like egg kichel or babka, and share with your book club.

2. Deborah's love of pop music was a shameful secret when she was growing up. Plan a group outing to a karaoke bar and belt out your favorite guilty pleasures.

3. James, Deborah's professor at Sarah Lawrence, suggests that she read some Yiddish poetry that has been translated into English. Have each member of your book group find a poem that was originally written in Yiddish and recite it to the group. Is there anything about the poem that reflects a particular cultural point of view or gives a hint of the Yiddish temperament or sense of humor?

A Conversation with Deborah Feldman

You say this book is "your ticket out" of the Hasidic world. Did going back over the details of your life in the Satmar community bring about any new realizations? What did you learn about yourself in the process of writing Unorthodox?

While I was writing *Unorthodox* I was going through that delicate transition period that comes after leaving, where I was struggling to figure out what kind of person I was going to be, and what kind of life I was going to lead. Being forced to reflect on the past made me realize I was never going to be able to erase it, and that the past will always be a part of who I am. I eventually learned that this was not necessarily a bad thing, and I grew to accept it. Without the book to help me, it would have taken me much longer to achieve that realization.

From the time you were a little girl you loved reading. What are some of your favorite books and how have they influenced you?

I mention many of my favorites in the memoir, but I've also been a huge Charles Dickens fan for as long as I can remember. Being an anglophile, I quickly familiarized myself with all the renowned English writers, but his books stood out because they often concerned young children who found themselves suddenly disadvantaged in life, and his writing was steeped in a sort of romantic melancholy. I think books like that allowed me to make my own life seem like an adventure. Of course, I can't forget about Harry Potter. I caught on to the series as a teenager and it was such an escape for me. To this day I credit J. K. Rowling for my surviving adolescence in the Satmar community. I remember a time when the next Harry Potter book was the only thing I had to look forward to. Recently I felt a similar excitement; I was reading a book by Lev Grossman that has been called the "grown-up Harry Potter," titled *The Magician King*, and it made me remember how I felt as a kid all over again. It's a great experience to recapture that feeling. If an author can do that, then they have really achieved something.

In the book you mention that you kept a journal. When did you start writing? Do you keep a journal now? Did you always know you wanted to be a writer?

I started writing as soon as I started reading. There's a reason writers write, and I think I understood that reason from a very young age. When I started writing, I felt like I had joined a club. I was engaged in an age-old process of reflection and creativity that tied me to the people I most admired: authors. In this way, writing made me feel less alone. It took me out of my small, limited world and made me feel part of the big picture. I still keep a journal; I think I always will. As I do this, I understand that it's not so much about creating content, but about what writing can do for me as a person. It aids both my creative and personal development.

Do you think there is any chance that the Satmar community can be reformed? Is there any way for people outside of the community to help?

I definitely think there is a chance for positive change to occur in the Satmar community. As a realist, I understand that the extent of that change may be more limited than I would like, but that doesn't negate its value. Change is created only when people demand it, though, and I am just one person. Others will need to stand up for what they want as well. I believe that there are people in the community for whom the lifestyle fits more comfortably than it did in my case, but I also know that there are many trapped on the inside who wish to be emancipated but have no tools to achieve that. When I was inside, I was convinced that there was no way out because I did not know anyone in the secular world, and my limited contact with it as a child had convinced me that no one would be receptive to my attempts at interaction. It would be nice if people could see past the costume to the person underneath it, and be more understanding as a result. If outsiders take notice, the Satmar community might be more inclined toward reform, as they are usually concerned with public image.

You write that you still consider yourself proud to be Jewish and that you still think it's important to have faith. How has your religion manifested itself in your life outside the Satmar Hasidic community? Do you belong to a temple, or do you find other ways to express your beliefs?

I think my Jewishness has stayed with me largely because of my son, who identifies very positively with his ethnic and religious identity. Seeing him take pleasure in Jewish holidays and customs has taught me not to reject the beneficial aspects of a culture just because it has negative associations for me. While I am still uncomfortable with the idea of "belonging" to a temple or community, I don't want to deprive my son of that choice, and so I try to stay as open and flexible as possible.

Now that you're free to delve into secular culture, what particular activities do you most enjoy?

That's easy. I love being part of a literary community. The fact that I don't have to hide my books, or my love for them, is the best part about being free. I spend time in bookstores and attend readings, and it always feels like a celebration to me, because I know I would never have been able to take part in this were it not for my escape. I also love to travel, watch independent films, and visit art museums. The fact that I can expand my intellectual horizons when I want to is still thrilling and new to me.

Food has always played an important role in your life. How does it feel to not keep kosher? What are your favorite things to eat?

Interestingly, I still keep a kosher kitchen at home, because I am raising my son as Modern Orthodox, something I agreed to in order to keep the differences between his father's lifestyle and mine as minimally confusing as possible. However, I consider myself a real foodie, and I love trying new dishes, especially when I'm traveling. I feel like the best way to get to know a new place is through the food it has to offer. Eating is such a sensual and indulgent activity, and I think I have an emotional relationship to food that was instilled in me by my upbringing.

Have you had any further communication with your grandparents or the rest of your extended family? Do they know this book is being published? Has there been any fallout?

This is a sensitive issue for me. When I left I changed my contact information and hid for a while because I was scared that they would force me to return. Later, when news of the book surfaced, I received a lot of hate mail from members in my family, and that was very hurtful. However, reading the abusive messages reminded me how lucky I was to have escaped the community and made me more grateful than ever that I had made the decision to leave it. I think my family and community will try to do whatever they can to hurt me, both to discount what I'm saying and to exact their revenge against me for betraying the code of silence. I am prepared for that eventuality, and I rely on the support of my close friends to get me through that.

Do you think anyone in the Satmar Hasidic community will read your book? Do you want them to?

I definitely think that members of the community will read the book, albeit in secret. There exists a certain curiosity about rebels; every time an article about one is published, it is discreetly circulated among a Hasidic audience. I certainly don't mind if they do read it, I expect a certain amount of public outrage, but I'm also confident that many women, and men, may be inspired by it. I think it will make them think differently about the lives they lead.

Would you like your son to read this book one day? How will you explain his heritage to him?

It's very difficult for me to imagine my son grown up and reading this book. I don't think anyone would be very comfortable with the idea that the intimate details of their parents' lives—and by extension, their life—are available to the public. I can only hope that he will accept me for who I am. Right now, we have a very close relationship and I answer all his questions honestly, and I can only continue to try my best to do so as he grows older and his questions become more complex.

What would you most like readers to take away from the experience of reading this book? What would you most like people to know about you, and about the Hasidic community in general?

I want people to think about how hard it can still be to grow up female in this day and age, because even though some of the experiences described in the book may strike you as extreme, I think all women can identify with the powerlessness I felt. A lot about how the Hasidic community conducts itself is a reflection on the greater society that allows it to do so, and I think attitudes toward multiculturalism need to change as a result. Justice for women needs to improve both in and outside of extreme religious cultures.

If you could talk to young girls from your old neighborhood who are struggling with their beliefs and feeling constrained by their community, what would you tell them?

I would tell them to reach out and ask for help. It's scary to make that first contact, but more often than not it pays off. I've been helped by some amazing people, and I would love nothing more than to pay it forward. I know I can't save the world, but I will certainly do everything I can to assist others like me.